Kenya Kaleidoscope

Agnes R. Shaw, OBE

Copyright © 2020

All rights reserved; no part of this publication may be reproduced, stored in a retrieval system, transmitted in any form or by any means, electronic, mechanical, photocopying, recording, or otherwise, without the prior written permission of the Shaw Family.

ISBN # 979-8558-8285-5-9

Published by Old Africa books
Naivasha, Kenya

FOREWORD

*"From quiet homes and first beginning
Out to the undiscovered ends
There is nothing worth the wear of winning
But laughter and the love of friends."*
--Hilaire Belloc

All my friends have told me I must write a book in order to commit to paper, while memory serves, my wealth of experience – happy, sad, gay, amusing, exciting, dull, but always deeply satisfying – welded together by family life in our lovely home 'Kipkebe' in the Sotik district of Kenya. I have called these reminiscences *Kenya Kaleidoscope* for I can think of no better description of the state of my mind: a jumble of recollections, incidents, and stories, chasing one another down the lane of memory.

My task, not an easy one, is to present to my readers a coherent pattern out of this tangle of light and shade. But though the more exciting events tend to stand out and catch the eye, like vivid pieces of coloured glass, remember that it is the whole which makes the pattern, and that without the more sombre shades our pattern would not be complete. I invite you to look at Kenya, that land of sunshine, through my kaleidoscope, and as you turn the pages see the events which go to make up the colourful pattern fall into place.

I have spent the greater part of my seventy-one years in the Colony and Republic of Kenya, having left Scotland, as I thought for a short visit, in 1927. In those far-off days, Kenya's claim to fame lay in its being the playground of the idle rich, their "Happy Valley" escape in the land of sunshine and safari. So Kenya achieved much undeserved nOturiety. In later years too, the spotlight of publicity has held Kenya in its glare, and she has been often much maligned and certainly much misunderstood.

Kenya does not owe me anything, for she has given me many years of happiness. If through these pages I can help my readers to a greater understanding of her peoples and their problems, then I shall feel that I have done something towards paying, in part, my debt to Kenya.

I have divided this book into two parts, the first dealing with my background, my early life on the farm, and the war years, and the second covering that reign of terror the Mau Mau Rebellion, which hung over the Kenya scene like a dark cloud. This part takes in my experiences over eleven years as a European Elected Member representing a province the size of Wales, perhaps the most interesting period of my life, including as it did attendance at the two Kenya Constitutional Conferences held at Lancaster House in London in 1960 and 1962.

I should like to thank my kind friends who through their encouragement, help and advice have made this book possible, which bears out the truth that "There is nothing worth the wear of winning but laughter and the love of friends!"

Agnes R. Shaw

Nairobi, 1973

INTRODUCTION

When Agnes Shaw arrived in Mombasa as a young woman in 1927, Kenya Colony had only been formally in existence for seven years. In the wake of World War I, and with the encouragement of the British Government, settlers were arriving in increasing numbers to take up farming in the areas reserved for white immigrants.

These settlers, a mere few thousand in a country of about three million people, were the inheritors of an Empire on which the sun quite literally never set, encompassing as it did roughly a quarter of the world's land mass. Many settlers believed not only that the Empire was an immutable fact of life but also that they were embarked on a noble purpose – something far beyond simply trying to make a living.

While such sentiments sound, at best, anachronistic to people living a century later, it is important in reading Agnes' memoir to remember that they represent the thinking of that era as well as of her race and class. It is also important to remember that Kenya's white settlers believed, with cause, that their efforts to establish an imperial outpost in Kenya had the complete backing of the home country. The betrayal of this belief (as the settlers saw it), as successive Governments in London responded to dramatically changed economic and political conditions after World War II, resulted in considerable bitterness among the settlers.

To be fair, Agnes was 'liberal' by the standards of her community. While African leaders for the most part rejected this kind of 'liberalism' as a rear-guard effort to hold onto white privilege, it did produce some genuine change, as, for example, the cross-race political friendships which she describes. By the late 1950s, however, the momentum for African rule was unstoppable. The British Government, buffeted by what Prime Minister Harold Macmillan famously called the 'Wind of Change' in a 1960 speech, decided shortly after that speech to hand Kenya back to the African majority.

It is greatly to Agnes Shaw's credit that – unlike many of the settler community – she accepted this turn of events and continued to live in Kenya for the rest of her life. Her memoir begins and ends with positive words about Kenya and Kenyans, and throughout the book she offers praise for African Kenyans with whom she worked and whom she came to admire.

What sort of person was she, this daughter of Scotland with an American grandmother, a fairly sheltered early life, and a sufficiently tough nature that she withstood years of hardship and ill health in one of the far reaches of Kenya Colony?

One of her neighbours, Patrick Walker, whose family owned a farm not far from the Shaw's property when he was a small boy, remembers Agnes as indomitable, taking herself quite seriously and could be quite intimidating. She was a superb organizer, whether of whist, tennis parties or political meetings. He confirms she was "ahead of her time" in terms of her moderate—in the context of European attitudes—politics.

Her daughter in law, Diana Shaw remembers her as a forceful person, a great character, tremendously hospitable, producing wonderful four course dinners, always preceded by drinks with 'first toasties.' She was a fabulous entertainer, usually telling endlessly amusing stories, although not averse to embellishing details every time the story was related! She was the one who held the floor on any conversation, while her husband Brian was a quiet, old-school 'English Gentleman.' Agnes also had a very good dress sense; despite being on the plump side, she always seemed well turned out, especially on formal occasions with silk dress, hat and gloves.

Agnes' oldest granddaughter, Tish adored her grandmother and recalls her as being "great, great fun," never at a loss for fun games for little people.

Diana also notes that although some of Agnes' writings might make her sound racially insensitive to modern ears, that was not at all how Diana remembers her. "She came from this background where one didn't socialise with other races, but over the years she mellowed and treated the new African members of the Legislative Council with respect." Moreover, Diana says, "She was a very fair employer" and enjoyed "immense loyalty" from her staff. For many years after her political forays into the African districts of Nyanza 'Mama Shaw' was remembered with love and respect.

That Agnes' many talents were recognized by the wider world is reflected in the fact that she was awarded the Order of the British Empire in 1960 "for public services in Kenya." Her political career spanned the period from 1951 to 1963. She was a major figure in Nyanza, a long way from Nairobi, but she only became known on the national stage after her attendance at the the two Lancaster House conferences in London in 1960 and 1962.

Then, too, she had to contend with the outright anti-women sentiments of the period. She was probably a feminist before her time.

In 1960 the Shaws turned the running of the farm in Sotik over to their daughter and son-in-law Ann and Don Bush, and moved to the suburbs of Nairobi, from which Agnes carried on her work in the Legislative Council until Independence in 1963. She and Brian continued to live in the Nairobi area for the rest of their lives where she created another garden and happy home. Agnes gave talks to the East African Women's League and other groups from time to time, offered cookery lessons to struggling housewives, and assisted Brian with growing roses for sale to help with finances. Their son Michael, after a few years coffee farming, became a lawyer, practicing in Nairobi.

Agnes died in 1978, aged 75, after suffering a stroke. Brian died a few months later. Both are buried in St Francis Church, Karen. Their son and daughter, Michael and Ann, have also died but their son's three children still live in Kenya, and together with Ann's two children have decided that the time has come when it is appropriate to release Agnes' story to a wider audience and hope that a remarkable woman may be remembered and admired for her contribution to the history of this lovely country.

Agnes Shaw's memoir is of historical importance for the insight it gives into the thinking of elected European office holders in Kenya in the key years leading up to Independence. It is also a vividly rendered account of the life of a tough and remarkable woman who was a true pioneer.

Appreciations

It was thanks to the efforts of Tessa McLellan, Agnes' youngest grandchild, and other family members, that Agnes Shaw's manuscript came to the attention of Old Africa magazine. The family would like very much to thank Shel Arensen of Old Africa magazine for his advice and very generous help with this publication. And also to Mike Adkins and Blake Arensen for their expertise in the layout and reproduction of the old photos, most of which probably were taken with a box brownie camera and therefore are not particularly high quality. We would also like to thank Karen Rothmyer for her expert skill in editing.

Portrait of Agnes Shaw taken by Lenare in London.

PART I

CHAPTER 1

Early Years

*"Home is the inner core, the core of the spirit,
The triple core, where Past and Present and Future
Are braided into one…"*
--Jan Struther

It is fashionable today to blame one's heredity for all one's faults and failings, but I am afraid that except for my streak of extravagance, a legacy from my pleasure-loving Virginian forebears, I cannot lay my shortcomings at my parents' door.

I was born in Glasgow, Scotland, on July 31, 1902, of mixed parentage, my father being a Scot and my mother, though of Scottish descent, an American. A more ill-assorted pair it would be hard to imagine.

My mother, Laura Bell, was born in Norfolk, Virginia. When my father, Charles Cree met and fell in love with her she was a pretty, blue-eyed, golden-haired girl of twenty-one, gay and irresponsible, with all the extravagance of her Southern background and upbringing. Photographs show her as an attractive and lovely young woman, and as she grew older her great charm of manner and love of humanity drew people to her. A vital and vivid personality, she impressed everyone she met. Her father had fought on the Confederate side in the American Civil War as Surgeon General on General JEB Stewart's staff, and all her uncles were in the Confederate forces.

The victory of the North brought ruin to my mother's family, as indeed, it did to most of the Southern planters. So after my grandfather's death my grandmother returned to Scotland, the land of her forebears, with her youngest and only unmarried daughter, to live with an elder brother who was then a flourishing general practitioner in Glasgow.

By modern standards my mother would be considered uneducated, but she had a great fund of energy and a natural gift for organisation, and was the working head of the Scottish-led Red Cross Stores and Despatch Department during the 1914-1918 War, winning an OBE as well as a French and Belgian Decoration for her services.

Laura Cree (nee Bell), Agnes's mother.

Agnes's father Charles Cree in 1918.

My father, Charles Cree, who came of a line of worthy Glasgow citizens, was respectable and hardworking, with all a Scot's natural caution, and an underlying sense of humour. His family had been ruined by a disastrous fire which destroyed their paper mill, and on his father's death shortly afterwards, my paternal grandmother, a courageous and talented Englishwoman, had faced the problem of bringing up her brood of eight children on a pittance. So my father left school at the age of fourteen to become the family breadwinner, apprenticed as an errand-boy to an uncle's paper and publishing firm, where he fetched and carried from dawn till dusk and then went to night-school in an effort to complete his education.

Gone were his dreams of becoming an engineer, for there was not enough money for an ordinary schooling, let alone specialised training. Was it any wonder then that he was swept off his feet by this gay American girl?

My parents met while playing in my great-uncle's amateur orchestra, where my father played the violin and my mother the big bass drum, playing her one note with great skill and precision, after counting up to one-hundred and thirteen! The suspense must have been terrific!

Ill-assorted as it was, the marriage was a very happy one, a matter of some credit to my mother. Still a young girl, she settled down to a life of drab domesticity on a small income, with the added burden of bringing up a delicate baby while nursing an invalid mother. My grandmother was a spoilt Southern belle. She lived in the past, recreating for us children, vivid tales of the Civil War, all the excitement of the times and the desperate courage of the Confederates. She lived with my parents for twenty years until she died at the age of eighty-one.

Being the first child in the Cree family [her father's side] for many years,

Agnes Cree as a young girl. Constance, Charles and Agnes as children.

I believe I was rather spoilt. I had a wonderful collection of over forty dolls of different nationalities, but none of these found favour; my heart was already given to a very ancient and dilapidated golliwog, later to be supplanted by a teddy bear who was my constant bed companion for years. In fact, my mother has told me that although a very gentle child in every other respect, I alarmed my parents by my horrid habit of pushing in the dolls' eyes, a sadistic streak which fortunately does not seem to have developed.

Except for a six-week visit with my parents to America, where I was led gloriously astray by an unbelievably naughty American cousin, I can remember very little of my early childhood. Looking back down the tunnel of the years, all I seem to see is a solitary little girl, living in a world of imagination. What I do know is that I was very delicate, and that my mother, who looked after me herself, gave me devoted care which forged a bond between us that made us very close throughout our lives.

When I was six years old my sister was born, and my whole life changed – not so much because of the birth of the baby, although that was exciting, but by the addition to the household of Nanny.

My father's financial position being improved, we moved to a larger house in the West End of Glasgow, where my brother was born three years later. We now had a nurse and a governess, the whole top floor being given over to a nursery flat, and although the governesses came and went, and made little impression, Nanny, who was with us for many years, had a great influence on my life. 'Ellen' was a very remarkable Scotswoman of great character, a tiny domineering figure in cap and grey alpaca dress, who hid beneath her rather grim exterior a warm and loving heart. The relations between mother and nurse were of armed neutrality, for Nanny resented any interference in her domain, where her word was law and where we lived and played, under her stern and watchful eye.

She came from a very poor Highland family in Wick and had little education, having been sent out to work at age twelve, but her early struggle only served to temper the fine steel of her character as it sharpened her native wit. So in her later years, in the place of education one found wisdom, relieved by a great sense of humour, and a foundation of God-fearing Presbyterianism impregnated with a mass of Scottish folklore.

As to my education, such as it was, from eight to fourteen years of age I went daily to an old-fashioned private school known by the high-sounding name of Miss Mac's Academy for Girls, where apart from lessons in the deportment of a young lady, all I remember learning was the satisfying historical fact that since James VI of Scotland ascended the throne of England, Scotland was never conquered.

The result of this somewhat one-sided curriculum was that at fourteen I was steeped in Scottish history and tradition, and a staunch Jacobite. This 'tribal' imbalance caused my more broadminded mother to ship me off to an English school, Branton Down, at the southernmost tip of Kent, where I found myself regarded with deep suspicion as the only Scots girl.

When I recovered from the shock of being in this alien world of Sassenachs, I settled down and spent four very happy years there. Our English mistress was a devoted classicist, and to her I owe my love and enjoyment of history, English literature, and the arts. My maths being correspondingly weak, however, I failed to gain my Cambridge Certificate, being ploughed in maths, although I gained Distinction in five out of eight subjects. In my first year I was very undisciplined, due mostly to home sickness, and being irked by the petty rules and regulations. However I was not unhappy for I shared a

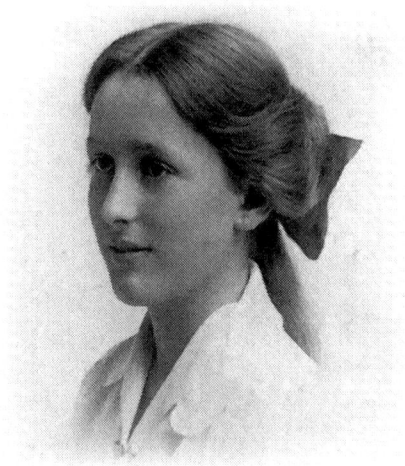

Potrait of Agnes Cree

room with three delightful girls, one was English, one Irish and one Welsh, so we were completely diverse in our national character, and therefore got on splendidly together. However, my conduct sheet was so black that I believe I came near to expulsion. Instead, much to my alarm and despondency, I was removed from my three delightful companions, and transferred to higher realms of being made a Prefect! Madame Kirby realized that some steady responsibility was what I needed rather than punishment. How I hated her at that moment, for I knew she had effectively stopped all my carefree fun, although in later years when I became Head Girl, I was grateful to her for her patience and farsighted understanding.

Two men who influenced my life during my early years were the Reverend Mr Dean, then Rector of St Mary's Cathedral Glasgow, and the Reverend Mr Elliot, the Rector of a church in Folkestone for many years. Mr Dean was a constant visitor to our home, but whenever he came to see my parents, he always had five minutes to spare for a visit to the nursery and a game of Bears around the nursery table.

Mr Elliot, a fine man too, was quite a different type, a very eloquent preacher who packed his fashionable church Sunday after Sunday. He was a spellbinder, who could even hold the attention of a lot of schoolgirls throughout his lengthy sermons, which lasted anything up to one hour.

When I left school I was perhaps something of a prig. In my tidy mind, people were divided into two classes, right or wrong, though I was prepared to allow that some of the latter at least meant well. For the next seven years, my life followed the pattern of that of any girl of the leisured classes. My mother, after her wartime Red Cross work was over, became the Girl Guide Commissioner for Glasgow, and later when we moved to Ayr she took over the work of the County Secretary. So it was only natural that I should throw myself into Girl Guide activities. I became a lieutenant in a well-to-do Guide company in a Presbyterian Church at Ayr until I started my own slum company.

Once a week, I would brave the terrors of the dark and dirty streets of Ayr in my Girl Guide's uniform. My worst fear was of the small urchins who let off firecrackers under my feet, shouting, "Here comes the capt'n." The annual camp was tremendous fun; it was so rewarding to give these town children a week in the country and see their enjoyment. I was very proud of my little troop. Over five years I brought them up until they were a top-ranking company, winning the Divisional Banner.

At nineteen I was made District Commissioner for Ayr. Six hundred Guiders and Guides came under my command. So Guiding became my main interest, and my training school for public speaking.

My daily routine included tennis, picnics and otter-hunting in our short

Agnes Cree on a Girl Guides camping trip.

summer, and in winter I played badminton, as I couldn't afford to hunt. (Even in those days it cost over £300 per annum to be mounted.) On the serious side there were lectures, music and cooking lessons, and, for lighter relief, amateur theatricals, Hunt Balls and other dances, race meetings, and an occasional visit to London. Thus the years slipped quickly and pleasantly by.

During this period the two outstanding events were my two trips abroad: the first in 1921 to the Riviera, where I spent the winter with my aunt and an American banker uncle in all the gaiety and luxury of the Monte Carlo of the Twenties; and the second a six- month visit in 1924 to the U.S.A.

Monte Carlo in those days was filled with a throng of wealthy people of all nationalities, trying to forget, in a round of hectic gaiety, the ghastly years of war. The only grim reminders were the disabled soldiers and the Russian refugees seeking asylum from the terror of their revolution, eking out a meagre living by doing fine needlework, teaching languages, or becoming gigolos in the Rivera's many night-Clubs.

Colonel de Basil's Russian Ballet, after fleeing from St. Petersburg, had made Monte Carlo their home, and so we had the joy of going to the ballet once a week. Thus was born my love of ballet. It was all the rage, and it was even fashionable to dress one's hair like the Russian dancers.

I had lessons in French conversation from a charming Baroness, and dancing lessons from Pierre, a delightful little Frenchman who taught me the foxtrot and tango. I became so proficient in the former that Pierre and I won a dancing competition at the Carlton Night Club, beating the Grand Duke Michael and his ballerina partner!

On the tiny dance floor at the Carlton, Monte Carlo's one and only night Club, one rubbed shoulders with the aristocracy of France, Britain and Russia (the Germans, like their operas, were banned); with American millionairesses seeking titled if impecunious husbands; with demimondaines; and with international crooks – all heady wine for a girl of nineteen.

It said much for my upbringing and native Scottish caution that I emerged unscathed, if a little heartbroken, from my three-month visit. I had fallen in love with a handsome Russian, Vladimir, an ex-naval officer. Our love was all the more romantic for being hopeless. Vladimir, having to support his mother and invalid sister, had to find an heiress, and although I was reasonably pretty, I was quite, quite penniless.

My six-month visit to America was totally different but an equally exciting venture. Travelling from New York with one of my mother's old friends, I left by train for Baltimore, where we sailed down the Chesapeake Bay to Norfolk, my mother's birthplace. I had a delightful visit in Norfolk, meeting many of my mother's relations, and then joined my uncle and aunt in Florida, where we spent a lovely lazy month at Miami Beach and then went on to Key West and Cuba.

After a week, on we went through the Panama Canal to sunny California, where we stayed for one month near San Diego at the Coronado Beach Hotel. Luckily, I was adopted by the local 'bright young things,' led by Randolph Hearst's son. All that I remember about young Hearst was that he seemed to have an unlimited supply of money, which he used with much generosity for the gang's entertainment, taking us across to Catalina Island in his yacht and aquaplaning behind his speedboats in San Diego's magnificent harbour, with masses of lavish barbecues on the beach thrown in for good measure.

The highlight of our stay at Coronado Beach Hotel was the Spanish Ball, organised in honour of the visit of Rudolph Valentino. The ballroom was transformed into the marketplace of a Spanish town, gay with stalls, with everyone in the most beautiful costumes, many of them old family relics of the Spanish occupation. Valentino's superb dancing in the Exhibition Tango is something I shall never forget for its beauty and grace of movement.

Before leaving California we visited Los Angeles and Hollywood, where we saw that great natural humourist, Charles Chaplin, filming *The Gold Rush*.

We returned to New York by train, taking five days to cross the huge continent. From there I went for a month to Hobart College in Geneva, New York, where one of my uncles was Dean. Great fun, as it did not involve much mental effort, for I found that the students at twenty years of age were doing the same work as I had done aged sixteen at my English boarding school.

If I had not known before my visit that we do not speak the same language as our cousins across the Atlantic, I learnt it then, and I found I needed an interpreter for all the college slang, but it was all great fun. One remark made to me by a young graduate stands out in my memory. He said, "Your British conceit is the most annoying in the world, for whereas we Americans boast that we are God's own people and give you something to contradict, you merely *act* as if you were." How true! Perhaps this is the reason why Englishmen are so often disliked abroad.

Spring came, and I spent a final, glorious nine weeks in Washington with my beloved cousin, Tom Talliafero, and his wife Janie. She explained that the numerous societies of which she was a member had been set up by the English-speaking communities in a desperate attempt to keep the hoi polloi of middle European ancestry from invading their Clubs and swamping their social life. It certainly was confusing for me, as a stranger, one day to attend a meeting of the Colonial Dames, my cousin proudly wearing her insignia with its ancestor bars (a distinction gained because her family had held land under the English King George), and on the next to meet with the stalwart Daughters of the Revolution, all decked out in their priest-like white frocks, chanting, "Down with the tyrant, George the Third."

If I saw Washington as the most beautiful of cities, remember it was cherry blossom time and I was young; and I admit I was sorely tempted to stay forever and become an American. However, the pull of Scotland proved too strong and so I sailed from New York with my banker uncle on the SS *Olympic*, then the Queen of the Ocean, in early June. So ended my American adventure.

My homecoming was sad. I found my mother very worried, as my dear father was far from well. Indeed, I was dreadfully shocked by the change in him, for he seemed listless, apathetic, and so unlike himself. We did not know it then, but this was the first sign of the disease of which he was to die some eight years later. It was a great sorrow to me, for I adored my father and to see him like this was heartbreaking.

In 1925, a young man and I visited the gipsy fortune-teller at a fair, agreeing to have our fortunes told together. He, a man of dark colouring, was

Agnes Cree as a debutante.

one of my most faithful swains, and when the gipsy foretold that I should marry a dark man I was overjoyed, only to be equally crestfallen when she said that it would be some time before I met my fate.

The old crone then forecast that in the near future I would cross a great expanse of water, where I would marry this man, settle down and have two 'bonnie bairns.' Many times during my life I should cross and re-cross this water, and should finally live to a ripe old age, dying in the land of the little yellow men at 81.

Of course, I did not believe her, but I was to remember her words only too well when two years later my cousins invited me to go out to visit them in Kenya.

CHAPTER 2

Out to Kenya

*"I am not afraid of tomorrow,
For I have seen yesterday
And I love today."*
--William Allen White

What a wealth of different pictures the name of KENYA conjured up. For me, escape to sunshine, adventure in a new land, fresh fields to conquer, and maybe, the beginning of a new life. For my mother, the fearful picture of her beloved daughter braving the dangers of the African bush, sleeping in a tent while lions and other beasts of prey prowled outside. For my father, remembering that year's Pantomime joke: "Are you married, or do you live in Kenya?" a rather different worry!

But finally the die was cast and I was to sail in the autumn. Then followed two months of hectic preparation with a fortnight in London, where, with the expert advice of the Army and Navy Stores, I was suitably outfitted for life in the tropics. Before I left their establishment I was the proud possessor of all the regulation kit, including a double terai [a wide-brimmed felt hat], a spine pad which buttoned on to my shirts, slacks, mosquito boots and gaiters for the bush, and worse still, undergarments which had to be of cotton as crepe de chine was said to have an unfortunate habit of melting in a tropical clime.

Then came the great day of departure. My excited happiness was only clouded for a moment as I said goodbye to my family. Fortunately, I did not know that I was never to see my dear father again.

To entrain for Africa from St. Pancras was the oddest thing: I could not believe that I was not just going North again as I had done so many times from this dreary station. It was not until we reached the docks at Tilbury and boarded the SS *Llanstephen Castle* that I felt the great adventure had really begun.

It was certainly an adventure, and, as it turned out, one that was to change the whole course of my life, although at that moment I did not think of the gipsy's words, nor realise that I had already met my Fate. My only thought on being introduced to Brian Shaw at the station was,

"Poor chap, he doesn't know what he has let himself in for." This was because I recognised the look in my aunt's eye which said as plainly as if she had spoken, "Here is a young man who will be most useful to exercise the bull terrier on deck." My reaction was to vow there and then that at least he should not feel obliged to be kind to me on account of knowing my cousins in Kenya. So every time he plucked up sufficient courage to ask me to be his partner, I was already committed.

I was going out with my uncle and aunt for a short visit to my cousins, Dick and Isabel Phillips, and taking out their small daughter Mary, aged four, while Brian Shaw was returning to his job as a farm manager at Njoro, along with his sister, Irene, after long leave in the United Kingdom.

Being used to the luxurious comfort of those Queens of the Ocean, the liners of the Atlantic run, my uncle and aunt thought the SS *Llanstephen Castle* a poor ship and found the voyage tiresomely long. Sir Donald Cameron, Governor of Tanganyika, returning from leave, shared this opinion. At the ship's concert, he referred to our gallant vessel as 'this old scow.' But for me the three weeks were all too short. The voyage was all that a voyage should be when one is young, the starlit nights are warm under a romantic tropical sky, and one is falling in love.

My first view of Mombasa, that island Eden, set in a sea of translucent blue and, on that November morning, shimmering with the portent of heat to come, was very beautiful. Our ship glided in past the Guardian lighthouse standing sentinel on the point, and past the dazzling white beaches and the strange baobab trees, their ungainly shapes emphasized by the graceful palms, to tie up at the dock in the new port of Kilindini.

Agnes Cree as a young lady.

From the noise and heat of the Customs sheds, we escaped to a delightful little beach hotel, the Tudor House, which still stands today. It was an enchanting spot, its little banda type cottages set in the cool shade of a coconut grove above a tiny sandy beach and overlooking one of Mombasa Island's many beautiful creeks. Here we bathed and spent a very pleasant evening, waited on by silent African servants clad in long white robes known as kanzus; they seemed to appear like the genie of the lamp whenever you clapped your hands.

Next morning, much refreshed by our short stay in this lovely spot, we drove in rickshaws to see something of the town. The streets were shaded by enormous mango trees, so that you passed through green bowers that made a good background for the jostling, noisy crowd who thronged the marketplace.

The vivid reds, blues and oranges of the clothing of these colour-loving people were thrown into relief by the sombre black robes of the veiled Muslim women, who were still living in purdah, poor things. Their dingy garments offered a sharp contrast to the glittering saris of their more fortunate Hindu sisters.

I was loath to leave the beauty of Mombasa, with its fascinating old Arab town and Fort Jesus, a relic of an ancient Portuguese civilisation. Re-visiting it, as I have throughout the years, I have never lost that sense of early enchantment.

That evening we all clambered into an antiquated type of train. My aunt and uncle were installed in one compartment; my cousin and her husband [who had joined us] and their little daughter and myself were in a four-berth one next door. Once under way, we were completely cut off since there was no corridor (although this did not deter a certain young man from climbing along the moving train and coming in through our compartment window to make up a fourth for bridge!).

Dressed suitably, as I thought, in spotless white, I was a sorry sight on arrival in Nairobi; I was red from head to foot from the red dust from the unmetalled tracks. Today, by contrast, women step out of a comfortable train, in the smartest of clothes, looking as if they were straight from Bond Street.

Nairobi, by then a town of some twenty-five years of age, was considered fairly civilised, though to me it looked exactly like its pioneering counterparts in the Western states of America – a one-horse town – though perhaps more colourful owing to the bright cottons of the African women's clothing, the Indian saris, and here and there a vivid red or orange shawl or turban worn by a visiting Somali. Even so, it had many points of similarity with the towns of the Middle West, with its ramshackle corrugated-iron buildings, the dust from its unpaved streets, the Model A Fords, and the cowboy-like costumes of the European men and women. Also, most of the business was conducted from the bars of the only two big hotels: the Norfolk, that habitat of the up-country settler, and the New Stanley.

As to the shops, I can only remember, apart from the universal small Indian dukas, (shops) two large general stores, one called 'The Dustpan,' run by Sammy Jacobs, and the other a firm found in most parts of the Empire, Whiteaway & Laidlaw's. There was a good grocery run by an old Scottish character named Duncan, Howse & McGeorge the chemist, and the offices of the *East African Standard*, until recently Kenya's only daily paper. Apart from those buildings, Nairobi seemed to consist of the railway station at one end of Government Road and a cluster of ramshackle wood and iron Government office buildings at the other. The Secretariat was up on the Hill beside the Nairobi Club, which was founded in 1901. This was and is still today the government and commercial club, for in 1927 you would only find the up-country farmers at Muthaiga Country Club, which had been started some eleven years later, in 1912.

Undaunted by the dust of the train journey, I set off on the 150-mile car trip up-country, arrayed once more in white, crowned by a double terai. Not trusting only to this to ward off the sun, I also carried a peach silk parasol.

My uncle went off with Dick Phillips in Dick's large and comfortable Buick car, while my aunt, cousin Isabel, her small daughter, myself and the bull terrier were left behind to come up in a dreadful old hired car driven by Maurice Vernon, an amusing ex-naval officer, who was later to become my brother-in-law. Looking back, I feel it was a most curious arrangement, only made perhaps with a view to ensuring the comfort of the male members of our party. For we, the females, could not have had a more dreadful journey. The springs in the seats of this antiquated open Ford had completely gone, and as we bounced and bumped from pothole to pothole, the small girl and the bull terrier puppy were, alternately, sick over our feet.

The plan to do the 100 miles to Nyeri by lunch and to reach the farm, six miles beyond Nanyuki, by tea-time, was upset by endless punctures. After the first one, these had to be mended by our unfortunate driver. He did his best to distract our attention from our worries by endless chat, and with every fresh disaster became more and more cheerful as my aunt became correspondingly more morose. It was all so very different from her luxurious chauffeur-driven Rolls and the tarmacadam roads of Britain and America.

We made the White Rhino Hotel in Nyeri by 5 p.m., the journey from Nairobi having taken eight hours, and were revived by the hotelkeeper, the well-known Sandy Herd, with tea and some welcome food. However, we were not encouraged to linger, for we still had fifty-odd miles, 'car willing,' to do. Maurice cheerfully assured us that the road was rougher than ever.

The sun set with alarming rapidity. The road got worse and worse and finally, just as daylight faded, we became hopelessly bogged down in a sea of black cotton soil masquerading as the main road. There was nothing to be done except for our driver to walk the five miles to the nearest farm to get help. By this time it was intensely cold. An icy wind was blowing straight off the snows of Mount Kenya, so although on the equator, we sat and shivered. We had no coats, rugs, or food.

Help did not reach us until 3 a.m., and those hours of waiting in the darkness seemed to us an eternity, stiff as we were with cold and fear, surrounded by the strange noises of the African night. So we were quite prepared to believe our rescuer, Jack Soames, when he said on arrival that it was a relief to find us unharmed, for it was at this spot that 300 rhino crossed each night. As the rescue car dared not come too near in case it, too, sank in the quagmire, we had to clamber through the loathsome mud to reach it, carrying our luggage bit by bit, by the light of a torch. What a sight we all were, caked and bespattered with black mud, and my much-prized peach silk parasol, which I was still clutching, completely ruined.

However, after a few hours' sleep and a good breakfast, we had quite forgotten the terrors of the night and enjoyed the beauties of the morning. As if to make up for the unpleasantness of our reception, Mount Kenya came out in all her glory, the peak dazzlingly white from a recent fall of snow.

The Phillips' farm lay facing this mountain, which in all its changing moods was a constant source of delight to us all. The small grey stone bungalow was set on a flat piece of land, bounded on one side by a wooded glen, through which a little trout stream tumbled over its rocky bed, fed by icy waters straight from the snows of Mt Kenya. Many were the happy hours I was to spend here, and it was in the waters of the Ontulili River that I caught my first Kenya trout.

My cousins ran a dairy herd of Friesland cows on this six-hundred-acre farm, as well as growing their own fodder crops. It was an uphill struggle, for not only were there the normal pests which plague the farmer in plenty, but many more only to be found in Africa. Even though all the arable land was fenced, they fought a perpetual battle against the depredations of wild animals. Leopard and lion attacked the cattle while elephant and zebra continually broke down the fences, indignant at the closure of what they considered their right of way. Then, too, there were occasionally giraffe, although they were more often to be found on the plains, where the telegraph poles had to be exceptionally tall to allow their passage underneath.

The Kavirondo cranes, those graceful birds, with their osprey-like crowns and magnificent plumage of black, white and red, marched purposefully behind the seed-sowing drills, picking out the maize seed as soon as it was planted. Also, there were all manner of buck, from the large and handsome waterbuck to the miniature dik-dik – death and destruction to a rose garden. It was in fact like trying to farm in an over-populated zoo.

It was all very exciting and I remember how thrilled I was on one of my first walks through the lush landscape with Mary, when following the frantic barking of the bull terrier we came into a little clearing to find that 'Buller' had treed a leopard. It was a beautiful animal, fat and sleek, but as it was hanging onto a burnt-out stump of a cedar tree not more than twelve feet high, and could only escape by jumping down, we decreed it imprudent to stay and reluctantly beat a hasty retreat to the house. When we returned with a rifle some twenty minutes later, both the bull terrier and the leopard had vanished. We were very anxious about the intrepid Buller, who had appeared quite unafraid of even such a dangerous enemy as a leopard. Happily, he returned unscathed.

Buller was a battle-scarred warrior, hero of many fights, and I remember another occasion when he was hanging onto the nose of a huge waterbuck, which he had in the famous bull-terrier grip, caught in its horns as the poor waterbuck thrashed from side to side. We had to shoot the animal before Buller would let go, even though by then the blood was pouring from the horn wounds in both his sides. He was a born fighter but the gentlest of creatures with children, adoring them and their parties, balloons, crackers, and all. Buller accepted me as one of the family and was our constant companion on our afternoon rambles through the bush.

My first few weeks were mostly spent in trying to learn Swahili, the lingua franca of Kenya – or rather learning the Kisettler version thereof, which was all I ever achieved in my many years in the country. Whereas at first my brand of Swahili was only used in the kitchen, it was gradually expanded and its vocabulary increased to cover farm and garden activities, and in later years it even had to be my medium for political speeches. The Kisettler version happily discards all tenses. This over-simplification, while perfectly adequate for ordering meals, makes conversation limited, description difficult, and political debate virtually impossible.

But in those early days I was not troubled by politics, only by the immediate problem of how to make the Kikuyu cook, who spoke no English, understand what I wanted for lunch. So armed with a Swahili/English dictionary, I set off to the kitchen each morning, only praying that there would be no repetition of the fatal misunderstanding which produced the chocolate sauce with the mutton, and the gravy with our ice cream. My early efforts caused much laughter amongst the good-humoured household staff, but soon the cook and I reached a large measure of understanding in a mixture of English and Kikuyu, bound together with Swahili words.

This understanding, however, did not help when it came to reading labels. I remember an occasion when we fell upon a delicious looking coffee cake. After the first mouthful, our expressions changed, as it dawned on us that instead of coffee essence, the cook had flavoured the icing with Worcester sauce!

Nanyuki, a tiny township, was obviously planned with an eye for future development, for in the year 1927 there was one mile of nothingness between its north and south ends.

At one end, with the equator running straight through its garden, was the Silverbeck Hotel and an estate agency run by a retired Army officer who was ably supported by Rene, his fierce but efficient wife. In front of the Land Office was the Fortnum & Mason of the town: a grocery store run by a most amusing young man nicknamed 'Cheese' Wilson, with the result that his shop, a tiny frame building perched on stilts, was known as 'Chateau Fromage.' Cheese's store was a popular meeting place for the settlers, where over a beer or ice-cream they swapped tales of their most recent farming failures, or more rarely, successes, while their wives discussed the latest scandal. Chateau Fromage was the social hub of 'brighter' Nanyuki.

At the other and perhaps less exclusive end was Younghusband's Garage and the large Indian general store of Osman Allu, along with a few smaller dukas, the veterinary office (all-important in a stock farming community), a post office housed in a duka, and the Club with its tennis courts and model racecourse. Next to it, a constant reminder of the danger of excess in any form, stood the whitewashed rondavels of the police. Even so, this warning was not always heeded for I seem to remember some bright young spark, after a particularly good Dance at the Club, suggesting a Bending Race in cars in and out of the Police Lines. The suggestion was carried out, to the terror of the Askaris, awakened from their peaceful slumbers at 2 a.m. A serious view was taken by the authorities of this escapade, and the Magistrate arrived on Monday morning with the warrants for the arrest of most of Nanyuki's leading citizens.

Everyone lived on a credit basis, for cash was impossible when your bank only came up once a fortnight. When it did, it was amusing to see everyone producing their IOU's in the hope of repayment. The wives got in first, knowing that by evening all the cash would be cleared out and everyone would have to resort to the IOU system once again.

There was only one place where credit was not given and that was the garage, where Major Younghusband wisely insisted on cash. He could afford to, for his was the only garage. The cash problem was solved by going across the street where one could borrow the necessary sum from Osman Allu, who was "always glad to accommodate such an influential gentleman and good customer."

The Club was a very friendly spot, where at weekends the farming community foregathered to play polo or tennis and run occasional race-meetings of the gymkhana variety, usually the excuse for a dance in the evening. All great fun, though it was only on the rarest occasions that funds ran to a proper band. When this happened, everyone turned up at the Club, for it was an event, but the difficulty was to get them home. I remember once when, after the Club Secretary refused to let the dance continue beyond 2 a.m., some stalwarts picked him up and put him out of the window, locking the doors before the band could escape. The members of the 'prisoner' band took it all in good part, and played even the most energetic enthusiasts of the then-popular Charleston to a standstill as dawn was breaking.

Then, too, there were the hunts. Always a rather timid horsewoman, I found the gallop flat out over the pig-hole pitted plains rather terrifying, and enjoyed my quiet rides round the farm much more. But what I really loved more than anything were the early morning shoots.

Dick and Isabel were both keen shots and very fond of going off early on a Sunday morning down to the Ewaso Nyiro River or Lewa Spring after guinea fowl, spur-fowl or partridge. The beauty of the mountain, with the sunrise glow on her snow-clad peak, is something I shall always remember, as well as the smell of wood-smoke mingling with the delicious cool of the morning as Mary and I scrambled the eggs for our breakfast, for that was our job. I loved the quiet of the bush, full of life and small sounds as it always was.

It was seldom that we were disturbed by other human beings during these early mornings, but on my first bird-shoot at Lewa Spring I was surprised by the sound of an approaching motor. It turned out to be a car and a lorry with a big crate on board, which to my astonishment housed a zebra. It was Mr Andrew Rattray, the well-known White Hunter (who was later to marry The Honourable Averill Furness), taking one of his Grevy's zebras to the train at Naro Moru en route for England. I believe he is one of the few, if not the only, man to have broken a Grevy's zebra to harness.

Before he sat down, Rattray looked in the bushes just behind us and said, "My dear girl, whoever left you and the child here as bait?" I told him that my cousins had left us to get breakfast ready while they went off bird shooting. Mr Rattray replied, "Oh, they did indeed," adding, "Well, you've had a damned lucky escape for I have just seen some fresh lion's spoor in the grass within a few yards of where you are sitting. But don't worry now for I am here, and I mean to stay and help you eat some of that delicious looking scrambled egg."

Perhaps today, when I know more about lions, I might not have been so calm.

About this time, after I had only been on the farm for a few weeks, Brian Shaw suddenly made his reappearance one Saturday to find me covered in posho, feeding Setter puppies. He had said goodbye to us in Nairobi, when our ways parted as he went off to the other side of the Colony to take up his new job at N'gongogeri, Lord Egerton's farm at Njoro. As I had not had one line since, I had decided that I must forget him as just another of these reputedly short-lived shipboard romances. But on that golden afternoon, I think I knew that ours was to be the exception that proved the rule. After a glorious weekend, he went back to Njoro – leaving me happy in the knowledge that he would return to spend Christmas with us. I trod on air through the intervening weeks.

On Christmas Eve Brian took me to a dance given by his stepsister, Miss Catherine Shaw, in Nanyuki. Catherine, who was considerably older than Brian, ran a small guest house in Nanyuki township. She was kind to me then, and remained one of my dearest friends until she died in 1949. This was my introduction to the Shaw Clan, en masse, which might have proved alarming except for the warm welcome I was given.

We, of course, had no idea that anyone knew we were in love, although it must have been fairly obvious, for Brian's youngest sister, Joyce, has told me since that when she met me for the first time, she knew I was the girl her brother was going to marry. Also, I believe that at that party, Brian's brother, Blair went up to Brian and said, "Have you asked her yet, for if you don't I will!" And on the way home in the small hours of the morning, he did, and I said yes, under a traditionally romantic moonlit sky, with the added Kenya background of a lion roaring.

We announced our engagement on Christmas morning, and received the blessings of our respective families. My uncle by marriage felt that standing in loco parentis he should make the usual enquiries into my fiancé's financial position, prospects, etc., but as the tiny bungalow did not possess a study and only one sitting-room, we all had to retire to bed early in order to leave the coast clear. As my uncle was an extremely wealthy man, Brian and I had 'great expectations' from this interview; but, alas, all that resulted from their two-hour session was, "Well, my boy, after you've made your first £10,000 the rest is simple."

In December, before the cables from Kenya had arrived, my parents had been mystified by receiving a studio portrait, from a Bournemouth studio, of a dark, good-looking young man, with no enclosed letter or clue as to his identity. But when they received the cable saying, "Am engaged to Brian Shaw everyone here delighted," they realised this must be the man I was to marry. But what has always puzzled me is how Brian could have been so sure my answer would be yes.

My aunt and uncle sailed for the United Kingdom shortly afterwards, having decided that although Kenya was a paradise for the young, it was a hell for the elderly.

After my engagement, life seemed to have a new purpose, and although we were not married for nearly six months, the days, full of delicious plans, flew by. We had agreed to wait in order to give Isabel time to make arrangements for little Mary to go to a kindergarten school and for my wedding dress and trousseau to be bought and sent out. For in those days the Kenya dress shops were very few and those there were, having a monopoly, were outrageously expensive. So my mother and sister were commissioned to buy my trousseau and wedding dress, which my sister actually designed.

After the excitement of Christmas, the household settled down to the normal daily routine once more and a very pleasant life it was. An early ride before breakfast, followed by housekeeping and usually some gardening, although the latter was rather disheartening because that year Nanyuki suffered one of the worst droughts ever known. Only 18 inches of rain fell in the year. I can remember planting a macrocarpa hedge, only to watch the poor little trees disappear down the cracks in the ground.

Thanks to Isabel's efforts, I learnt a lot about the duties of a farmer's wife. Although I could cook, I found it very difficult to learn to weigh out the exact quantities required for each pudding or cake. For petty pilfering is rife in Kenya and if one doesn't look after the store [larder], the grocery bill will be doubled. So every morning, the prudent housewife doles out the day's allowance of soap, blue, starch, tea, coffee, sugar and flour, while a close watch has to be kept on bread, butter, milk, drink and cigarettes. Although the major domo might be completely honest, and above petty pilfering, there was always the floating population of kitchen and pantry totos [young boys] who, working for a few shillings a month, considered any pickings which they came by as their legitimate perks.

I also taught my little cousin Mary, and though lessons only consisted of simple reading and writing, it all added up to a busy morning and it would be time for lunch before one could turn around. As our days began at 6 a.m., it was usual to have a siesta after lunch from 2 p.m. until our early tea at 4 o'clock. Afterwards Mary and I, accompanied by all the dogs, would go off for our walks, for this was playtime, and many's the house we built in the secret places of this wild and beautiful spot.

Sometimes we would fish the stream, which was well stocked with trout, or sometimes play tennis. Then there were the bi-weekly shopping expeditions to Nanyuki Township. Everything one bought had to be covered, or it would be ruined by clouds of dust raised by the cars from the unpaved dirt tracks which passed for streets. Add to this the week-end visits to the Club and other social activities – my cousins being a most hospitable and popular pair who entertained a good deal – and no wonder the months flew by.

Two months before we were married, Brian took a team of seventeen to Kitale to play in a rugger tournament over the long weekend. The

Agnes Cree and Brian Shaw in Nanyuki before their marriage.

games were hard fought and the celebrations that followed were equally tough going. Late on the Sunday night, two carloads were returning to Njoro when suddenly the second car almost ran into the back of the first, which was stationary without lights in the middle of the road. The driver, Ian Robson, got out and found all the occupants of the stationary car asleep. Arousing them from their slumbers, he enquired what was the matter and was told that there was no air in their tyres. However, on examination, the tyres appeared to be all right, and Ian told the sleepy occupants that there was plenty of air in their tyres, whereupon Brian replied that unfortunately it was the wrong kind of air.

But, alas, there was a more serious side to this weekend, for thirteen of the visiting team went down with malaria ten days later, and the unfortunate man who found my husband very ill and took him into hospital in Nakuru died himself of blackwater fever within two days, in the next bed to Brian.

During their visit, their host had never appeared as he too was ill in bed with malaria, although they did not know this until afterwards, nor were they warned to sleep under mosquito nets. Kitale, in the Twenties, was riddled with fever, but the settlers there would rather have died than admit that they were in a malarial district. If the local graveyard is anything to go by, quite a few of them did.

Later, the Government's anti-malarial gum planting drained the swamps and the malaria disappeared, but the tombstones in the Kitale Cemetery are a tragic reminder of what happened to some of those early settlers. They, poor things, certainly paid dearly for their refusal to face facts, and although luckily it did not cost Brian his life, it lost him his hair. For on leaving hospital he told Dr Tennant that he must get the malarial bugs out of his blood, as he was going to be married in a month's time. The doctor prescribed an arsenical tonic, which killed the bugs but nearly killed Brian as well.

When he came up to Nanyuki for a weekend after a fortnight's treatment, he was obviously suffering from arsenic poisoning, for although he had a voracious appetite, eating was followed by intense vomiting. I made him stop taking the tonic and he gradually recovered, but what was our horror and dismay when, after three months of married life, all his hair fell out and his nails came off, leaving him completely bald. It was not until some years later that we realised that Brian's loss of hair was the direct result of that tonic, although being an ardent reader of detective fiction I should have known, especially when his nails came off. And Dr Tennant might never have known, had he not once again prescribed a similar tonic, which Brian flatly refused to take.

An open-backed car in Nanyuki.

We had chosen my father's birthday and my parents' wedding anniversary, June 27th, to be our wedding day as, alas, they could not be with us in person, though I knew they would be in spirit. It was sad for them, especially for my mother, as all their three children married abroad, my brother and I in Kenya and my sister in Hong Kong, and they were not able to attend any of our weddings. A great sorrow to me too, for although my mother paid us a number of visits and lived with us for the last twenty years of her life, I never saw my father again, nor did he know Brian or ever see his grandchildren, for he died before we managed to get home on leave.

Dick Phillips was a great stickler for etiquette, and when I asked what dress would be correct for Brian and the Best Man to wear, I was told a morning coat. So I wrote to Brian to that effect and received a wire from the Best Man, Ronnie Lane, saying, "Received dreadful ultimatum, spent sleepless night, am going Nairobi to borrow Governor's." The situation was saved though, when the week before our wedding, Lord Delamere, the leader of the European community, was married in a lounge suit.

As there was no church in Nanyuki, we decided to be married in the tiny guesthouse, but first it had to be inspected by the Bishop, whose permission must be gained. A special Governor's Licence had to be obtained and, as well as this, Brian and I had to appear three weeks before the actual wedding in front of the District Commissioner, thirty miles distant in Nyeri. So Brian came the one hundred miles from Njoro and we dutifully presented ourselves at the District Commissioner's office on a Saturday morning.

The District Commissioner, a tall, broad-shouldered man, well over six feet, wore a monocle in one eye, while his wife, half his height, wore another. He was known as 'Long John' Llewellyn or 'Long Lou' and was a popular figure amongst the Somalis and the tribes of the Northern Frontier District, where he had spent many years.

Long Lou was obviously not very well versed in the duties of a Registry Office and from the number of times the Book of Instructions was consulted, I decided that we were the first couple he had ever married. He made Brian solemnly swear he had not been married by Native Custom, or any other method, only to discover that as I was the one who was the resident in his parish, it was I who should have done the swearing, so we had to start all over again. This was necessary because Nanyuki had no church, so there was no way in which our banns could be called, and yet we had to show "that there was no just cause or impediment."

From that moment, apparently, we were legally man and wife, but in spite of all the swearing we did not feel the knot was well and truly tied. So after an excellent lunch, Brian took me back to my cousins' in Nanyuki and went off sadly himself to Njoro, returning three weeks later on June 26th for the proper ceremony.

Shortly after our engagement Dick Phillips had announced at a party given in their house that now everyone must remember I was an Engaged Girl, and that he and he alone, as my cousin, standing in 'Loco Fiancé,' had special privileges.

In immediate to response to this, Cheese Wilson formed the 'Cousins Club' and then elected himself President. The Club, whose sole object was "cousinly behaviour rewarded by privilege," was only in existence for less than six months, for 'the cousins' gave a dance for me at the Phillips' house the night before my wedding, at which time the Club was formally disbanded by the President. A wonderful dance, but one which nearly proved disastrous when the huge bonfire built on the roundabout to give the Cousins Club a decent burial endangered the surrounding cars.

At last the great day dawned, sunny and warm, though all I can remember is that everyone worked unceasingly – cooking, laying out our lovely presents and banking the converted guest-house-cum-chapel with flowers, as well as making the bouquets for the bride and my tiny bridesmaid. That morning, the padre who was to officiate called to reassure me, saying, "Don't be afraid for I am used to marrying the highly nervous." But he need not have worried, for I was so tired that after lunch I went to rest and slept to within half an hour of our wedding.

On being awakened I dressed Mary first, sitting her on the bed, where this old-fashioned little girl of four made a charming picture in her full-skirted white organdie dress, with its blue sash and crown of tiny pink and blue flowers and matching Victorian bouquet. As I was putting the finishing touches to my veil, Mary said, "Agnes, you are beautiful, but I think that I look rather sweet, too?" which, bless her, she certainly did.

She was a very self-possessed little girl, but I think she had grown fond of me, as I had of her, during our six months of constant companionship, for we even shared a bedroom. When I told her that I was leaving after my marriage, she said in a sad little voice, "Why must you go to look after Brian and leave me?" adding, "I suppose it is because he can't look after himself, while I can." Out of the mouths of babes!

In all the preparations there were only two disasters. One was that my beautiful undies, hand-worked by Vladimir's sister in Monte Carlo, were stolen in the post, and the other that the bottom half of my three-tiered wedding cake, a triumph of confectioner's art from Galbraith of Ayr, Scotland, was destroyed by Customs, who cut it open searching for opium owing to the fact that a month previously a cake had been used as a vehicle for the smuggling of drugs.

Brian and I both enjoyed our wedding and reception in the garden backed by our beautiful mountain. Here under the shade of the great cedar tree, we cut our cake and received the congratulations of family and friends, with my faithful companion, Buller the bull terrier, sitting on my veil.

Agnes and Brian on their wedding day 27th June 1928.

So ended for me six very happy months under my cousin's roof and began for us what has proved a long life of mutual trust, love, and respect, the only basis for true wedded happiness.

CHAPTER 3

From Coastal Idyll to Nakuru Rugby

*"Serene will be our days and bright,
and happy will our Nature be,
When Love is an unerring Light,
And joy its own security."*
--William Wordsworth

We were married at 4 p.m., but it was 6 o'clock before we left in Brian's open Chevrolet box body for Nyeri, and dark by the time we arrived at the Outspan Hotel. The hotel, considered very modern and up-to-date, was built by Major Sherbrooke Walker and Lady Betty Walker, who kindly lent us their private cottage for our first night.

We had a sitting-room, bedroom, bathroom, and veranda, with a wonderful view of Mt. Kenya. There was also a most intriguing fireplace, which by pulling a lever could be in either the sitting-room or the bedroom. This fascinated Brian so much so that we nearly missed our dinner. At 9 p.m. a message was sent across saying that the dining-room was closing. So at five minutes past nine, we self-consciously entered the large dining-room, hoping that at least by our lateness we would avoid the other diners.

Imagine our dismay, however, when an all-male party including Long Lou, who had married us three weeks previously; the bank manager, Sidney Parker; and Rex Johnson, a well-known coffee planter, all dining at a nearby table, stood up and raised their glasses to us in a silent toast.

Next morning, we travelled to Nairobi by the old Fort Hall Road, which wound through the patchy cultivation of the Kikuyu Reserve to Kiambu, one of the best coffee-growing areas in Kenya. Here, our Best Man, Ronnie Lane, was managing Kiora, the estate belonging to the CV Whites, and lent us his house for the night.

After the wedding, Ronnie, with great tact, had stayed on in Nanyuki, so we had the whole of the enormous house and garden to ourselves, except for a well-trained staff of servants including a Goan cook, who produced the most superb dinner complete with a wonderful confection of ice-cream, spun sugar and petit fours. As we never saw another European, we imagine that the Whites must have been on overseas leave.

After a leisurely morning in this delightful spot, we caught the 4 o'clock train for Mombasa, to spend the rest of our honeymoon at the Tudor House Hotel.

We arrived in Mombasa on a Saturday morning and decided we would go to early service in the Cathedral next day. As we were dressing, Brian said to me, "Hurry up, for there is just one thing I don't like and that is being late for Church." So we set off, as we thought in plenty of time, for the 7 o'clock service, only to be greeted as we walked into the Cathedral by the final blessing. Summer Time had been introduced that day and all clocks had been put forward by one hour. The padre, realising what had happened and seeing that we were young and rather upset, took the service again just for us. Perhaps we had 'newly-wed' written all over us and, seeing our disappointment, he may have guessed that it was our first Communion together. I often wonder who he was and hope he knows how grateful we were.

For us, time had little meaning. Brian had hired a most luxurious Buick car, and day after day we went off with our gramophone, picnic basket and bathing suits, exploring the many lovely beaches which lie to north and south.

We spent our days in this tropical Eden, lying in the shade of the great coconut palms. The hours passing unheeded as we watched the busy little crabs scurrying about on the dazzling white sand and were lulled into timelessness by the lapping of the tranquil sea, its translucent water shading from palest turquoise to the deepest of emerald greens. For lunch we bought fish from the African fishermen as they came ashore with their catch in their outrigger canoes. Combine freshly caught and grilled fish, fresh baked bread, butter and mangoes, and you had a meal fit for a king. So it happened that one day we did not notice how the hours had slipped by, and suddenly realised that we had to do fifty miles in as many minutes if we were to catch the last ferry at 6 p.m. back to Mombasa Island. Brian drove the Buick along the narrow sandy track like the wind. Neither of us relished the idea of a night on the mainland, which was a paradise by day but a mosquito-infested hell by night.

When Brian hired the car he did not realise that a tiny Arab boy was part of the bargain, but every evening when we came back he appeared as if by magic to wash and polish the precious Buick. We called him 'the genie of the car.'

Some days we spent in Mombasa in the shops, full of beautiful and tempting things: ivory carvings, brooches, beads and bangles, beautifully embroidered Indian saris, lovely Chinese silk – in fact all manner of fascinating Eastern goods. As well, there were plenty of African wood carvings, leather beadwork, and skins of all kinds, from the handsome black-and-white colobus monkey to the soft silky pelts of the dik-dik. I fell in love with these and Brian gave me enough to make a coat. The finished garment was beautiful and I enjoyed wearing it for many years. Finally, what was left of it made a delightful little shoulder cape and muff for my eighteen-year-old daughter.

Had I known then that these charming little creatures, whom one almost always sees in pairs, are so faithful that if they lose their partner in life they never mate again, I should not have felt so happy about the 180 skins it took to make my coat.

In those days Brian had a delightful Bunyoro boy as a personal servant; the boy did everything for him, and being completely trustworthy, was even keeper of the family purse. As well as washing and ironing all our clothes, he kept us supplied with delicious mangoes and other fruits for our early tea. But he had not adjusted himself to the arrival of a memsahib and when we went to our banda the first night in Mombasa, I found Brian's clothes filling all the drawers, while mine still lay unpacked in my suitcase. Unfortunately, having married an expensive wife, Brian could not afford both, and he had to forego the efficient service of this well-trained servant for the inefficiency of an untrained wife.

During that blissful fortnight, we spent money like water and enjoyed every minute. Their memory has remained evergreen throughout the years of our lives together.

Brian, the seventh in a family of twelve, had come to Kenya in 1920 and, with two brothers and an Australian brother-in-law, had started the family farm, Lamuria. The farm was twenty-six miles north of Nyeri. It had been father Shaw's ambition, since the early days of the century, to take his large family overseas, to settle and farm in the great open tracts of the Empire. With the support of his family, he went to London to draw Land Reference Numbers from a bag. He was allowed to draw out three numbers, thus getting a choice of the farm offered. There was little information to be had, so he based his choice on what looked like a good-sized river. He drew, in all, 3,600 acres.

After a few years, the family started a creamery. Their cream,

The Shaw family before they emigrated from England to Kenya. Brian is on the top right.

together with the cream from the surrounding farms, was turned into butter. This was marketed in Nairobi, a chancy business as regards payment. Later, the famous 'Lamuria Cheese' (a type of cheddar) was made, originally from a formula in Mrs Beaton's cookery book. It was soon sold all over East Africa.

In addition to shorthorn grade cattle and merino sheep, they kept a large herd of pigs. To reach the bacon factory at Uplands, the baconers were first driven into Nyeri, a distance of some twenty-six miles, on their feet, followed by a further forty-five miles through the forests over the ten-thousand-feet high Aberdare Mountains, down to the railhead at Naivasha. There they were trucked, and went the last thirty miles by train to the bacon factory. The trip took over twelve days, but did not seem to harm the baconers, for the exercise tended to harden the pig's fat, which from a diet of maize and skimmed milk tended to be soft-setting. At any rate, Uplands seemed to like the pigs and always demanded more. Later, a bacon factory was built on the higher reaches of the farm, but elephant proved a nuisance, smashing up the water supply and damaging the factory buildings.

As Lamuria was under-capitalised, it was necessary for some of the Shaw brothers to go out to work as farm managers, so after my husband had built a large cedar frame house for his parents, he left to find a job. Meanwhile, Lamuria was run by Gladys Mathias and her husband, Walter Mathias, assisted by the two youngest brothers, Ridley and St. John. Walter had served with the Australian Forces in Flanders, and during the war had been gassed and wounded several times, being awarded the Military Medal for bravery. Gladys and Walter met while she was nursing at Addenbrooke's Hospital in Cambridge. After the war, he followed the family out to Kenya, where he and Gladys were married in November 1920. His lungs gave him endless trouble, while a piece of ivory did duty in his arm for a bone. Poor Walter suffered a great deal, although no one but his wife would have known, for he had a quick mind and lively imagination, was full of fun, and beloved by all. It was to Walter that the success of Lamuria was largely due, and it is fitting that when he died in the middle 1930s, he was buried on the farm he loved and had done so much to build.

For the first two years after we were married, we joined the large Christmas family gathering at Lamuria. The house, although large, was so full at Christmas time that the only way we could be housed was for all the visiting wives to sleep together in the two big bedrooms, while the brothers took over the Manager's house. More fun, perhaps, for the brothers, who were free to go off shooting and fishing, while their wives were tied to the house by babies and baking. The Shaws were a very united family and Walter Mathias was the life and soul of these Christmas parties.

Although Brian always intended to farm on his own, he felt it wise to gain experience by managing for some years. He initially found a job as Manager for Major WAC Conduit, and started work in January

Lamuria, the Shaw family house in the Nanyuki area.

1923. The Conduits had bought Equator Farm, part of Lord Delamere's original holding.

Both WAC and Lady Viola, daughter of the Earl of Shrewsbury, were experts with horses and kept a large stable where polo ponies were trained. For this purpose, they employed an Indian ex-Cavalry man from the Viceroy's bodyguard named Shere (tiger) Khan. There were over seventy horses in their stable and WAC rode around the farm on a large grey gelding named Castor. His wife rode a mare called My Dear. Both horses were well-known on the polo field.

While my husband was there, he supervised the building of their large cedar house, little thinking that one day after it was sold and became a preparatory boarding school, his own daughter would go there.

The farm was under a large acreage of flax, 700 acres of wattle, and many hundred acres of maize, and also had a small planted acreage of coffee. To decorticate the flax they had a scutching mill, and many were the prizes won by their flax exhibits at the Nakuru Agricultural Shows.

The farm backed onto the forest; in fact part of it was uncleared forest land, where the Kikuyu squatters who made up most of the farm labour lived. The Kikuyu are a forest people, but even so they lived in fear of the small herd of buffalo which shared this part of the farm with them.

Brian left the Conduits to go on overseas leave. On returning to Kenya, he took a temporary job for just over a year managing N'gongogeri, the neighbouring estate of Lord Egerton of Tatton. While there, he was amused to receive a visit from his successor on Equator Farm, asking him if he could tell him where the coffee (over 200 acres) was, as he couldn't find it. He could not very well go to his employer and admit that he could not find the coffee!

At first Brian was given the Manager's house, a miserable little shack where the bathroom was only a partitioned-off portion of the veranda, possessing no door. But on returning from our honeymoon, we moved into the big house, as 'Egetat' was in Great Britain and was not due back until early in the new year. This was a long barn-like building, ugly and badly planned, but a perfect palace compared with the Manager's bungalow.

It was decided that during Lord Egerton's annual visits to his estates in Kenya he should live at N'gongogeri, and so the wife of his then-general manager was entrusted with the task of redecorating the house. In an attempt to brighten the rather dreary, green-painted sitting room, Doreen Wright had turned to colour, providing curtains of a cotton material with a design of vivid multi-coloured stripes on a black background. This produced an effect that was more garish than gay. The story goes that Lord Egerton's first reaction was one of horror, which he expressed rather forcibly, much to his decorator's dismay. Expecting expressions of surprise and pleasure, she had hidden herself behind the stripe-covered sofa and now did not dare to emerge.

We wished that Doreen had spent less on colour and more on comfort, for the beds were grim, especially the one in the main bedroom. It was a black iron, brass-knobbed bedstead, of what was known as three-quarter size, which means in fact that it was too big for a single bed, yet not big enough for a double bed. In the place of springs were plaited iron slats, many of which were missing. It was second-hand, and the previous owner must have been a very heavy man, who through his habit of sleeping in the centre had formed a deep groove. This meant that every night we each clung to our edge trying not to be the first to lose consciousness and roll into the centre.

It is, in these days of modern stoves, difficult to imagine the appalling conditions in the kitchen imposed by those early wood-fired stoves, which belched smoke from every pore, and whose temperature was directly dependent on the dampness of the kuni (firewood) used. Keen to show off my culinary skill, I often tried to make cakes to grace our tea table. Alas, lunchtime usually found me with weeping, red-rimmed eyes, gazing at the ruin of all my morning's work. For just when a slow steady heat was required, the wood flared up and your cake rose to a tremendous height, only to fall equally flat when the wood burned out. My 'by the book' cookery told me to weigh joints, giving them twenty minutes to the pound and twenty minutes over, but, again, all my timing would be upset by damp wood and we would have to lunch off the inevitable scrambled egg, as our roast was not nearly done.

The Kenyan *mpishi* (cook), well versed in the vagaries of these stoves, evolved a fool proof, or possibly a fireproof, method. The experienced African cook stokes his Dover until it roars like a furnace, and rapidly cooks his joint before the fire dies, so your roast and two veg are all ready by 11 a.m., from which time on they sit on the shelf above the stove until Bwana calls for *chakula* (food). In this way the cook, who is probably the houseboy as well, is never caught out. Should his unpredictable bachelor employer return early or late, food will always be ready.

My memory of those early days is of men, men, men! My husband resumed his bachelor life with me attached, so my social life was a round of Rugger 'dos' and dances, with an aftermath of bars and banjo.

All great fun, though not so easy when one is expecting a baby, for car trips over rough roads and meals at all hours are not the best recipe for pregnancy. Neither of us realised what was wrong with me when I first began to feel sick. Brian diagnosed liver problems and prescribed an active game of tennis at the Club. However, this did not seem to cure my trouble and, after a little, the cause dawned on us and from thenceforth, a box of digestive biscuits, kept in the car, was my lifesaver.

At that time Brian's first love was the Goddess Sport, although she was a hard task mistress. As she demanded a high standard of fitness, every night before dinner Brian set off in singlet and shorts to run his training two miles. At the time of our marriage, he was captain of the Nakuru rugger team and that year, under his captaincy, the team was all victorious.

A typical weekend programme would be a rugger match on Saturday afternoon, followed by a rugger dinner and dance. Sunday morning, as a cure for any stiffness or hangover, a hard game of men's singles on the tennis courts at the Rift Valley Sports Club, and after lunch we would leap into our old box body Chevrolet and tear the twenty-seven miles to Gilgil, where Brian would take part in that murderous game, mixed hockey.

Brian should have married one of those tough hockey-playing girls from Roedean. I with my plump figure was definitely not that type, and here I was married into a family of sporting Shaws. All Brian's brothers were good athletes, excelling as runners, while his sisters had all played hockey for their school, if not their county. How out of place I was, although my delightful brother-in-law, Walter Mathias, said, "If farming fails, the Shaw brothers could make their fortune as a team of acrobats and I would do as the lady in pink tights who introduces the act."

I was supposed to fit into the masculine regime and play my part by sitting on the touch-line every Saturday and shouting, "Feet, feet, feet, Nakuru," or hooting the car-horn when the team scored a Try. When after a month of this I rather plaintively asked, "When do I play tennis?", Brian answered in surprised tones, "But I thought you would like to watch me play games; my sisters do."

The rugger matches were played on the Nakuru Athletic Club ground and, after a session in the bar, where the players either celebrated victory or drowned their sorrows, Brian and I would repair behind the Rift Valley Club, where by the light of a torch he would practice his speech for the Rugger Dinner. John Stanning sometimes refereed and his attractive and charming wife known as 'Vi Darling' (her maiden name) would act as mother to all the young rugger wives, inviting us all to dine with her at the Club whenever we lost our husbands to a Rugger Dinner.

The hardness of the sun-baked grounds made rugger a very dangerous game, for a tackle could result in a serious injury, and often my bandaged guests on a Sunday morning made our home look more like a hospital than a house party.

Strangely enough, in those days, even in Kenya, women were not encouraged in bars, and I can remember many hours of waiting outside after the rugger matches were over. I could have been bored and lonely if it had not been for Brian's pals who were so charming to me and kept me entertained.

Their Captain was one of the first of the Nakuru Rugger Team to acquire a wife, though this was soon remedied by an influx of girls from the United Kingdom. Amongst these was an attractive girl called Margot who had come out on the boat with us and caused me certain qualms. For on one or two occasions, when I was returning from spending the morning with a female friend, I would pass Margot in a large Lancia car just leaving N'gongogeri after presumably lunching with Brian.

Many were the tales of Margot and her Lancia, for she was the enterprising young lady who, on the occasion of the visit of Edward, Prince of Wales, offered to drive the Prince home after a dance at Muthaiga Club. The Prince accepted, for she was a most attractive girl, but when the car unaccountably broke down, the story goes that Edward P got out and, putting up his umbrella, walked back to Government House in the rain, rather ungallantly leaving his chauffeuse in tears. That visit, in the autumn of 1928 to open the Agricultural Show, was a big event which brought the settlers down from their farms by the hundreds.

I must admit that I don't remember much about the Show as such, for I was more interested in the occasion as a social event, even though it proved to be a disastrous one for me, which I have always remembered with a sense of shame. The day was hot and sunny and by lunchtime, having walked miles over the rough ground, I was very tired. So when we discovered that we had lost our party, who had all gone back to Muthaiga Club for lunch, leaving us car-less and stranded, I was very near to tears. At that moment, up came a tall, good-looking man whom Brian introduced as Captain Hugh Barclay. Hugh in his kindly way offered to drive me anywhere, but by then nothing Hugh or Brian suggested pleased me and to make matters worse, the heavens suddenly opened and without warning down came a heavy shower.

With great ingenuity I had refurbished my mud-bespattered peach silk parasol, dyeing it with the best Stephen's blue/black, but alas, while all right as a parasol, it was a complete failure as an umbrella, for instead of keeping off the rain, it rained ink! Covered with ink, confusion and shame I fled. Every time I met Hugh Barclay for many years afterwards, I was to remember my bad-temper and this humiliating experience. However, rest and the resilience of youth worked wonders and by evening I had recovered my usual good temper. Dressed in my simple three-quarter length white satin wedding dress, I thoroughly enjoyed our dinner, followed by a dance at Muthaiga Club.

It was my first of many lovely evenings there, for the Muthaiga dances resemble the Hunt Balls of the United Kingdom more than any others, having the same quality of friendly informality. The Muthaiga dance in 1928 was memorable for the presence of the Prince of Wales, as the guest of Lord and Lady Delamere, and also because of the scandal caused by a certain lady escaping her Lord. The aftermath of the latter was a request from the highest quarter next morning that the said Lady with her escort should leave the Colony immediately. Which goes to show that, contrary to popular belief, Kenya's Happy Valley days were over, and that as far back as 1928 there were the first signs of the existence of public opinion, the only real guardian of the moral rectitude of any country.

Like many a young wife starting out not only in a new district but in a new country, I was homesick and missed my mother and family more at this period of my life than at any other. There were not many young wives nearby and I was too shy to ask advice from older women whom I hardly knew. My cousin in Nanyuki and I had always been very close, for although Isabel was six years my senior, wherever she led I used to follow, and we had been through many childish escapades together. But now she was on the other side of the Colony.

Fortunately, I made a true friend in Kay Morton, who was later to marry Len Spiers, a forceful, sandy-haired Scot with a shrewd business brain and a tough exterior which hid the kindest of hearts. We were introduced by Dick Phillips, who spent his first year in Kenya at the Conduits, Brian's first employer. Kay was a great friend of Brian's, too, and indeed it was with her that I stayed when I came over with Brian's brother Blair to visit Brian during my engagement. This was to be the first of many visits I and my family spent under Kay's hospitable roof, and the beginning of a long and enduring friendship.

The 'other' Kay whose friendship meant a great deal to me, especially in my middle years, was Brian's stepsister Catherine. Our friendship was born when I stayed with her in her guest house the night before my wedding. Dear Catherine, so understanding and so wise, it was to her that I confided all my hopes and fears, and throughout those early years she was my Mother Confessor. It was she who was the first person to suggest to me that I should enter Legislative Council. Alas, she never knew I had taken her advice in 1951, for she died of cancer in 1949, dying bravely as she had lived, with thoughts only for others.

The two Njoro bachelors who came most frequently to our house were Rex Schofield and Hugh Coltart, both charming men and a very popular pair. Hugh, with a natural and ready wit, was the greatest fun, and although very deaf even as a younger man, he rose above this handicap in the most splendid way. Lord Egerton's home farm was run for many years by Hugh, and after Sandy Wright's retirement he became Bwana Lordy's right-hand man.

Out of gratitude, Lord Egerton, when he died, left him all his Kenya estate, which I believe consisted of a large parcel of land, an equally large overdraft, and a castle at Njoro which he had built for himself but seldom occupied. For of all his ventures, and many foreign investments, Lord Egerton used to say that "the only one which really paid was a small shop in Vancouver, run by a Chinese." Perhaps this was because Lord Egerton, himself a bachelor, was more of a philanthropist than a businessman or practical farmer, his especial interest being the training and welfare of young men. The Egerton Agricultural College, founded as a Memorial to him and now thrown open to young farmers of all races, bears witness to this.

I cannot leave Njoro without a mention of a few well-known settlers, for instance, General and Mrs Colville, an elderly couple with an old-world charm and graciousness of manner of a bygone age. Then there were Major Jocelyn and the Hon Mrs Nellie Grant, Elspeth Huxley's parents, who had by then moved from Thika, buying one of the pipeline farms and building their thatch-roofed bungalow in the forest behind Njoro. Nellie Grant, a very gallant lady, lived alone there in retirement until 1962, surrounded by dachshunds, if such a questing spirit as hers can ever be said to retire.

Another couple of stalwart women who come to mind when thinking of Njoro in the 1920s were Mrs Naithsmith-Jones and Mrs Morton, Kay's mother, who lived with Kay until 1929 when Kay married Len Spiers. Kay, who was an accomplished horsewoman and knowledgeable trainer, had bought the land for her stable while Len built the house, and they both lived there while Mrs Morton acted as duenna. Then they married and so was born the partnership out of which was to grow one of Kenya's most successful racing stables.

Another colourful Kenya personality of those days was Captain

Edward Caswell Long, known as 'Boy,' a tall good-looking man, who lived the life of a cowboy and saw no reason why he should not dress the part. He was often to be seen in Nakuru in his ten-gallon sombrero, a brightly coloured Somali shawl sitting over his shoulders. He spent long hours in the saddle, often dossing down for the night outside a thorn sheep boma. He spoke fluent Maasai and they regarded him as their friend.

To watch Boy Long counting a mob of hundreds of grade sheep on the open plains was a fascinating sight. The count was done with the aid of ten sticks, and the sheep were made to run between Boy and a Maasai herder posted some twenty feet in front of him, with three other assistants: one to drive the sheep forward, one to corral the counted sheep, and one at his side to see that none went behind him. The speed with which the operation was carried out was remarkable.

Then would follow a most amusing conversation. If the count was short the herder would attempt to make excuses, and after some time Boy Long would turn to him and say, "Tell me the truth: did this animal die because it was sick, or because you ate it for your supper?"

No account of the 1920s in Kenya would be complete without further mention of Lord Delamere, that pioneer statesman who had blazed the trail for white settlement early in the 1900s. Delamere, when I first came to Kenya, was a middle-aged man of some 57 years, but although his head was almost bald, his eyes were still as piercingly blue as they had been when he was a young man. Also, he was still hasty of temper – impatient of fools – but possessed of great charm of manner. As long as he lived, he was the undoubted leader of the Kenya Europeans, though by then regarded as an elder statesman.

Three weeks after we returned from our honeymoon, we went to Nairobi to play rugger against the Nairobi Nondescripts, staying with our Best Man, Ronnie Lane, then a bachelor, and I acting as chaperone to an engaged couple. The matches were usually played after tea when it was cooler, and were invariably followed by a session in the bar, so by the time everyone had bathed and changed it would be very late and we rarely dined before 9 p.m.

On this occasion we did not arrive at the Norfolk Hotel until after that hour, when the dining-room was quite empty except for Harry Watts, an old Kenya character who was sitting with a crony at a table on the other side of the large room. They may or may not have dined, but there was no doubt that they had wined extremely well, and every few minutes they would thump the table and shout in furious tones, "Down with Delamere." What 'D' had done to them we never discovered, but they insisted we support them and, as they were very belligerent, we responded each time with choruses of, "Hear, hear." This seemed to satisfy the old boys and so we were left to finish our dinner in peace.

In January our carefree six months at Njoro came to an end and Brian, having packed our goods and chattels, went off to the farm he had bought in Sotik. He was to come back to fetch me later, so I stayed with my friends Dick and Delphie Guthrie.

Before starting my new life in Sotik I had a most restful three weeks with this charming pair in their comfortable house, which was just as well. For "that was pioneering, that was," and a far cry from the fun of rocketing around attached to a rugger team. Nor, perhaps, was my delightful life at Njoro the best preparation for what was to come. But I was not to know that and on that bright January morning in 1929, I went off with Brian full of excitement and high hopes.

CHAPTER 4

First Years on the Farm

*"If you have built castles in the air
Your work need not be lost.
That is where they should be,
Now put the foundations under them."*
--Henry David Thoreau

Sotik, where is it?

That is what I was about to discover, although the question was not asked in Kenya's only daily paper until 1934, nor adequately answered until two years later by the publication of Sotik's first brochure. Even as late as 1948, Peter Hill, one of the most successful of the post-war farmers, writing in the *East African Standard*, headed his article, "Sotik – A Remote but Prosperous District in the White Highlands."

By 1948, the 135,000 acres of bush which comprised Sotik in 1902 had become a flourishing district, with well-planned and laid-out farms where high-grade cattle grazed in fenced and cleared paddocks. Many acres were under maize and fodder crops. The coffee *shambas* [farms]

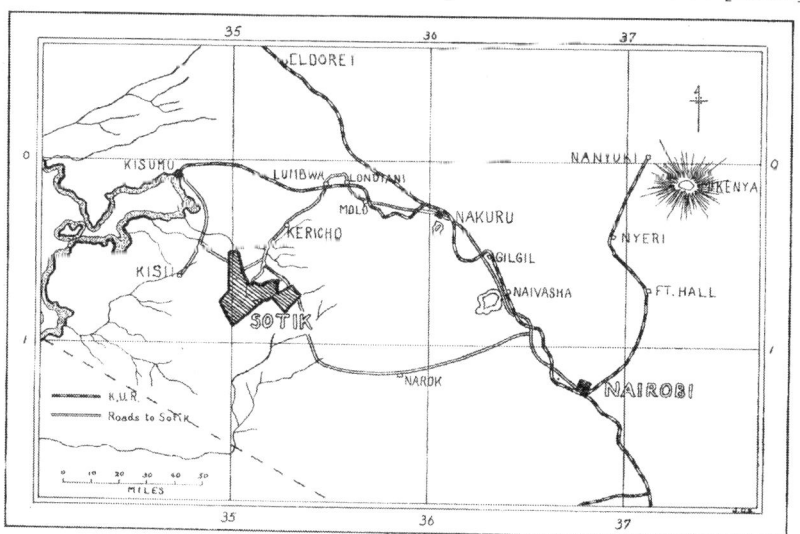

A map of the Sotik settled area, that appeared in the booklet issued by the Sotik Settlers' Association in 1936.

of the 1920s had mostly gone, replaced by grasslands, for with the control of the dreaded East Coast Fever by regular dipping, dairying had become the district's main industry. Tea was first planted by WG Dawson about 1935, and although he proved that it could be grown successfully, it was not until 1941 that Brooke Bond bought the N'goina Estate and established the first plantation in North Sotik.

But all that was in the future. To quote from that 1948 article by Peter Hill, he began with a question: "On looking at the map one wonders just why Sotik was ever included in the White Highlands at all, for lying as it does south of Kisumu, and due east of Lake Victoria, it is an isolated block apart from the main European Settled Area."

The answer was conflict. The Sotik district was a Y-shaped strip of land some fifty miles long and in some places not more than three miles wide, carved out of the African Land Units as a buffer state to keep apart four warring groups: the Kipsigis, Kisii, Maasai and Luo. Government hoped that the advent of the Europeans and the establishment of farms in this buffer state would prove of benefit as a civilising influence, which in time it certainly did, although the immediate result was that the farms became a battleground, and the scene of many raids.

Brian had first visited Sotik in 1927 to look for a farm, with the intention of going in for coffee. It was an area of good rainfall, and coffee seemed to do well. As it was 60 miles from a railhead, the land was reasonably priced, and there was a fair chance of the railway being extended through Sotik towards Kisii and Lake Victoria in the foreseeable future. The road south to Sotik from the railway station at Lumbwa was 60 miles of earth track, which was fair travelling in fine weather but sheer hell when it was wet. It led through the Kericho district, a region of very heavy rainfall which extends as far as the Mau Forest. The larger tea companies, Brooke Bond and James Finlay, were developing Kericho fast, so it was no wonder that this earth track could not stand up to all the heavy traffic in the rains but collapsed and turned into a veritable slough of despond.

After a second visit, my husband found a piece of land he liked at the southern end of a 5,000-acre farm, for which the owner wanted £5 an acre. Brian only had £3,000 with which to purchase land, and he spent the whole morning sitting on the top of Kipkebe Hill, mapping out the acreage he wished to buy to fit his financial cloth. Having made his decision, he offered the owner £3,000 for that piece of land, no matter what the acreage proved to be, although he thought it was approximately 1,000 acres. After much hesitation, the offer was accepted on that basis. Two years later when a survey was done, the acreage turned out to be slightly over 1,300 acres. Although under no obligation to do so under the terms of the agreement, my husband paid out a further £500 for the land in the interest of good neighbourliness.

On my first visit to Sotik in September 1928, we could not drive onto the farm but had to leave our car at the boundary, walking the rest of the way through the tall grass, for there was no road. I remember trudging over the uneven ground of the low-lying vleiland, up the gentle slope, until we reached the plateau which made up the floor of the larger of the two valleys. There we were met by Kipsigis men, bearing gifts of chicken and eggs.

To me, unused to the ways of Africans, this welcome was strangely touching, and throughout the years I have never failed to be amazed at the generous way Africans give of the little they have. I realise now that they were men who were already squatting with their families on the 1,300 acres we had bought, and so, hoping they could remain, it was in their interests to placate the new owners. But whatever the motive, it was a kindly gesture, and since that day I have liked and trusted the Kipsigis, who were our friends and neighbours for many years.

I was delighted when, years later at a cocktail party given in Kericho by the District Commissioner, the General Manager of the Standard Bank asked me, "Mrs Shaw, do you know Senior Chief arap Tengecha?" I replied, "Yes, indeed, I am an old friend of arap Tengecha's." But the Chief corrected me with a charming smile, saying in Swahili, "Mrs Shaw is not my friend but my brother."

Our task that September day so long ago was to choose the site for our house. This was not easy, for in some places the grass was over our heads, which made it difficult to see what the land was like. It would have been unwise to choose a low-lying site because of the danger of malaria, but it was equally foolish to go too far up the hillside, knowing that we should have to cart all our water from the stream below.

At last a site was chosen and pegged out, and it has proved to have been an excellent choice; the bungalow we built there, a long low house with a thatched roof, a cross between an African hut and a Devonshire cottage, nestled under the protection of Kipkebe Hill. How many of our countless visitors told us on arrival that it was the prettiest house they had seen in Kenya, and someone once said in an article that of all Kenya homes, it was the only one which looked as if it really belonged and was happy in its setting.

The house sits on a little raised terrace of lawn, supported by a dry stone wall, edged with gay herbaceous borders. The same flagstones have been used to make the wide steps and path leading between standard roses to the open veranda which does duty for the front entrance. From

The house Brian and Agnes built at their Kipkebe farm in Sotik.

there you look over brightly coloured flower beds to the cool green lawns below, now edged with great trees of our own planting.

Where once under the glare of the relentless mid-day sun we chose our site, now beautiful jacarandas, Nandi flames, tall graceful gums, and the stately cypress cast their shade. The rough grass has given way to velvet lawns, bounded by the gorgeous colours of bougainvilleas and other tropical shrubs. No one can ever know how much love and care went into the making of that garden, nor how much homesickness lies buried there. And if the house could talk, what tales it could tell, for it has seen a lifetime of happenings.

Within its sheltering walls, one baby was born, six were christened, and four young couples 'plighted their troth,' while in the garden, beneath the bridal bower, four brides have stood beside their grooms and a fireworks display was staged to celebrate an eightieth birthday. The house has also been the scene of countless church services, dances, political meetings, fund-raising garden fetes and tennis tourneys, and of one serious operation when life and death hung in the balance. Kipkebe was occupied by our family, after it was built in 1929, for 36 years.

To skip briefly to the end of my story, the Sunday before we left in 1960 to move to our new home at Langata, near Nairobi, I was in the garden with my little grand-daughter, aged four years, and I said to her, "You know, Tisha, tomorrow granny and grand-daddy are leaving, and this won't be granny's garden any more, but your mummy's."

Another view of the Shaws' house at Kipkebe.

The little girl ran up the lawn, and when I called out to her, "Where are you going?", the answer came back, "To tell mummy the good news!" So there was no sadness in our going, for we went in the knowledge that the old garden would ring with the happy laughter of our grandchildren, at least for some years to come.

This is continuity in this fast changing world, and whatever fate may befall the old house and garden in the future, Kipkebe has fulfilled its purpose of providing the safe security of a happy home for four generations - and that is a great deal more than can be said of most houses in these changing days.

To return to our arrival at the farm: My husband's youngest brother had gone up to Sotik in September 1928 to begin the development of the piece of land Brian had bought, and by the time we arrived in January he had built several huts, and done a lot of bush-clearing and even some ploughing.

When I followed three weeks after Brian, I found that the two brothers, having had no one to cook properly for them, had lived off a diet of *posho* (porridge), Christmas cake, and Kei-apple jelly, as a result of which Brian was suffering from a bad go of indigestion. They had not unpacked as they had nowhere in the grass hut to put anything, but they had rooted through every case, so that the carefully packed trunks were in a terrible jumble. Our grass banda had a partition down the centre, which did not meet the ceiling, and a length of cotton 'amerikani' [cloth]

Agnes and Brian in front of their Kipkebe house, showing the farm behind it to give some perspective

did duty for a door. The sitting-room was on one side and on the other, our bedroom – not much privacy for a young married couple, although it is true my brother-in-law did sleep in the office hut.

Upon my arrival as a bride, the Kikuyu labour held an *ngoma*, or tribal dance, in my honour. This was a most colourful and exciting experience, held after dark by the light of three huge bonfires. These were completely encircled by a double ring of dancers, the maidens facing their male partners with their backs to the bonfires forming the inner circle, while the men formed the outer. We, as the guests of honour, were placed in the centre, which we shared with the Master of Ceremonies, who intoned the narrative song between the oft-repeated chorus.

The dancers were naked except for their feather head-dresses and the bead and wire ornaments with which their waists, necks and ankles were adorned. Their bodies glistened with oil and sweat as they stamped out the rhythmic beat, the whole resembling a bronze frieze against the leaping flames. As we were the guests of honour, the narrator sang of my *bwana's* exploits and of his *bibi's* beauty amongst other topical subjects.

Although the dance appeared to our Western eyes as highly immoral, the Kikuyu had their own set of standards. Should any of the young warriors overstep the bounds of Kikuyu propriety, one of the guardians of their tribal moral behaviour would smartly beat two lighted bits of wood over the offender's backside. The shower of burning sparks would serve to remind the offender of the limits of moral propriety.

The whole scene stands out as one of my most vivid memories of those early days.

Our first few weeks were hot and dry, and the dust was appalling; then the rains came and our farm, which had been a dust bowl, became a quagmire.

Most Sunday mornings we would go off with our dogs and picnic basket, and walk along a hillside track which led us into the back valley with its uncleared bush. Here, under the shade of a thorn tree, we would cook our breakfast and settle down to read our books. If we were lucky, before long we would hear the war cry go up. This meant that someone had seen a leopard, and the hunt was on.

The young *moran* [warriors] running up with their *simis* [short swords] and spears would divide, some going upstream and some downstream. Both parties would then beat back through the thick bush, closing in on the unfortunate animal until it was surrounded. Then, standing shoulder to shoulder, they would form a circle and wait with upraised spears. The terrified beast, knowing it was trapped, would spring out, to be met by a hail of spears.

Once, when they failed to kill a leopard, the wounded animal sprang at one of the men, and with his claws tore a large gash in the man's head. As there was no doctor nearer than Kericho 40 miles distant, the victim was brought to our house, and Brian sewed up the gaping wounds with surgical gut, putting 26 stitches in the unfortunate Kipsigis man's head. We then gave him a sedative and locked him in our farm store so that we should be able to give the terrible wound constant dressings and the care it required and keep it clean. At the time, the warrior was anything but grateful, but at least he lived to fight and hunt again.

Being so far from a doctor we carried a good supply of surgical dressings, as well as a few simple medicines, and many's the emergency we had to deal with. Brian served as a dentist as well as a surgeon, though I never let him pull out any of my teeth!

Meantime, the house grew day by day, as it had to be ready for the great event, which was expected early in May, although my baby daughter nearly defeated all our plans by hurrying into the world a month before she was due.

We moved into our home on 10th April and my sister-in-law, Brian's sister Irene MacDougall, a trained nurse, arrived the next day and I went to bed with a temperature. On the morning of April 12th I felt better, but my time was on me, and Irene sent Brian off to Kericho, some 40 miles distant, to fetch the doctor. But my little daughter was too impatient to wait for any doctor, and by the time he had got back with my husband, the tiny five-pound baby was safely tucked up in her cot.

What I should have done without my sister-in-law I can't think, for she was wonderful, and although she had no aids such as chloroform, she coped in such a calm manner that I felt completely safe in her competent hands. The worst moment came just as the baby was appearing in the world. The kitchen *toto* came into the adjoining bathroom, sent by the cook to ask "if Memsahib would like the chicken hot or cold for lunch."

After three weeks Irene could stay no longer, and poor Little Ann, so tiny that she had to wear my doll's clothes, was left to the tender mercy of her ignorant parents.

Our first year in Sotik was very happy, although perhaps we had more than our fair share of worry and sleepless nights. Ann, having been an eight-months baby, was very delicate. But in between bouts of teething, we had lots of fun, for our neighbours were delightful, and mostly young married couples like ourselves with babies and all their attendant problems. We played tennis, laughed and gossiped, and occasionally danced, making our own amusement in this little known part of Kenya.

Because Sotik was such a long district, it divided naturally into two parts. This division gradually became accentuated because of the fact that all the more sober and respectable married couples seemed to settle

Irene MacDougall, Brian's sister and a trained nurse, who came to Kipkebe to help with baby Ann.

in the one end, while the wilder types of bachelors seemed naturally to gravitate towards the other. So the opposite ends inevitably became known as 'the Snobbery' and 'the Slums.'

Perhaps the North End, where we lived, earned the name of the Snobbery because our tiny community, consisting of ten families all told, was led by the 'Duke and Duchess.' This elderly couple, two of the earliest settlers in Sotik, arrived to take up their 5000-acre farm 'Moneiri' before World War I, in 1910. He was dubbed Duke because he told everyone that he ran his estate on the feudal system – although they both lived up to their titles, for our gracious Duchess was undoubtedly the doyenne of our district.

"Mrs Moneiri,' as she liked to be known, was kindness itself, taking all newcomers under her wing, although one was apt to feel rather like a cottager's wife being visited by the local grande-dame when, on arrival, she uncovered her basket and said, "Just a little butter and some home-baked bread, my dear." She came of a generation who were inclined to gush, and to describe everything in the superlative, which until I got used to it had a paralysing effect on me.

But this couple's most tiresome trait was their belief that they had every right to know what was going on, which made everyone else equally determined that they should not. Such is the perversity of human nature. We all went to the greatest pains to prevent them from finding out even the simplest and most unimportant of happenings; but had we only known, we could have saved ourselves many prevarications, for their intelligence service was as well organised as MI5.

As there were no telephones then, the only method of communication between farms was by runner, and many were the notes which flew back and forward between our farm and the Moneiri estate. I was forever answering these effusions, and thanking the good lady for some kind thought. The masterpiece of blessings and good wishes arrived one day shortly after Ann was born, in the form of a little heifer calf with a beribboned neck whose label bore the words, "To start the baby daughter's dairy herd." We found such a handsome gift embarrassing, but I hope my reply made up for what it lacked in effusiveness with very real gratitude.

After that, on the frequent occasions when we were visited by the ducal pair, the Duchess always enquired for the calf, saying, "And how is the dear little calf?", to which I invariably replied, "Very well, thank you."

That was the truth, until one night our houseboy called excitedly, "Bwana, there are buck in the maize!" This was an opportunity not to be missed, for the only meat we ever had was what we were able to shoot ourselves, and lately we had not been too successful.

My husband seized his rifle, ran to the car, and with the aid of the spotlight, successfully accounted for three pairs of eyes, much to the general rejoicing of the household. What was our horror next morning to discover that what Brian had shot so successfully were our own calves, and that the poor little gift heifer lay amongst the slain. Our hearts were heavy, although that did not prevent us from enjoying the first veal we had had for ages.

We debated what we should do, and decided that writing was too difficult, but that the next time we saw the 'Moneiris,' Brian would pluck up his courage and confess to the Duke. The dreaded day came, and they arrived at 6 p.m. along with two strange female visitors. It would not have been easy for me to compete with two total strangers with a fractious baby in my arms, even had I not been possessed of my guilty secret. The inevitable moment came, and I heard the Duchess ask her usual question, "How is the calf?", and with horror heard myself give the stock answer, for I completely lost my nerve. I dread to think what they must have thought of me for, of course, they knew all about the tragedy.

The Duchess thought it her duty to be the guardian, in this outpost of the Empire, of a British way of life, and every Empire Day she organised a sort of miniature Ideal Homes Exhibition where each one of us was expected to demonstrate that we were keeping up standards by exhibiting the biggest and best of our produce. As Mrs Moneiri's birthday conveniently fell on Empire Day, and as she always received our exhibits and our good wishes with such profuse thanks, most of us didn't have the nerve to reclaim our produce after the Show. But there was a well-known Scot who did not see why he should be forced to give a present, and marched off carrying his one exhibit, a pound of butter, under his arm.

I have been told that on an earlier occasion the Duchess had appeared draped in a Union Jack, with a brass coal scuttle on her head. A very impressive Britannia she must have made, for she was a massive woman.

Perhaps we were unkind, but youth in its search for laughter is no respecter of persons, and although we certainly got a great deal of fun out of the fads and foibles of our feudal friends, they were a grand couple. Think of the courage of this remarkable pair who, nurtured in the safety of suburbia in the Britain of the late 1800s, left it all behind to seek their fortune in 'Darkest Africa.'

The ducal castle, suitably perched on a hill, was a rambling rabbit-warren of smallish rooms. But while inside it reflected the owners' English background, it had one odd feature, a peculiarity shared by many Kenya houses of that period: there were no ceilings, and the inside walls did not meet the roof. In fact, they were only partitions, in this case not more than six feet high, and although this did not make for privacy, it had its uses, as we found out on our first overnight visit.

While dressing for dinner, we were astonished to see a head pop up over the wall from the next bedroom. It disappeared as quickly as it had appeared, and later we learnt the explanation. Sotik's evening dress ranged from dinner-jackets and suits to pyjamas and dressing-gowns, and our fellow guests had forgotten to enquire that evening what the form was. So when the wife asked, "What shall I wear?" her husband replied, "Wait a moment, dear, and I'll look over the wall and see."

There is another incredible but true story on the same theme. In this case, for the convenience of plumbing, the kitchen and bathroom were side by side, and before dinner the husband had occasion to go into the kitchen. To his horror he saw the small kitchen *toto* standing on a stool on top of the table, looking over the partition into the bathroom. When he asked furiously, "What the hell do you think you're doing?" he got the calm reply, "Mpishi tells me to do this every evening, for when Memsahib gets out of the bath, I call the cook to dish up the soup," – a sensible labour-saving arrangement from the cook's point of view.

It was rather terrifying being so far from the nearest doctor, and Ann, who was a very delicate baby, gave us many anxious moments, most as the result of our own mistakes. Poor darling, I don't know how she survived. First of all we overfed her, until one dreadful night she had convulsions.

The Truby King Baby Book said that hundreds of babies die of convulsions in New Zealand each year; you must call in a doctor immediately and put the baby in a warm bath. But we had no doctor and no hot water - the wood was wet and the fire out. I was in tears and sobbed out, "If only she'd stop screaming I could think what to do!" And Brian was frantic between the two of us.

After that horrifying experience, we were so terrified of convulsions that every time the child cried we cut down her food. Also, the Kipsigis watered our milk regularly and we parboiled it because of the fear of typhoid, which meant that the child got no vitamins at all. After two or three months, Ann was suffering from starvation, and the poor mite never stopped crying from sheer hunger.

We were at our wits' end, exhausted with lack of sleep and worry, when fortunately for us all, Kenya's only Mothercraft Nurse, the wonderful Miss Ford, arrived to stay in the district and kindly came to us for the weekend. The first thing she did was to take over complete charge of the nursery and the baby, and told us that after we had had a good night's sleep, we should go out and enjoy ourselves. "I don't want to see you until Monday, when I shall give you both a baby lecture," she said, adding, "You look much worse than your baby."

After a glorious carefree weekend, we were given our baby lecture by 'Fordi.' She taught us how to weigh the baby and to find out the calorific value of its body weight, and how to give the babe the equivalent in food calories. As I was no mathematician, Brian worked out the sums after the weekly weighing, giving me the correct answer. This, of course, would depend on whether the baby was being fed on mother's milk or cow's, or on one of the better-known patent baby foods. Many were the amusing conversations I have heard down the party-line telephone during Brian's 'consulting hours.' For my husband became the baby expert of the district!

Ann recovered, though the harm had been done, as we were to find to our cost later, when Fordi, bless her, again came to our rescue and without doubt saved Ann's life. But that was still in the future, and fortunately one did not know what disaster was going to overtake one next week.

In those early days, farms were almost entirely run by squatter labour under a sort of feudal system which, although it had many

Oxen and farm equipment at Kipkebe.

disadvantages, possessed one great advantage outweighing all else: namely, the bond that was created between the European farmer and his African employees. To your squatters you were father and mother, and responsible for the physical well-being not only of the man himself, but of his wife and family. This made the relationship between master and man a much more personal one, and although under a bad employer the system was open to abuse, on the whole it worked well. Out of kindness and fair treatment grew loyalty and liking, and it was just this, the loyalty of our old squatters to my husband as their Bwana, that enabled me to run the farm with no labour troubles during Brian's absence on active service in World War II.

Alas, that loyalty born of mutual respect tended to disappear when the squatter system gave way to the larger force of casual labour, and the farmer lost the personal contact with his employees and their families.

By law, squatters were allowed to cultivate one acre of land and keep ten head of cattle and twenty goats. In return they were expected to work for six months of every year, and the farmer could also call on them and their families in times of emergency to fight a bush fire or some other threatened disaster. However, it was seldom that the contract was observed to the letter, and what they were supposed to have on paper bore no relation to what they had in practice. Every squatter would soon be the proud possessor of two or three huts, the same number of wives, and in a very short time there were hundreds of head of livestock on the back portion of the farm, where the bush was literally alive with children, cattle, goats and sheep.

After a few years of this regime, our Kipsigis squatters were farming half our land. But as long as we did not need the back valley we did not mind, for their cattle and goats kept down the bush, and they cleared the land to plant their shambas. The disadvantages were that they cut down all the timber to build their houses, make their cattle *bomas* [enclosures], and to provide firewood, and also their methods of cultivation harmed the land. But these disadvantages were far outweighed by the advantage to a young farmer with limited capital of having a cheap labour force over whom he had some control.

So for more than 12 years, while we lived, worked, played and had our being in the front valley, our African squatters worked for us but lived, played, and with their wives and livestock had their being in the back valley, where the population of man and beast increased daily in the most alarming fashion. Yes, I said 'played,' for life was not all work and worry – far from it.

The Kipsigis thought Brian was lucky, for he did not have to pay a bride-price of so many head of cattle and goats for me, and instead I brought with me a dowry. This they could not understand, and thought my father a fool for allowing his daughter to be carried off without some compensating factor.

My dowry consisted of some beautifully fine Robinson and Cleaver linen, which was completely unable to withstand the pummelling on a soapbox which was the local method of washing, and was ruined by rinsing in our brown unfiltered water. As well as this, I gave Brian a magnificent sum of £100 in the Highland Railway. We immediately converted this into a wagon and team of oxen, with which Brian carted the material for the building of our excellent murram tennis court, which as far as I know, is still in action today. We were all keen tennis players, and my £100 has given us a great deal of pleasure down the years, especially before the building of the new Sotik Club in 1948.

We were lucky in that we had two courts in our end of the district, and so every Saturday the Kipkebe court became the meeting place for tennis enthusiasts, while on Sundays, Colonel and Mrs Matheson kept open house at Kivoga. While we enjoyed the simple pleasures of a game of tennis, followed by an informal dance, the warm nights throbbed with the beat of drums and the rhythmic singing of the African *ngomas*.

During our first years at the farm we employed only Kipsigis, for they considered the Sotik farms their country, and the right to work on them entirely their prerogative. They still do, although nowadays they graciously allow other tribes such as the Kisii, Luo, and even the

Team of oxen and wagon at Kipkebe.

Kikuyu to work on the farms. Many of the Kipsigis, having grown rich over the years through cattle increase and good husbandry, are men of substance and have no need to work. In fact, many of them employ Luo to work for them. But they regard with grave disfavour any scheme which allows other tribes to buy land and settle on the Sotik farms, which they still look upon as theirs by right.

It is this which may cause the trouble when the fenced and cleared farms of the settlers, which proved a most effective buffer state, have all gone with the going of the Europeans. All that is now left of the Sotik district which we knew and helped to build out of the bush are four or five tea companies in the north end of Sotik, Kipkebe Limited amongst them. The buffering influence will have come and gone. Has it served its purpose? Only time will tell.

CHAPTER 5

The Kindness of Friends

*"Friendship improves happiness and abates misery,
By doubling our joy and dividing our grief."*
-- Marcus Tullius Cicero - Roman Orator

Life at Kipkebe flowed along in the Twenties, and nothing upset the even tenor of our ways, although Pax Britannica was rudely shattered now and then by tribal wars. So frequently did these "wars" break out – almost every week – that they were looked upon as an annoyance rather than a danger. For it was very inconvenient if, after one of these forays, your entire labour force was absent without leave on Monday morning, being incarcerated in the local gaol. Given any option by the District Commissioner, the farmer always plumped for a fine all round, rather than a prison sentence. This was just as well for the unfortunate warriors, who had spent the night in the local Black Hole of Calcutta where, after a battle, there would be standing room only.

It was equally maddening for me to have my cook suddenly off to the war, leaving me with a luncheon or a dinner party on my hands. On one occasion, my gardener was in the middle of planting a row of young carnation plants when the war cry went up. Before he could down tools, I said, "No you don't – go on with your work."

With only a blanket draped gracefully over one shoulder, he drew himself to his full height and said with much dignity, "But Memsahib, I am a warrior, not an old woman," to which I firmly replied, "You finish planting those carnations and then you can go to your war," and he did.

The war cry, a high-pitched wail made by the women, might be heard at any hour of day or night, whenever they wanted to collect the tribe for some purpose ranging from a full-scale attack to a leopard-hunt, or even a burglary. A dismal sound even in broad daylight, on a moonlight night the effect of the cry echoing through the hills was eerie in the extreme.

On one such night, in 1930, we were awakened at about 2 a.m., by the war cry. We dressed hurriedly and ran out into the back road, where an astonishing sight met our eyes. An endless stream of warriors dressed in their war-paint flowed through the farm, carrying their beautifully painted shields, while their small sons ran beside them carrying their fathers' spears. It was an exciting moment, for the air was full of the sound of the cry and the thud of warriors' feet as they sped along.

By 6 a.m. there was no one left on the farm except old men, women and children, for all able-bodied men had answered the call to arms. As soon as it was light, my husband was all for dashing off in the wake of the warriors to find out what was happening, for it was the first time that the call had been on such a big scale. But before he went he thought he had better park me and our babe at the pre-arranged rendezvous for women and children if there should be trouble. This was Kivoga, where the coffee factory was the only two-storey brick building in the district, though otherwise an unsuitable choice, as it lay in a hollow.

On arrival we found only a handful of women with two or three babies collected there. Colonel Matheson, the owner, had answered the call sent by a runner from a woman on the most northerly farm, saying that she had been told that the Luo were going to take advantage of the Kipsigis men's absence from home and stage a cattle raid. Our hostess begged Brian to stay to give us moral support, which he did until the return of her husband after lunch. There was an amusing incident during that meal, which showed the tension, for we were all wrought up. The lack of news coupled with the lack of sleep and the excitement of the night had played on our nerves more than we realized.

Brian was the only man amongst women and suddenly, just as we were about to sit down to lunch, there was a terrific bang. Our hostess leapt from the table and with a shout of, "Revolver," dashed down the veranda steps, closely followed by Brian, while the rest of us flew to our stations at our sleeping babies' side. When we found out that it was nothing more than the bursting of a soda syphon bulb in the pantry, we all felt excessively foolish.

Shortly afterwards, Jimmy Matheson returned and we crowded round to hear the news. But 'JK,' having been at the opposite end of the district from the zone of war, had little to tell us. He and Brian set off together to find out what they could, but it was not until much later that we were to hear the full story.

The district had been plagued for some time by robberies, carried out by armed gangs, and several loyal night watchmen had been badly injured defending their masters' property. The thefts were nearly always of arms and ammunition, for in those days the farmers were not yet security-conscious, and their guns were normally kept on the veranda, with ammunition on the shelf above. This was so that they were in easy reach for a quick shot at any passing buck, for the pot. The *laibon* [seers and leaders of the Talai clan] had organised these raids, and built up an efficient "intelligence" service to help them do so, by placing their agents in employment with the farmers as *nyaparas*, or headmen.

Perhaps this was an attempt to build up an anti-European force, perhaps even a forerunner of the Mau Mau. No one really knew, but whatever the plan in the mind of the *laibon* it went off at half-cock.

The Administration's investigations into these robberies were at first unsuccessful. It was known that gangs of young Kipsigis moran were responsible, but not who they were, until some of the loyal *nyaparas* informed against them. Before they could be rounded up, the Maasai, sensing trouble in the wind, gathered some 7000 men on the hills at the end of Sotik to be ready for any eventuality; they were itching for a fight.

The Kipsigis knew this and as soon as they heard the war cry, thinking it was a call to fight their hereditary enemies, the Maasai, rallied and streamed southwards ready to do battle.

It turned out that it was not the Maasai but the *laibon* who were at the bottom of the trouble. In revenge for the betrayal of their plans to the police, they had decided on a certain night to fire all the huts of the loyal Kipsigis, who had informed against them on the Sotik farms, and also the police lines. It was the terrified victims, awakened rudely from sleep and trying to escape from their blazing huts, who put up the cry for help, thinking that it was the work of marauding Maasai.

The situation was serious. A major tribal battle, sparked off by this series of crimes, intrigues and misunderstandings, was imminent. Warfare on this scale would have led to further bloodshed and possibly necessitated a campaign by the King's African Rifles to put down the trouble among the warring tribes. However, Major Sooner, one of Sotik's older settlers and a veteran of the East Africa Campaign in the First World War, realised the danger. Disregarding the District Commissioner, who showed more aptitude for golf than government, he sent a most peremptory wire to the Governor, saying: "Sotik situation serious – come at once." Awakened by the news at 4 a.m., Sir Edward Grigg lost no time, getting straight in his car and setting off on the 250-mile journey to Sotik.

As luck would have it, on reaching the trouble spot his car ran right into a huge gathering of Kipsigis moran, war dancing and hotting themselves up for battle. A rather amazing coincidence when you consider the many hundreds of square miles covered by the Kipsigis Reserve.

So the battle, thanks to the prompt action of His Excellency the Governor, was stillborn, and the warriors returned to their homes much sadder and wiser, and later a lot poorer, for the Government, as a punishment, imposed a fine of £6,000 on the Kipsigis tribe. This was to pay for the levy force of KAR, stationed in the district for six months, who saw to it that at least as far as Sotik was concerned, the King's peace was preserved.

As to the *laibon*, just retribution overtook them at last; for as well as these measures a new District Commissioner was appointed, Government entrusting the task of unmasking them and their evil activities to Mr Brumage. He successfully rounded them up and with many curses and lamentations they were removed – men, women and children, the whole 700 members of the clan – to a detention camp at Gwassi, on the shores of Lake Victoria, where they lived under restriction for many years. One hundred and thirty firearms were recovered in this operation. This was done at the urgent request of the Kipsigis tribe.

Shortly afterwards, I was dancing in Kericho with, as I thought, a young Tea Assistant, and when he remarked, "I believe you've lately had a little tribal war," I replied, mimicking the District Commissioner, "Oh it was nothing, a little blood-letting is so good for the tribes, don't you think?" Then seeing his face, I asked, "What is your job?" only to be told, "I am the new District Officer." "Well," I said, "I've not been too tactful, but at least you know what the Sotik settlers think of the District Commissioner," adding, "an opinion shared by the Administration if the change of District Commissioner means anything at all."

Writing of Mr Brumage reminds me of an entertaining Court Case heard by him, in his capacity as Magistrate, in which we were the chief witnesses for the prosecution. This was the case of a 'Peeping Tom.'

Finding it very difficult to judge how much food we were likely to consume in a month, at the end of that time Brian and I were always on very short common, and so we awaited the arrival of the monthly stores with some anxiety. The lorry usually left Kericho in the afternoon, by which time it was probably raining and the roads in a dreadful condition, so the stores never arrived until late, although I must say they usually got through somehow.

One night when the lorry was later than usual, we were bathing when I thought I heard it. As we were out of sugar and several other vital necessities, Brian, wrapped in a bath towel, went into the bedroom and looked out of the bow-window to see if he could see the lorry's lights. What he saw instead was an African crouching down in the flowerbed and looking into the bathroom through a crack in the curtains.

Brian rushed back into the bathroom saying, "Good God, there's a boy looking in the window." He seized a dressing-gown and tore up to the servants' quarters, looking in the kitchen en route to see who was there. As he reached the servants' hut, a panting black figure came running up saying, "It wasn't me, Bwana." Convicted out of his own mouth! Brian locked the culprit in the farm store overnight and in the morning we preferred a charge against him, and handed him over to the Police.

It was usual to charge the Africans in cases of this sort, to act as a deterrent and keep the youth from going from bad to worse. In due course, the case came before the District Commissioner, acting as Magistrate. The Assistant Superintendent of Police, prosecuting, was a Scot, and his cross-examination of us was conducted in the broadest of Scots accents.

It went something like this: "At 8 o'clock on the 8th of June, where were you, Mistress Shaw?", to which I replied, "In the bath." He then turned to Brian, asking him the same question, to which Brian gave the same reply, "In the bath." He couldn't believe his ears and turned back to me saying, "But I thought Mistress Shaw said that she was in the bath," to which I replied rather indignantly, "So I was!" He shook his head in disbelief and turned back to Brian with the same question.

This farce continued until very slowly and deliberately the Magistrate said in the most profound tones, "I take it that at eight o'clock on the 8th of June, both Mr and Mrs Shaw were in the bath." At this shocking revelation, the ASP flushed crimson, for it was obviously not done in the best circles for husband and wife to bath at the same time. Nor, it would seem, had he ever suffered from a water shortage.

No account of the 'good old Sotik days' would be complete without mention of our postmistress, 'Ma Collett.' I believe her early life had been spent in the barracks square in India, where presumably her spouse was a Sergeant Major, although her only reference to him was, "I 'ates me 'usband with an un'oly 'atred." Most of us had some sympathy with the erstwhile Mr Collett, for 'Ma' was an expert in the use of invective, and it was more than your life was worth to lose your parcel slips, for to commit any such crime might mean that your mail was withheld for several posts.

She lived, as was fitting, in a witch's hovel, which did duty as a post office, village store, and her living quarters. She shared the dark and musty interior with a pack of half-starved mongrel dogs, several cats and some hens, who found the post boxes made the most convenient nests. She was a holy terror and we were all more than a little afraid of her, but at least our letters, etc., were secure, for she slept with the keys under her mattress and no one dared beard her in her den, let alone in her bed.

April 5th, 1930 was a day of disaster. Brian came in during the morning complaining of severe stomach pains. In the nursery the baby was crying incessantly with earache and a bad go of teething. The day was grey with overcast skies, and by two o'clock it had started to pour, and the rain fell incessantly all through the afternoon and well into the night. By tea-time Ann was no better, while Brian was definitely worse, and when the post brought a cable telling me of my dear father's death, I felt that I could not stand any more.

Brian agreed to my sending off a note by runner to Jan George and Teddy Sharp, friends from their Cirencester College days, who owned a farm some four miles away, asking them if they could come over. Then followed hours of anxious waiting. They finally arrived at 11 p.m. after a terrible trip, having had to leave their car on the main road and walk the last mile up our farm track, which by then was almost impassable.

I shall never forget what I owe to these two young men, and indeed to so many of my Sotik neighbours, who through their prompt action helped to save my husband's life.

After seeing the patient, Jan went back, as his wife Mary was expecting her first baby, leaving Teddy, who was then still a bachelor, with us. I had found that the only thing that seemed to ease Brian's pain was a really hot compress, and so Teddy spent the long hours throughout the night stoking the sitting-room fire to keep the two kettles continuously on the boil, while I, in my ninth month of pregnancy, lay on our big double bed beside Brian, fully dressed, ready to shout for Teddy whenever a spasm came. Then Teddy would come tearing in and we'd clap another boiling hot compress on the groaning patient.

This gave great relief, although I was to discover later that there was no surer way of hastening the growth of the abscess. But although our ignorance nearly caused his death, it certainly saved Brian a good deal of pain during those long hours.

Between bouts of pain, Brian dozed and I pored over my Homeopathic Materia Medica. From what I gleaned, we decided that Brian's symptoms were those of acute appendicitis, and as soon as it was light, Teddy drove the eight miles to the police post to telephone to the doctor in Kericho. Major Caddick, the doctor, realising from Teddy's description that it was a matter of life and death, in his goodness came down straight away in spite of the dreadful state of the road. Fortunately for us, although the Major could not operate himself, having lost two fingers of his right hand in the Boer War, there was nothing he did not know about appendicitis.

Meantime, some more kind neighbours, Ted and Elaine Gunning, had come over to see if they could help in any way.

After examination of the patient, the doctor diagnosed, as we feared, acute appendicitis with peritonitis. We held a conference at which the doctor told us that there was no hope of taking Brian to hospital, for even supposing we were able to get through the one hundred miles to Nakuru, the jolting of the car would be sure to cause the bursting of the abscess, which could mean certain death. He said that in the normal course of growth, it would be unlikely to come to a head for another forty-eight hours, and stressed that the only hope of saving Brian's life was to bring a surgeon to operate on him in Sotik within that time limit.

How was this to be done? It seemed impossible with the heavy rains and the roads in such a state.

There was a moment's complete silence, and then Ted Gunning volunteered to go for the surgeon, and Teddy agreed to accompany him. Without waiting to collect money or food they set off, with a tree trunk strapped on to the side of their car and a couple of *jembes* [hoes] to dig themselves out of the potholes and ruts that did duty for a main road to the railhead at Lumbwa.

Meantime, the bush telegraph had been buzzing, and North Sotik, hearing that an emergency operation was to be performed, rallied round. Gifts of brandy, food, cotton wool, *debes* (cans) of rainwater and even a long kitchen table poured into Kipkebe. Car spotlights were fixed up on the lawn, their beams trained through the window of the bedroom which was to act as a theatre, in case the surgeon had to operate immediately on his arrival.

To me the hours of waiting seemed an eternity, for although we knew the doctor would eventually arrive, the question uppermost in my mind was whether he could get there in time. Praise be he did. But after taking some fourteen hours to travel the 120 miles, his hands were so shaky that, being satisfied with Brian's condition, he decided not to operate until the morning.

They had left Kericho at 2 p.m. but had spent over nine hours on the last forty-mile stretch. The road had completely collapsed and was a sea of mud. The surgeon's car had had to be abandoned, over its axles in mud, and the car to which they transferred also became hopelessly bogged down. They were finally rescued and came on in an Asian lorry. The surgeon, Dr Tennant, a dapper little man, had left Nakuru immaculate in a pale grey suit and matching spats, and his theatre sister in spotless white; but what a sadly bedraggled mud-bespattered pair they were on arrival.

By then my band of willing helpers had grown, and we sat down nine to dinner and slept six in our two-bed roomed bungalow. The tremendous relief of the surgeon's timely arrival, and the lifting of hours of anxious strain, caused such a reaction that we had the most hilarious of dinner parties. As our laughter rang out, the poor patient lay supperless in the next room, waiting to be carved up the following morning.

The operation was fixed for 7 a.m., but it was not performed until four hours later, for it was discovered that in the hurry of departure, the theatre sister had forgotten the chloroform. This meant another eight-mile trip to the police post telephone and an SOS to the District Commissioner, who sent off a young District Officer post-haste to Sotik with the necessary anaesthetic.

During the operation, I occupied myself by getting the garden boys to dig a pit to receive this troublesome appendix, but it was a very nerve-racking hour.

After the operation was successfully over, the surgeon discovered that tubing, too, had been forgotten, and so the wound was kept open for draining with a piece of old cycle tube. But worse was to befall, for Dr Tennant left for Nakuru, taking his theatre sister with him, before the patient had even come round. It was a terrible blow at the time, for no trained nurses had yet arrived, and none of us had ever dealt with an operation case before. Dr Caddick, who had given the anaesthetic, realising this, saved the situation by agreeing to stay and take over the daily dressing of the wound. Although Brian suffered from much inexpert nursing during the day, at night he had his ministering angel in the shape of a Miss Thomas, governess to the Young children. Her claim to professional training was that she was a failed probationer from her namesake's hospital, but she was a kindly soul as well as a born nurse.

Thank goodness the theatre sister did go back with the surgeon, for on the drive down to Nakuru she was in pain and that afternoon she went down with appendicitis and had to be rushed to the theatre and operated on that night – a most extraordinary coincidence.

As we could not get any trained nurses, Brian's eldest stepsister, Kay (Catherine Shaw), a retired matron from the Queen Alexandra Military Nursing Service, came to us for a week, taking charge of our willing band of amateurs, so we managed somehow.

My second babe was due towards the end of April, and two nursing sisters, one for each of us, came up together by train to Lumbwa on Ann's first birthday, April 12th. WG Dawson, another of our kind bachelor neighbours, went to meet them at railhead at Lumbwa. With the continuous rain, not only was the road in a terrible state, but the Kipsonoi River had risen some fifteen feet and was flowing over the N'goina Bridge. This bridge had no guard-rails, and a crossing could be very alarming when the river was over the top, for there was always the danger of being swept over the edge. On this occasion the girls were so terrified that one of them threw her arms around the driver's neck, a gesture which nearly proved disastrous for them all since to drive onto a bridge submerged by a river in flood required a cool head and no distractions!

Miss Sherlaw took charge of Brian and my one-year-old daughter, although Ann did also have Damaris, her Kipsigis *ayah* [nanny], to whom she was devoted. I initiated Miss Sherlaw into the ways of the household, and on the 20th April, Miss Carter and I departed for Kelunet, a coffee farm some seven miles distant, the doctor having insisted that the risk of infection was too great for the baby to be born at Kipkebe. Again, my wonderful neighbours came to the rescue, for without a moment's hesitation, the Gunnings turned their guest-wing into a maternity ward, and there Michael was born, a week late, on April 29th.

The day before, a telephone had been installed, and Brian had spoken to me, having evaded his ministering angel – a great thrill. Early next morning he was awakened by the lowing of the cattle and felt sure that his son and heir had arrived. He crept to the telephone, although he was not supposed to get out of bed, got through to Ted Gunning, who was frantically ringing the doctor's house in Kericho, and so heard the great news.

Michael made up for his lateness by rushing into the world in two hours, long before either his nurse or I was ready for him; and as the doctor did not come until the next day. Both my babes were born without benefit of doctor. But as Brian had reassuringly told me when we had decided to have our first at Kipkebe, it would be quite all right, for he had often seen calves born. Brian was right and after ten days I returned in triumph with my nine-pound son. It was just three weeks since I had left Kipkebe, and five weeks since Brian's operation, but it was safe for me to return as the peritonitis had cleared up and the wound was closed.

By this time the road system had completely collapsed under the incessant rain, for the 1930 long rains were the heaviest on record. We were completely marooned, for nothing could get through the last twenty-two miles to Lumbwa, where in places the mud was now over the oxen's thighs. So there we were, both convalescent, no longer in need of nursing, with two nursing sisters ticking up a guinea a day like waiting taxis. With our slender resources we could ill afford this financial burden. So when Dr Caddick rang up to say that he had heard that a Public Works Department breakdown lorry, fitted up with winches, etc., was going to try to get through to Lumbwa, we seized the chance to send them back to Nairobi.

But first we had to get them to Kericho over forty miles of appalling road. Another of Sotik's young bachelors offered to make the attempt, and they set off in our box body Chevrolet. After a terrible day which they spent digging the car out of pothole after pothole, dark descended and as the car lights failed, the Chevrolet gave up its valiant struggle. The young man spent the night with a girl's head on each shoulder. Awaking cold, wet, stiff and hungry, they discovered that they were only two hundred yards from the house of a Mr Lee, the General Manager of the African Highlands Produce Company.

The breakdown lorry did not even manage to do the first two miles out of Kericho next day before it became hopelessly bogged down, winches and all. The nurses, stranded, decided to walk the last twenty miles by hillside tracks, with African porters carrying their bags. An heroic effort, for though Miss Sherlaw had been in Kenya for two years, Lucy Carter was straight out from the United Kingdom.

So ended 'Operation Appendix,' which became an epic in the annals of Sotik.

The aftermath was two of the most depressing years I have ever spent. The rain, coupled with lack of supervision, had wrought havoc with the *shamba*, and bills which could not be met poured in from all sides.

The operation cost us over £600. This was such a shock that, the next year, I decided that an appendix on the farm was a financial risk we could not afford and had mine out in Nakuru Hospital for the meagre sum of £25.

Neither of us was allowed to drive a car for six months – had we had a car to drive. The garage told us that it would take £70 to make ours go again. Added to our financial problems was the constant worry of poor little Ann, who was continuously ailing, so that we hardly ever had an unbroken night's sleep.

The weary months of Brian's long convalescence dragged by, and it was Christmas again and we were off once more in our repaired box body to join the Shaw family gathering at Lamuria. Not so much fun this time, for Ann caught a chill on the way over and was ill the whole time, while on arrival I went to bed after an attack of the most appalling pain.

Dr Doig of Nyeri came and gave me morphia, diagnosing gallstones. When I asked him, "Doctor, can I die of this?", he replied, "No, my dear, but you can pray to." I was to remember his words often in the next six years, during which I had an attack of gallstones on an average of one every two months, for every time I went for a long trip in the car the rough roads bumped out another stone. The pain was agonising, and I would rather have a baby without chloroform any day than an attack of gallstones without morphia, and I am in a position to know.

Going over to Lamuria, we got stuck on the plains and as there was no one in sight, we had to take down the local signpost to prise the car out, while on the way back we found that the bridge over the Sugarol River had collapsed. This held us up for over three hours. After several abortive attempts, Brian managed to drive the car down one steep side, across the river, and up the other, while the ayah and I with the two babies crawled over the rubble and broken tree-trunks which were all that was left of the bridge. To cap it all, I had an attack of pain and had to lie down for an hour at the little hotel at Thomson's Falls before I could go on.

After that, we vowed we would stay at home for Christmas.

We reached Nakuru by dark and stayed there for the night so that I could see Dr Tennant the next day. Tennant did not advise an operation, for he said few of these operations were performed in Kenya and as I was young there was a reasonable chance that the gallstones could be dissolved by the correct treatment.

Another disastrous prescription: he put me onto such an acid diet that within two months I went down with rheumatic fever. That it was artificially introduced was the considered opinion of our Dr Caddick, by then our next door neighbour, kind friend, and standby. For the disease did not come on suddenly in the normal way, but over a period of a fortnight I grew stiffer and stiffer, until one day kneeling down to bathe the babies I found I could not get up. In the light of the present knowledge, I realise it might have been polio, but whatever it was I was completely paralysed for six to eight weeks and suffered agonies from the intense cold aching of all my limbs.

It was during the first two weeks of my fever that Ann became seriously ill. The government doctor in Kericho diagnosed colitis, or malaria, but was obviously stumped, and when in desperation we sent for Fordi, the poor wee girl was losing four ounces of weight a day in spite

Agnes with her two children, Ann and Mike.

of forcible feeding. Miss Ford, in whom we had complete faith, said she could not take the responsibility, for in her opinion, if Ann was not taken to Nairobi immediately she would die. I was the problem, for paralysed as I was, I could not be left alone, and once again the Lady Grigg Nursing Service had no nurses available. Finally, we got a nurse from the CMS, and off Brian drove to take Fordi and baby Ann down to Nairobi. On the way to Nairobi, the train had to be stopped to revive the baby with brandy, as Fordi thought she had slipped away.

The next day, not knowing anything was wrong, my brother-in-law, Ridley, arrived to spend his local leave with us. Thank God he did, for the nurse turned out to be a drug addict and I, paralysed as I was, and completely at her mercy, had lived through a night of terror. It was so bad that Ridley phoned the District Commissioner and asked him to send down someone to remove this maniac of a woman at once. This he did, and my brother-in-law nursed me devotedly, talking to me endlessly about anything and everything all through the night, in an effort to keep my mind off my pain and other worries. One of our near neighbours' wives, Mary George, nobly came for several hours each day to give Ridley some rest. Three days later, Brian returned with his sister, Gladys Mathias, who left her home and family to come over 200 miles to nurse me for several weeks.

Ann's case perplexed even the Nairobi doctors, although finally it was diagnosed as Tetany, a wasting disease then little known in Kenya, which was due to the atrophy of the parathyroid glands, caused in this case by septic absorption from the abscesses in her ears during teething. The cure was to restore the lost vitamins by a diet of raw foods and sun-bathing; a very slow process though mercifully successful.

In the nursing home, the only way Ann could be got to sleep was for Miss Ford to hold her in her comforting arms, rocking her and crooning continuously. Every time Fordi stopped, the child, too weak to speak, would pat her arm with her thin little hand until she sang again. Fordi, Ann's guardian angel, sat hour after hour singing with the baby cradled in her motherly arms, and so through her goodness our little daughter's life, hanging by the slenderest thread, was saved.

Realising that Ann was missing her mother and her family surroundings, Miss Ford insisted on bringing Ann home to convalesce, although she was a skeleton of a child, weighing only 18 lbs at two years old, her poor little body so thin that she had to be carried about on a bolster. She had lost control of her nerves and forgotten how to speak, although she whimpered continuously like a hurt animal. She never slept for more than twenty minutes day or night.

Once Ann had turned the corner, Fordi left and I looked after Ann, while the treatment was supervised by the remaining trained nurse. Slowly but surely the poor mite regained her strength, and I, after six weeks, began to get back the use of my legs. So Ann relearned how to talk and I relearned how to walk again.

Ann and Mike standing.

Ann and Mike with their animal toys.

Michael was the one bright spot, for he was a beautiful boy, whose health bore witness to the fact that thanks to the Mothercraft lectures, Brian and I were now experts in the matter of childcare and feeding.

Thus ended our two years of trials and tribulations; although Brian, Ann, I and the farm were to bear the marks of those misfortunes for many years.

Sometimes during this period I rebelled and, feeling that I must escape from it all, I'd run away after putting the babies to bed and leaving a 'farewell note' for Brian on the mantle-shelf. I'd usually climb up Kipkebe Hill and there, under the starlit sky, in the silence of the warm night, sanity would return and I would decide to go home. For I had no one to run to and nothing to run with. Back I'd go, only to find my note still on the mantle-shelf, unread, for Brian had not even noticed that I'd gone. Nothing could have been more humiliating, and I usually wept from sheer rage.

Brian would then be very distressed and would offer to sell the farm and take me back to the United Kingdom. But we both knew this was only a gesture, for no one would have bought the farm in that half-developed state and, having sunk every penny we possessed into Kipkebe, we did not even have the price of our passages, let alone capital to start again. In fact, we were well and truly bogged down in the Sotik mud.

With an average rainfall of some sixty inches a year, how could any earth road hope to stand up to the heavy lorry traffic it had to carry? There is no doubt that much of the settlement in the 1930s came as a result of a survey carried out in 1927 for the extension of the railway from Lumbwa, through Kericho and Sotik, to open up the Kisii Highlands. Certainly, Brian would never have bought land in Sotik had he not thought that there was every chance of the railway coming. After a meeting at Jamji in 1929, when Sir Godfrey Rhodes, the General Manager of the Kenya Uganda Railways & Harbours, spoke on this extension, we thought our hopes would soon be realized; but alas, the slump in 1931 put paid to any more branch lines.

Now, in 1973, Sotik still lies sixty miles from the railhead and is likely to remain so, I fear, for the foreseeable future. But we were not to know that and so, like JC Snaith's sailor, we "just kept on keeping on" in the firm belief that tomorrow would be better than today.

Such is the resilience of youth that a fresh disaster was almost always the signal for another dance. Encouraged by the success of our first, held at Kipkebe on June 27, our wedding anniversary, we decided to hold another in 1931 to celebrate our joint return to health and strength.

At our first big dance, we had served an excellent, though potent, brandy/rum punch, which we had first learned about in Nanyuki. We followed the recipe faithfully, but forgot the weakening effect of ice in Nanyuki, so ours was 'potent punch plus,' and as a result the dance went off with a bang. We were pleased though somewhat surprised to see one of our more elderly settlers swaying to the strains of the tango in a manner that would have done a Spaniard credit.

But our surprise turned to alarm when the husband of Sotik's most correct of matrons came to us and said, "What have you put in your punch? My wife has just asked the young man she's dancing with why he never came to see us, much to his astonishment, for he is actually staying with us for this dance." Brian and I, realising what had happened thanks to the absence of ice, hurriedly reduced the strength, diluting the punch by the addition of soda water.

At our next dance, encouraged by our success, we courted disaster by being over-ambitious and attempting a cabaret. It was definitely not a success. Perhaps we were all, with one exception, too sober? Or was the one exception the cause of the trouble?

Here is the story and you shall be the judge. We had written a short sketch, a skit on pioneering, and just as we were about to begin, a young American pushed her way into the bathroom-cum-dressing room, announcing her intention of dancing a hula-hula dance. My husband and I tried to dissuade her, but without success, feeling that she was in no condition to dance. But there we were wrong. Clothed simply in a bright orange Spanish shawl, she danced the most realistic hula-hula, much to the horror of her unhappy husband and the stunned fascination of the other guests.

After it was all over, with the uncertain applause ringing in her ears, she fell into the dressing room, where my husband, along with Teddy Sharp and his young brother, were standing beside a stuffed tiger propped up in the bath, awaiting their 'call.' Dressed as house servants, they stood with their blackened faces discreetly turned to the wall, on which hung a mirror. So they, too, were fascinated when our hula-hula girl, having danced away all inhibitions, abandoned the shawl and stood plaintively asking, "Oh where, oh where, are my panties?" She finally put her arms around the tiger's neck, saying in the most coquettish of tones, "A girl should never trust a tiger with her panties!"

What a jumble of events go to make up my Pioneering Patchwork! But in laughter or tears, dances or disasters, what stands out in memory above all else is the wonderful kindness of our neighbours who never failed to come to our aid at any time.

It is sad, but alas only too true, that when civilisation comes in, neighbourliness goes out, for the need for it no longer exists. While memory serves, Brian and I shall not forget that our darkest days were lit by the light of "laughter and the love of friends."

CHAPTER 6

Visitors, Locusts and Witchcraft

"The lowest Ebb is the turn of the Tide."

--Henry Wadsworth Longfellow

In September 1930, the autumn before my rheumatic fever and Ann's illness, a young cousin aged eighteen came out from London for a year's visit. Why poor Connie Cree was asked to exchange a rather frivolous life of boyfriends, cinemas and dances for one of hard work and pioneering in Kenya, 1 have never understood. For although her father was my favourite uncle, I hardly knew Connie at all. The poor girl was sent out to total strangers, with whom she had nothing whatsoever in common.

Brian's youngest brother, St John, who did so much to start the development of our farm, was still with us, and a more dissimilar pair could not be imagined. Connie, with her love of frivolity, her light-yellow hair, high-heeled shoes and pretty painted face, was anathema to St John, at that time a very censorious young man, who disapproved of many worldly things and hated paint and powder above all.

Poor Connie, teetering about on the rough, uneven ground on her high heels, could not have been very happy. She was teased unmercifully and sometimes rather unkindly, as for instance when one of our elder settlers said to her, "What I'd like to do with you is to wash your face, throw away those silly shoes, burn your clothes and make a woman of you." Perhaps he had glimpsed the character beneath the make-up, for Connie certainly had guts. Much could be forgiven her when one knew how she had spent her early childhood.

She was born in Baghdad, where she and her little brother lived until they were two or three years old. Then came the war and her father (my uncle) left his family in Baghdad to join the British Forces as political liaison officer on General Townsend's staff. He was taken prisoner with Townsend at Kut al-Amara, and passing through Baghdad with the other prisoners he could find no trace of his wife and family. He discovered later that, together with all the non-combatant civilians of Baghdad, they had been rounded up as prisoners and marched to Mosul. This must have been a horrifying experience, aggravated by the fact that their march took them through Armenia in the wake of the massacres. My courageous aunt spent the next two years traipsing around Asia Minor with her two babies, sometimes as prisoners, sometimes free, but always short of food, money and clothing, trying to find out where her husband was imprisoned and, through the good offices of the American Consuls, to alleviate some of the hardships of his dreadful captivity. The courage of Connie's parents, which withstood all the horrors and ill-treatment of being prisoners in the hands of the Turks, was lying just under the surface in their daughter, and life at Kipkebe brought it out in good measure.

Connie's advent not only set the district talking, but nearly set our house alight. In order to see to powder her nose, she once turned up the oil lamp so high that it caught the thatched roof, whereupon she flung open the sitting-room door and rushed in screaming, "Fire!" St John, who had just come back from his bath, tore in and, seizing the blazing lamp, flung it out of the window and beat out the flames with his towel, just before they caught the main roof.

St John and Connie, what a contrast in character, but how good they were for each other. It says a lot for this young girl that, thrown into what must have been a most uncongenial household, in a strange land, with few of the creature comforts to which she was used, she settled down, taking her share of the work, joining in our simple pleasures, and, during my illness, stepping into the breach by taking care of nine-month-old Michael. Thus Connie proved her mettle, and having grown fond of her, we were all sorry to see her go.

We decided to give a farewell dance for her. My uncle had sent us £100 to pay for the building of the small guest room which made her visit possible, telling us to keep the balance, if any; as we were so broke, we decided to use the money to pay for the farewell dance.

The dance, which was great fun, this time preceded disaster. For just about two months later, we suffered from the worst visitation of locusts that we had ever had.

That year Kenya was infested with swarms of locusts which came down from their breeding grounds in the north. To protect the crops, Brian had organised perimeter smudge fires on the farm, which were to be lit on the approach of a swarm. On this particular occasion, a huge swarm measuring some ten miles square was flying up the Kipsonoi

Valley about two miles distant from the farm, in an easterly direction. Had they continued they would have missed us, but unfortunately, about mid-day, the swarm altered course and soon the farm was enveloped by locusts like a dense fog. The fires were lit and all the labour turned out shouting, yelling, whistling and beating tin cans, in an effort to turn the swarm and keep them from settling. But all our efforts were in vain, and as the lines of beaters moved ahead, millions of locusts settled behind them. They lay six inches deep upon the ground while the shrubs, coffee bushes and the trees were weighted down by the loathsome creatures.

Connie and I, acting as beaters, were unfortunate enough to get some inside our cotton frocks. She made off to the house and released the imprisoned locusts, but not before they had eaten a row of holes in her dress. I, not being so modest, took off my dress on the spot. They ate everything in sight, from the maize in the shamba to the clothes hanging on the clothesline, cropping the lawn bare and even the thatch on the roof. When at last they moved on, they left behind them a scene of desolation.

It was a bitter blow to us, for until our coffee was old enough to bear, we were entirely dependent on our maize crop for our income. That year Brian had estimated a return of some £500 from maize, but after the locusts' visitation, all the maize we salvaged from the 100 acres planted brought us in only £100.

Faced with the expensive operation, hospital, and doctors'and nurses' fees of the preceding two years, we were in despair, not knowing what we should do. Although we had gone teetotal as a necessary economy, we found a little drink in the cupboard, left over from the dance, and decided to drown our sorrows.

It was this disaster that forced us later to apply to the Kenya Land Bank for assistance.

The next member of my family to visit us was my brother, Charles, my junior by nine years, who arrived in October 1932. He came down from Oxford during the early Thirties in the years of the Depression, when jobs were few and far between. He had taken a degree in Forestry, but as the British Government had embarked on an economy drive, there were no Forestry appointments that year throughout the Colonial Empire.

My poor young brother was at his wits' end and accepted our offer of a home and came out to Kenya hoping to slip into a forestry job in Uganda, through the back door. This he did, taking a second-grade job as a Forester. From this beginning he has had a very successful career in Forestry, which has taken him from Uganda to Northern Rhodesia, British Honduras, Tanganyika and finally to Australia. But before this happened, he spent eighteen months with us at Kipkebe and, after six months of apprenticeship, he ran our farm while we went home for a much-needed overseas leave, our first in six years.

My good sister-in-law, Gladys Mathias, took the two children, now three and four years of age, under her wing at Lamuria, with the Haslehurst's eighteen-year-old daughter, Lavender, as their governess. This was a very real kindness, for Ann was still a delicate child and I, after such a long period of nursing her, awoke at the slightest bleat of every goat, thinking it was Ann's cry, and was badly in need of a complete rest and change. Great was the general rejoicing, and although we could only afford to travel German Third Class at a fare of £33 to the United Kingdom, we found to our horror that we had spent double that sum in celebration between Nairobi and Genoa.

In those days, most of the young Kenya settlers travelled Tourist on the German boats, which were out to catch the tourist trade, so the service was courteous, the food ample, and the accommodation cramped but clean. We had an inside cabin, which became an inferno in the Red Sea, but this did not worry us as we slept on deck. The person it did worry was the large and rotund Chief Steward, 'Herr Apel.' To take mattresses and bedding up on deck was strictly *"verboten,"* but each night we managed to do so, by the simple ruse of my engaging Herr Apel in conversation about the growth of his carefully tended hyacinth while Brian nipped up on deck with the bedding. It was all great fun, as the whole of the Third Class was taken over by Kenya settlers and so we had many of our young friends on board.

My sister had married a Gunner and as they were stationed at Gibraltar, we had arranged to see them on our way home, for the German boat called at Malaga. I knew her husband, Gerald Wolfe-Barry, who had been a constant visitor at our house in Ayr before I sailed for Kenya, but they had not met Brian. Determined that Brian should make a good impression, we had decided to be up and dressed and ready for them by 8 a.m., never thinking that they would arrive before then, as Malaga is some seventy miles from Gibraltar by road. But our plans went awry: In order to see as much of us as possible, they had left Malaga in the early hours and were on the quayside as we, dishevelled in our rumpled night attire, leant over the rail of the top deck.

My mother's introduction to her son-in-law was amusing too. We were so broke on arrival in London that the first thing Brian did was to bound up the steps of her London hotel and ask her for 7/6d to pay the waiting taxi. Far from being astonished, my mother's reaction was magnificent. "Of course, Brian dear," she said. "Now I know you have joined the family."

I was very excited, for although I had been happy, the years of separation from my family had seemed long. With no air mail, no radio, and letters taking five weeks each way, one is apt to feel exiled, especially during the bad patches.

My mother, I have since realised, was shocked at our appearance. We had no new clothes, and indeed we must have looked awful. Brian was wearing a grey suit which was yellow with age, and I the tweed coat in which I had set sail six years previously, with its then fashionable waistline around my hips and its sleeves badly shrunk from repeated washings. Mum did not let us see how shocked she was, but merely took us to a nearby London store, where we shed garments on every floor and emerged completely re-clothed.

We had a glorious, carefree leave, then set off for the return journey to Kenya. My mother was to come with us, joining us at Genoa. But first we took a P & O boat as far as Gibraltar to visit my sister for ten days. There we enjoyed a round of picnics, polo and parties which seemed to make up the life of the British Garrison in the 1930s, afterwards going on to Marseilles in another P & O boat for three days with my aunt and uncle in their Monte Carlo villa. My aunt sent us down in her Rolls Royce Phantom to Genoa, and as there had been a landslide on the coast road, we had to go by an inland route which took us up into the Italian Alps. Here in 1933 the fortifications and troop movements were an eye-opener.

So we arrived by Rolls Royce to travel back to Kenya as Third Class passengers on a German boat. What a change of atmosphere, unbelievable in such a short time, for Hitler was on the march. My mother was awaiting us on board and told us that the officers and stewards were distinctly unfriendly and even rude. We immediately noticed the change ourselves and were fascinated by the Heil Hitlers and the heel clicking, for a very important high-ranking Nazi was amongst the First Class passengers, going out to organise Tanganyika for the Third Reich. Alas, he had infected the whole ship with the Nazi spirit, and the anti-British feeling ran so high that an international incident was nearly caused by a young Nazi being pronounced winner of the greasy-pole event after biting Brian so as to loosen his grip.

On arrival in Mombasa, we naturally took the train to Nairobi. What a contrast between this trip and my first rail journey in 1927. By 1933 the tracks had been metalled, so the passengers were no longer smothered in red dust, and we travelled in the comparative comfort of the new coaches. I say comparative, for many of the early settlers preferred the old non-corridor compartments which were far more roomy and gave one the privacy of one's own bathroom.

On arrival in Nairobi, Brian went straight to the agent who was selling our coffee. Samples of the different grades had been sent down by my brother, to be in the agent's hands on our arrival. My husband was shown into a very lush office, with a deep pile carpet on the floor and the agent sitting behind an enormous desk. After an exchange of the usual courtesies, the agent proceeded to damn our coffee right, left and centre, ending by saying that for such a poor quality coffee he could not possibly offer more than £40 per ton. Brian was furious, as he could see nothing wrong with the coffee. He told the agent politely to go to the devil, saying he could not accept his offer, but would ship the consignment home and let it take its chance on the London market.

It was a great blow, for having just had a most expensive leave, we were dependent on getting a good price for this our first crop of twenty-five tons. We believed the agent was attempting to put over a fast one, but we could not be sure, so a general aura of gloom hung over our return, as well as a feeling that young Charles had somehow slipped up in processing the coffee. What was our delighted relief when two months afterwards, a cable arrived from JK Gilliat & Co. saying that our coffee had topped the market at that particular auction, realising the price of £131 per ton. So much for the Nairobi agent! Today, under the organised marketing of the Kenya Planters Coffee Union, the individual planter is not at the mercy of the unscrupulous agent as he was in the old days.

JK Gilliat & Co. handled the bulk of the coffee crop at that time. It was a wonderful feeling to be able to go into the London office of these Merchant Princes to collect a cheque for several hundreds of pounds as an advance against the crop. That was all right when the crop materialised, but the trouble began when hail or Coffee Berry Disease, then prevalent in Kenya, caused a crop failure, or when, because of a fall in coffee prices, the crop only realised half its estimated value.

During the 1930 Slump, many planters were so indebted as to be at the mercy of their agents, as they had taken advances not only in respect to the harvested crop, but even against crops not yet on the trees. For there would be a crop loss unless cultivation were maintained and the necessary manuring and spraying against such diseases as Coffee Berry Disease, as well as pest control, were continued. Thus the unhappy planter was in a cleft stick, for with his indebtedness, he could not risk crop failure, so he applied for yet another loan, often mortgaging his farm to do so, and getting ever deeper and deeper into debt.

JK Gilliat certainly fulfilled a need before organised marketing came into being, but we paid dearly for their services. While Kenya coffee sold at anything from 2/- to 2/8d per lb in the London shops, the planter only got a meagre 2d or 3d per lb on the plantation. Without the middleman, the profit figure on the plantation would have risen to a steady 3d per lb after all costs of production, transport, marketing, etc., had been deducted – a very different figure. But to do this would have required capital. Also, such was the tyranny of the powerful Coffee Ring that once a planter became a blackleg, he had not a hope of selling again under the same mark in the Mincing Lane market.

Amongst other services Gilliat's provided for their clients, they sent out a monthly social column, which read rather like a Court Circular. With no BBC News, we all much enjoyed this breath of London, but the price paid for this as well as for their other services was far too high.

The prices realised at the auctions of 1933 were a flash in the pan, for we were on the verge of the great coffee slump of the Thirties, when the lower grades fell to £22 per ton, a price which did not even cover the cost of production, let alone transporting, marketing, etc. A tragedy for us, as our coffee was about to come into full bearing, and one which caused the bankruptcy of many Kenya planters. Gone were our hopes of an early retirement as coffee barons to a delightful little Queen Anne home in Somersetshire; what we faced was a struggle for survival.

Perhaps you wonder why we chose coffee, but our reasons were sound enough. Who could have foretold that world overproduction would cause the bottom to fall out of the coffee market, in spite of Brazil's burning its crop? At that time the condition of the link main road made the marketing of fresh produce quite impossible. Coffee could lie in one's stores over the period of the long rains, when the mud roads became impassable, and the good prices then obtained could bear the cost of the long haul, sixty miles by lorry, to the railhead at Lumbwa. So it did not appear a foolish choice when we started out in 1929 to plant our coffee at Kipkebe with such high hopes.

True, we managed to survive the slump, but only with the assistance of the Land Bank, and the crippling interest of $7^{1}/_{2}\%$ was to prove a millstone around our necks. But we were lucky; the disastrous fall in prices spelt ruin for many coffee farmers.

They disappeared, leaving their once well-tended plantations to become a tangled mass of vegetation, which bore witness to the extent of the damage done by the slump to the whole coffee industry in Kenya. Those who survived were forced onto the Land Bank, and although it is true that the loans made it possible for many to by-pass bankruptcy, the Bank certainly took its pound of flesh.

It took us fifteen years to repay our loan and we paid back in interest as much again as the original loan. A long hard road to solvency, which was only achieved as a result of turning the farm into a small private company.

Twice during our years at Kipkebe I was to see the terrifying power of witchcraft. The first occasion was when my brother Charles was helping us on the farm. As Brian had gone off for the day to some Defence Force meeting in Kericho, Charles, completely baffled, came in to ask me what he should do: Lying on the back road was a poor little girl, writhing in agony, her stomach dreadfully distended, surrounded by the farm labour who said she had been bewitched and would surely die at four o'clock. They were most definite about the hour and as it was then 2 p.m., we did not have much time to lose.

The culprit who had cast the spell was a boy of fourteen, son of a witchdoctor, who no doubt was trying out the power that would one day be his, for the craft was handed down from father to son. The spell had been cast as they were picking coffee together and started to quarrel. The boy then let his shadow fall on the little girl and cursed her, saying she would die, and from that moment the pains started.

We carried her into the shade of the farm store, but were at our wits' end, for she seemed to be getting worse. The culprit was threatened with a beating and with being handed over to the police if the spell were not removed, all to no avail. In desperation, with only one hour to go, we sent for the farm elders and they called an emergency meeting of their tribunal.

The boy was handed over to them and after a very short time was led back to us. Arap N'yige, the Chief Elder, asked that he and the boy be left alone with the little girl. We agreed and they disappeared into the store, while we waited outside, but we saw and heard nothing beyond a low murmur of voices. What was our amazement when about a quarter of an hour later, the door opened and arap N'yige called us in, and there was the little girl sitting up, her stomach having returned to its normal size. She seemed to be quite well in every other respect, and within half an hour was back in the shamba coffee-picking.

Arap N'yige explained afterwards that the elders had not wasted time in idle threats but had just told the boy that he was to remove the spell immediately or he would be killed. The boy saw that the elders meant what they said, and so, wishing to live a little longer, he agreed to use his power to remove the spell. An astonishing affair, but apparently quite simple to an experienced practitioner.

The other case of bewitching with which I came in contact personally was that of our milk recorder, Musa, an educated, English-speaking Luo. This happened much later, during the war, when I was running the farm.

After the coffee slump we turned to mixed farming, including dairy cows. When our first twelve cows arrived, I asked our old Luo Obilo, who had been one of our head *nyaparas* on the coffee side, if he would like to be my milk recorder. He accepted the post with alacrity. All went well at first when we were only milking 12 cows, but when all our cows calved and eventually there were over 100 to be milked, trouble began.

Obilo's elementary knowledge of the three R's was not sufficient to cope with dairy records. The only answer was for me to employ a younger man, a trained recorder from the Maseno School, as assistant. This I did, but after a year, just as he had worked into the job and was becoming really valuable, he came to me and said he wanted to go. When I asked him why, I was assured that nothing was wrong, but that he must leave at once. Although I questioned him closely, begging him to tell me what was the matter, he only rolled his eyes and looked profoundly unhappy. Not one word could I get out of him.

After losing two excellent assistants in this way, I engaged Musa, but after a year he, too, came to me and said he must go. Again I was assured that he liked his work and that there was nothing wrong. I insisted that there must be, for a sensible man does not throw up a good salary and a job without reason. He agreed that that was true, but said, "If I tell you what is troubling me, Memsahib, you will laugh at me, for I am a Christian and I know I should not believe these foolish things, but the truth is that I and my family are being bewitched."

I did not laugh, for I discovered that they had been living their days in fear and their nights in terror, lying huddled together in their house, listening for the footsteps and muttered incantations that they knew would inevitably come. In the morning, there was proof of these nightly visitations, for there were footprints in the flower beds surrounding their little cottage, and bags of bones, pebbles, and other items known to be the stock-in-trade of a dealer in magic and spells were found buried in small holes in front of their door. Poor things, the dread of these sleepless nights of terror was making them all ill. It was not very reassuring to learn that everyone on the farm knew about the bewitching, and were all convinced that Musa and his family would die before the year was out.

Musa admitted that he knew who was casting the spell, but refused to speak the dread name, in case worse might befall. Finally, he was persuaded to write it on a bit of paper, which he folded and handed to me. When I opened the paper I could not believe my eyes, for there was the name of our good and faithful Obilo. Alas, after a lengthy investigation it was proven without any doubt to be Obilo, nor did he deny the charges. We were in a dilemma for we had had no quarrel with this old Luo, who had served us loyally for over seventeen years.

My husband, who was home on leave, decided to call in the District Commissioner and to ask his advice. The District Commissioner came down from Kericho and, having had all the facts of the case presented to him, he said that we must get rid of Obilo immediately, as once a Luo became proficient in the art of bewitching he could never give it up; it gave a person such a sense of power over his fellow men. With a degree in witchcraft, the removal of anyone who stood in your path was simple, as Obilo had found. Fearing that the trained dairy assistants would oust him from his post, he had got rid of them one by one.

So on the DC's advice, Obilo was summarily dismissed, being paid a month's wage in lieu of notice, as well as compensation for the value of his standing crops, etc. All very sad after such years of faithful service. He returned to his home some sixty miles distant with his wife and goods and chattels, and Musa and his family appeared to recover.

All went well until six months later, Obilo returned to Sotik, taking a humble job as a turnboy on a lorry. Although he lived somewhere in the township, a distance of eight miles, he started to bewitch by remote control. His hatred was such that he determined to get Musa out of his position of head dairy recorder at Kipkebe, resolving that if he could not have the job, neither should Musa. So, in the end, the unhappy Musa had to leave, although he did return when Obilo finally left Sotik, and he remained with us for many years.

After these two experiences, never again shall I doubt the existence of witchcraft, or its terrifying power.

Arriving back from home leave recently, my daughter-in-law was surprised to find only one of her mother's servants there to greet her, namely the ancient cook. On enquiring where the others were, she was told that they had all, including the Kikuyu *ayah*, been taken off to the local witchdoctor by the young man who rents their bungalow, as his wireless set had been stolen and they had been accused of the theft by his house servants. Fortunately, the *ayah* and my daughter-in-law's head boy were proved innocent, and the theft pinned on the renter's servants by the witchdoctor. This may be done by some ancient ritual such as walking over hot charcoal, but more often the culprit's own guilty conscience gives him away in the face of discovery, for Africans believe implicitly in the witchdoctor's clairvoyant powers.

A modern tailpiece which shows that even now, witchcraft still plays an important part in the lives of the Africans.

A house party particularly famous in Sotik's annals was held in 1934. It was announced that HE The Governor, Sir Joseph Byrne, would visit the district, and he was to stay at a large estate in East Sotik. The news of the impending three-day visit spread like wildfire and Sotik hummed with agitated speculation, for no one knew if this visit was to be of an official or purely private nature.

His Excellency, nicknamed 'Jaunty Joe,' had met his hostess-to-be at a Government House party, and, being a susceptible male, had fallen under the spell of her beautiful blue eyes. Hence, a three-day visit to our back block was included in one of his first tours. Sotik, unused to these attentions, was surprised, but naturally delighted, and although the Committee had not been consulted officially as to where the Governor was to stay, it decided to recapture some initiative by staging a gymkhana and dance for the visit.

In order that His Excellency should be suitably entertained, a house-party was arranged and the locally invited guests, who consisted of our great friends and near neighbours the Sharps, along with ourselves and a gay young bachelor called Hurleigh Hopley, were asked to bring some of their household goods to fill in gaps in the furnishing. We arrived as bidden with our rugs, coffee cups and even a pair of long black gloves for our hostess, an hour before the Government House party were due.

It consisted of the Governor, his daughter Mrs Stewart Smith, and his Aide-de-Camp, Captain Maitland Edye, soon to be our next-door neighbour. Our beautiful hostess, looking too lovely in a blue silk dress matching the deep blue of those wonderful eyes, met us saying in the most impressive of tones, "I hope you won't mind but I've decided to run this house-party on the lines of one in an English country house by having a dressing-gong rung half an hour before the dinner-gong." We said we did not object and would pay heed to the gongs. But on being shown our quarters, we did not feel that they measured up to country house standards, as the Shaws and the Sharps were in one bedroom, with only a small blanket, which did not even meet the floor, suspended from the ceiling between the four single beds. In fact, the only place you could not be seen was on top of the beds.

Before leaving us, our hostess gave us our orders, saying, "I must be in charge of His Excellency, while you, Agnes, can look after Mrs Stewart Smith and Brian can go ahead to prepare the crowds." Her final words were, "Now you can change and when they arrive, you will be playing tennis, but stop when the Governor reaches the pavilion and come forward to be introduced."

After her departure, we collapsed in helpless laughter, deciding that our quarters, with our iron bedsteads and one tin basin between the four of us, resembled life in a tenement rather than in a country house. However, we obeyed our orders and went forth to play tennis and, as His

Excellency crossed the back of the court, my husband's serve hit him, a quite unrehearsed effect.

Another unrehearsed effect was when the electric light plant failed after dinner, during a game of bridge. Emmie Sharp swore that some male toe tried to play 'footy-footy' with her and she was equally certain that it was not her husband's. We had never been guests at a more extraordinary house party, and have often laughed since about the many ridiculous things which happened, for our lovely hostess did not possess one grain of a sense of humour. For instance, she solemnly said to George Maitland Edye, "I do hope His Excellency won't mind walking down the garden path, for I'm afraid our house doesn't run to modern conveniences." To which George replied, "Well, if he does mind he'll be a very unhappy old gentleman, as we are staying here for three days."

CHAPTER 7

Putting Sotik on the Map

"Wha does the utmost that he can Will whyles do mair."

--Robert Burns

In the years between 1934 and the outbreak of war in 1939, Sotik went through a period of change and development, and our lives, so closely bound up with the district, changed too. At first the change was slow enough. Until 1936 coffee was still our main crop, and slump conditions held us in their grip; but in 1934 the District Association made its first concerted effort to start Sotik on the path of real development by a campaign of publicity to put Sotik on the map.

In 1935 the Morris Carter Commission report was published, and the borders between native lands and the White Highlands were fixed, which enabled more farms in Sotik to be taken up, and in 1936 a new farming policy was presented to the district by an Agricultural Commission. From then on Sotik began, literally, to pull itself out of the mud, and the new impetus given to food production by the war put many of the struggling farms on their feet. But it was still a slow and hard struggle.

The story of Sotik's awakening begins in 1934. Up till then, pioneering, not publicity, had been the district's preoccupation. My mother, visiting us in 1933, complained that she was tired of trying to explain where Sotik was, as when she told people she met in other parts of Kenya that her daughter lived in Sotik, their immediate question was, "Oh, where is that, I've never heard of it."

As a result, we put the need for publicity to the District Association and my husband and I were given the task of forming Sotik's Publicity Committee in February 1934. The first "Sotik Notes," published in the *East African Standard* of that month, started like this: "Sotik, where is it? Yes, we do really exist, are very much alive and think that it's time the rest of Kenya knew something more about us than, 'Oh, Sotik, I believe that's a place somewhere beyond Kericho.'"

Our Committee consisted of Colonel Matheson, the 'First Citizen' of North Sotik, a successful coffee farmer with a bent for business; Mr and Mrs Royston, leading personalities and stock farmers of East Sotik; and Mrs Evans, a woman of character with an original mind. Our first task was to write up the district for advertising purposes, and the publication of our little brochure *Sotik* was welcomed by the tourist Travel and Publicity Association in these words: "A brochure entitled *Sotik* which is issued by the Sotik Settlers Association is a very excellent tribute to local energy and enterprise."

Whether or not it was a tribute to the veracity of the Sotik Committee is another matter, for it needed quite a stretch of the imagination to recognise Ma Collett's filthy hovel as "Sotik boasts a modern Post Office and up-to-date European store." But we felt justified in some wishful thinking when we had the will to work and only time was needed to make it all become a reality.

Re-reading the glowing description of what Sotik had to offer, I think that our Committee was definitely taking a chance. It was true, however, that Sotik had some undoubted advantages, for due to its inaccessibility (not mentioned) and the high cost of transport (glossed over), its undeveloped land, although very fertile with one of the best rainfalls in the Colony, could be bought for as little as from Shs 15/- to £3 per acre, according to whether it was suitable for grazing or for the planting of coffee. The brochure states that there were some 4,000 acres of coffee planted in 1936 and that there were as many as eighty to ninety Europeans settled in the district by then, on thirty-five farms. In North Sotik, by 1937 our ten families had grown to nearly twice that number of householders.

In 1935 the Morris Carter Commission presented its report. This was of vital importance to all those who had taken up land in Kenya, and was in fact the main political event of the year. As a member of the Sotik Publicity Committee I commented on the Commission's findings. In the light of later events they were interesting and in fact foreshadowed the setting up of the Highlands Board [set up in 1939 to protect the rights of the inhabitants of the White Highlands] on which, as an Elected Member of the Legislative Council, I later served.

The conclusion of the Sotik Publicity Committee was that there can be few in Sotik who look on the passing of 1935 with any regret. Produce prices were such as to make farming a mockery. But the lowest ebb was to prove the turning point of the tide of fortune. The year 1936 laid the foundations of a new prosperity for the farming community. New farm policies were formulated and began slowly to be put into practice, and Sotik's total reliance on coffee as a cash crop was gradually ended.

There were two events in 1936 which I remember with pleasure: One was the Coronation of King George VI and Queen Elizabeth, and the other the spread of radio communications. The second greatly enhanced our enjoyment of, and sense of participation in, the first. Indeed, wireless made the greatest difference to our lives in Kenya. Going through some old papers, I came across an article I wrote in 1937 called "Wireless Connections" for a magazine sponsored by the Overseas League. It is now out of date, since later development in the science of radio and electronics has been so tremendous, but as it describes what the coming of radio meant to us in the outlying district of Sotik I shall quote the first paragraphs:

"Our far-flung Empire. How often has that phrase been used, and do the people of England ever stop to consider what it means for many of the King's subjects? Those words still spell for some, and used to spell for many more, exile, isolation, and a life spent away from one's own people in a new land. I say 'used to', for now that is all changed. The exile may still exist for many, but the sense of isolation is no more.

"This wonderful change has been brought about by the invention and gradual improvement in radio. This improvement has been so great in the last few years that it is now possible for all the King's subjects to be connected by wireless with London, the centre of the Empire. That it is now possible for our King to speak directly to his subjects in all corners of the world may have far-reaching effects and will surely be the means of welding the great Commonwealth of Nations together in a stronger bond than ever before. That is the wider aspect of radio. But let us take a more personal view: Think back a few years and then compare the change brought about by broadcasting and the speeding up of communications by air travel.

"Ten years ago in Kenya in the outlying district where I live, mails took nearly a month from London to Nairobi, then on by train, lorry and, for the last forty miles, by native runner. There was only one mail per week and this, which was awaited with impatience, often arrived sodden with rain and smelling of kippers, which the Postmistress had thoughtfully put in one's mailbag, the result being that both kippers and mail arrived in a rather high condition! Apart from the mail boy there was no direct connection with the outside world. No wonder a sense of exile and isolation existed and made the reverses that are too often the daily lot of the Settler doubly hard to bear.

"Today, the conditions are very different. A letter and answer can be received from England within two weeks. Mails are brought by lorry to within a few miles of the farms, three times a week. It is possible to step into a luxurious airliner and be in London within five days. Someone once remarked that the rapid transportation from the solitude of darkest

Africa to the terrifying hubbub of London was almost too great a shock for the average mentality. Air travel as yet is only within the reach of the wealthy, but wireless is within the reach of millions."

During the war, because I had the only radio in the area I would take notes from the daily war news bulletins and relay the news at once to all my neighbours on the party telephone line. I remember hearing the church bells of England ring out, all those thousands of miles away, after the victory of El Alamein.

Today, TV has brought us the marvel of visual sight, and with TV and radio one can, like Puck, that prophetic sprite, "put a girdle round the earth in forty minutes."

In order to mark Coronation Day in 1936, Sotik, by reason of its length and the bad state of roads owing to the heavy rains at the time, had to hold two celebrations, one at either end of the district. In this way everyone was able to take part in the general rejoicing.

In the south end, settlers foregathered at the Club, where a very enjoyable day was spent. The proceedings were opened by Lt Col Donald McLeod, DSO, who held a parade of ex-servicemen, together with a squad of *askaris* [African police]. The flag having been saluted and "God Save the King" having been sung, he made a short speech in which he said that the welding together of the British Empire on this day by the crowning of our King and Queen would be a step along the path of world peace.

After the parade everyone adjourned to the Club, where the King's health was drunk and Mrs McLeod presented Coronation Medals to the children. The presentation was followed by a tree-planting ceremony, the planting being done by the younger members of the community. There was golf or tennis for those who felt energetic, followed by luncheon, and a wireless set made it possible for everyone to hear the Coronation broadcast. In the evening a dance was held, followed by a display of fireworks, and the celebrations were brought to a close with a colossal bonfire.

At the north end of Sotik, everyone was invited to foregather at a local estate, and enjoyed an excellent lunch provided by Mrs WG George. The King's health was drunk and the wireless set enabled everyone to hear the broadcast from London. In the evening most of the settlers again braved the roads and, assisted by oxen, arrived to dine at a nearby farm; an interesting evening was spent listening in to the Empire's homage. This Coronation broadcast culminated with the King's speech, which in its sincerity was deeply moving.

We felt that it was the dawn of a new era, but it was more surely the passing of an old, as celebrations of this kind, where the speeches refer to the welding together of the British Empire, have passed into history. No longer today can you see the brave sight of the Union Jack flying proudly against Kenya's azure sky. But who was to know then that the gentle breeze that stirred the flag was to become a hurricane of change?

So, undisturbed, we forged ahead, for although conservative in our political outlook, the Kenya settlers were go-ahead farmers and under such men as Colonel Matheson, George Maitland Edye, RC Royston, and WG George, Sotik's planning in the middle Thirties was imaginative. In their search for prosperity, no crop potential was left unexplored.

Looking back over the eighteen years after 1920 when the 'Soldier Settler' arrived to augment the real pioneers, my husband wrote that "it is probably safe to say that those who placed their faith in stock are those who have weathered more successfully the trials and stresses of the intervening years." He well remembers his disappointment on his arrival in the country to find that his 1,200-acre Soldier Settler farm was not in the flax or coffee belt, but only a stock farm in West Kenya, 120 miles from the railway.

Had Sotik gone in for stock instead of flax and coffee, it would have quite a different story to tell today. But at that time with coffee and flax booming, and the absence of roads and marketing facilities, stock hardly came into the picture. When flax faded out, coffee was practically the only commodity produced. When the railway to Sotik was surveyed, more settlers arrived and maize growing increased, but when the plans for the branch line were dropped, farming operations largely reverted to coffee, with the result that in the ensuing years of declining prices, planters became deeply indebted.

In 1936 there came to the district an Agricultural Commission preaching mixed farming, with stock as the key to future prosperity. Unfortunately, in many cases there was little or no money left to take advantage of this advice, and incredible as it seemed to the would-be borrower, the Land Bank was shy in advancing money for this development.

Mr Thornton was Secretary to the Land Bank for many years, and I remember with gratitude the understanding kindness of that very humane man. 'Papa' Thornton, with all a Cockney's native wit and humour, helped many a Kenya farming lame dog over a stile. What he said at a Sotik meeting was typical of his sense of humour. Opening his remarks by stating that the Kenya Land Bank was run as a business institution and not as a Government Department, he congratulated the

Sotik settlers on their enthusiasm, which had resulted in his being here with this clutch of experts, and gave an assurance that the Land Bank would look kindly on any schemes to broaden the basis of production and produce a monthly cheque which, he added, the Bank would then have pleasure in taking off the producer with great promptitude.

Alas, Mr Thornton's kindness and foresight did not pervade the whole of the Bank, and loans were difficult to get. But the seeds of mixed farming had fallen on fertile soil, and bit by bit money was scraped together somehow, and areas of uneconomic coffee were cut out and small acreages of pyrethrum, high nicotine content tobacco, granadilla, maize and beans substituted. Production was small at first, but in the end all these lines brought in their monthly quotas to the farm budget. Given a period of stable prices, they were bound to have a revitalizing effect on the district.

I cannot leave this account of the change of farming policy in Sotik without mentioning two men who did a lot to establish the district's prosperity. One was Major CJ Caddick, a pioneer in cattle farming who lived in Kenya for 20 years, of which he spent the last eight in the Sotik district as our next-door neighbour. He moved to Kapsasura Farm in 1931 and lived there until he died in November 1939. He was quick to see the potential of the rich grazing, which he used to say was Sotik's greatest asset, and of dairying as a basis for a mixed farming economy.

After clearing, fencing and cleaning up one or two paddocks by the dipping of native cattle in this tick infested area, he introduced some high-grade Jersey cows, as well as a pure-bred bull which he imported from South Africa. In spite of heavy losses, he persevered and that his faith was more than justified was borne out by the splendid herds of high-grade cattle, sired by pure-bred bulls, which grazed those fertile pastures for twenty years and more thereafter. For more than anything else, it was the monthly cream cheque which pulled Sotik out of its Slough of Slumps.

To us he was a kindly neighbour and many's the evening he spent in our armchair, reminiscing about the Boer War. Our difficulty was to dislodge him at bedtime, and when we reached the point in the story of "...and there stood Smith Dorien up on the bridge and I said to him dammit, Sir..." Brian and I knew it was time to attract his attention to the lateness of the hour by beating up the cushions, etc. He would then rise, saying, "Good gracious, I'm afraid I've kept you up a bit," and depart. Dear old man, we missed him after his death, and Kapsasura without him never seemed quite the same.

The second man who had a great influence on the district was Mr

GR Morrison, a well-known Nakuru farmer. He visited Sotik in the years just before the Second World War and saw the great potential of the district for tea growing. At that time, Government restricted the planting of tea by individual farmers in order to protect the vested interests of the big tea companies. Mr Morrison wrote a well-publicised article attacking this policy, from which I quote: "In at least two ways Sotik must be unique. No comparable community is farming at so great a distance from railhead and no other area has been created as a buffer state between two fighting tribes."

As Mr Morrison wrote, "Every prospect pleases except the financial one and only the transport facilities are vile!" He went on to describe the Sotik settlers' search for a stable foundation crop to take the place of coffee, which though once thriving, was ruined by Coffee Berry Disease. In this connection, he said, "It must seem ironical to those who are struggling under a burden of debt that much of their land is eminently suitable for tea, one of Kenya's most profitable crops, and I couldn't help feeling surprise that the restriction on planting was so complacently accepted by the Sotik settlers."

Mr Morrison's article had the desired effect and jolted the Sotik Settlers' Association into action, for they realised that tea and cattle were the two industries that could restore the district's prosperity, which had suffered so grievously from the failure of coffee; tea in the wetter areas, dairying in those with a moderate rainfall, and ranching in the low-lying, hot, dry parts bordering on the Maasai Reserve.

As a result of pressure, the Government lifted the tea planting restrictions and the first tea was planted on Kipkebe in May 1940. Now, both at Kipkebe and on much of the land that was Kimoru, many hundreds of acres are under tea, forming a part of the flourishing tea plantations of North Sotik – the only area of the development in Sotik which has remained in a recognisable form since Independence.

Mr Morrison's article did much to change the face of farming in North Sotik. We were also pleased by what he said of our house, Kipkebe, which he described as follows: "I saw the most delightful house of the joined up rondavel type that I have ever seen. It was built of mud bricks and thatch and I dare say did not figure very high in the farm's valuation, but it had a happy and individual air about it – I liked it and I felt sure the garden liked it and the hillside thought it just fitted in, and surely no one can think for a moment that all gardens like the houses they surround!"

To the changes going on in Sotik during those years was added yet another: A new Elected Member to represent us. The Member for

Nyanza had been the Hon Conway Harvey, but in Sotik we hardly ever saw him. Now the district was becoming more politically aware, and a new candidate offered herself to the voters of Nyanza. This was Lady Sidney Farrar.

Once before, in 1934, Conway Harvey's membership had been challenged, but since on that occasion he met his opponent's car around a blind corner, forcing him off the road and down a steep bank into a ravine, he might be said to have won that contest before it came to polling day. Lady Sidney Farrar's challenge was a much more formidable affair, and as the poor old boy was quite unable to compete either with her charm or capabilities, he was defeated, albeit by one vote.

Colonel Maitland Edye, the Chairman of our Sotik Settlers' Association, welcoming Lady Sidney on her first visit after her victory, said he was in rather an invidious position as at his last meeting he had taken the Chair for her late opponent. But he was glad of the opportunity to recant his narrow-minded prejudices in regard to the feminine influence in politics, adding that the very sincere and efficient manner in which Lady Sidney was tackling all the district's problems had won everyone's admiration. After hearing her speak, Colonel Edye said the fact that our new Member was a working farmer and not a politician was a point in her favour, and to have someone representing the constituency who had our interests at heart would be a new experience.

Sir Robert Brooke-Popham was Governor during those halcyon days, so the welcome given to the Brooke-Pophams on their first two-day visit was of the warmest, best summed up by the words of "Robbie", the stalwart Master of the Sotik Hunt, one of the oldest settlers, a warm-hearted and charming Cockney who said he "'oped that 'is H'Excellency would 'ave an 'appy time with the 'ounds!"

CHAPTER 8

War

> *"You that have faith to look with fearless eyes*
> *Beyond the tragedy of a world at strife,*
> *And trust that out of night and death shall rise*
> *The dawn of ampler life."*
> *--Owen Seaman*

September 3rd, 1939. War!

That Sunday was punctuated with wireless bulletins and calls from the Sotik Commandant to stand to, stand to!

At 10 p.m., I remember telephoning him to know if we still needed to stand to, or could we go to bed. We were given permission to retire, but told that next day Brian must report with three days' iron rations at the local bridge. I had no idea what an iron ration was, but it sounded a very indigestible diet.

A few days before, how happy and excited we had all been, for we were on our way to Mombasa. The children, aged nine and ten, had never seen the sea, but at last we had saved enough in the Holiday Fund and the much-planned fortnight at the Coast was about to become a reality. But alas, Brian was in the Kenya Defence Force and he got his call-up notice, sent on by telephone from Sotik, as we reached Nairobi. So back we went, in spite of tears, for the disappointment was intense – so great in fact that poor little Ann developed an attack of shingles.

On the Monday, Brian pinned on a Kenya Defence Force armlet and we repaired dutifully to Kijaur Bridge complete with iron rations. There we were joined by another three members of the KDF, looking extremely unsmart in khaki shorts and open-necked shirts, the tribal dress of the settler. Suddenly, up drove a large limousine and out stepped a most military figure, all glorious in the uniform of the 17th Lancers: chain mail, epaulettes, spurs, and all. Our local Gauleiter had arrived. He promptly fell-in in the scruffy squad of four for the purpose of reading the orders of the day.

A site was found for a small corrugated iron hut, a slit trench and a machine gun emplacement, to command the approaches of the bridge.

For Kijaur, we were surprised to learn, was a post of great strategic importance. It was through this back door that German infiltrators from Tanganyika were expected to sweep to catch Kenya unawares. Had not the Count and Countess Doenhoff, a German couple, supposedly farming in the Maasai Reserve, charmed everyone with their Continental ways, and turned out to be Nazis and been recalled to Germany only a week or two previously?

The Commandant departed, leaving behind on that Sotik road a most dejected looking working party to man the Kijaur Post, our bulwark against surprise attack.

The orders were four hours on and four hours off, later to be changed to eight on and eight off. This did not make matters much better, for periods of rest had to be spent in the tin hut where it was impossible to get any sleep owing to the ringing of the party line telephone. Fortunately the weather was dry, a deck-chair just fitted into the deep flood drain which served as a trench, and as nothing passed during the whole operation except for one Indian-owned lorry, I suspect that the squad, aided by a drop of 'Mother's ruin,' found the hours on duty spent in the trench more conducive to slumber than the periods in the hut. Even so, Brian said it was the most exhausting four days he had ever spent, for although at the end of the second day the BBC News announced that all Germans in Tanganyika had been interned, this news did not officially reach Headquarters, Nairobi, until two days later.

Ann and Mike with Granny Cree.

As to rations, iron or otherwise, the wives fed the camp, and the Army rations came up two months later, together with our daily allowances of Shs 4/- for a wife and Shs 2/- for each child.

Our Commandant had his worries, for although most of the local farmers were veterans of the 1914-1918 War, that was a long time ago, and it was not easy to be a peaceful farmer one day and to become a militant soldier the next in a place so far removed from the theatre of war. So perhaps it was understandable when, on his rounds of inspection of these newly set up guard posts, Colonel Maitland Edye found all members of one of the posts dining in their hut and no one on guard. On asking where the machine-gun was, he heard to his horror a rather ashamed voice reply, "In the box, Sir." So much for our introduction to World War II.

Brian joined the 1st Pioneers and went off to camp on the Kano Plains after hurried preparations for me to take over the farm. He was there for two months and we were able to visit him once or twice in camp before the Pioneers were transferred to Garba Tula. After that, except for short and infrequent periods of leave, he disappeared from our lives until the Autumn of 1945, when he was demobbed on the grounds of ill-health, the result of over three years' service in the northern Frontier District and the unhealthy climate of Mogadishu.

My mother, who had come out for a year to run my house and look

Local Kenya Defence Force guarding the Kijaur Bridge

after the children while I had an operation for gallstones, told us that she would stay on to keep me company while Brian was in the Army. And she did, bless her, giving me her companionship, counsel and comfort during those four long and lonely years.

As to the children, Michael and young David Edye had just gone to the excellent preparatory school of Pembroke House, where Michael was to spend four happy years, and the Edyes, our kind neighbours, offered to let Ann live with them to continue having lessons with their daughter, Penelope, from their darling old Scots governess. As I had neither the time nor the petrol for the daily transport, Ann stayed with the Edyes, coming home for weekends only.

Miss MacKay, or 'Kiki' as she was called, was a splendid Scotswoman of the old school, an excellent teacher, who, although the greatest fun, stood no nonsense during school hours. The children, who had been her pupils already for two years, loved her, and I have no doubt that they owe a lot to her wise rule and training.

The month of September 1939 was one of turmoil and change, after which my mother and I took up our new pattern, which was to be our daily routine for those war years. For the first twelve years of my married life I had been dependent on Brian for everything, sticking strictly to my department of babies, house, garden and hens. Now, jolted out of my happy humdrum rut, I was entirely adrift in an uncharted sea. My Swahili did not go beyond kitchen requirements and my knowledge of farming was limited to dealing with a labour force of four outside the house, namely the hen *toto* who looked after the poultry and the three garden boys.

Somehow I muddled through those first three months, learning by my many mistakes, though my over-spending brought a stern letter with a threat of foreclosure from the Land Bank, asking me to come and see the Secretary in Nairobi at once. This occurred in January 1940 and I was in bed with influenza. But 'flu or no 'flu I got up and dressed and shot off to Nakuru in the car, where fortunately Brian was on a course at the OCTU. He got leave and together we set off for the dreaded interview. It couldn't have been worse, for the Chairman, a successful businessman, was one of the hardest and most unsympathetic men it has ever been my misfortune to meet.

We pleaded the failure of our coffee crop through hail, for in one hailstorm we estimated that ten tons had been knocked off the trees, and the rest was hail-damaged, along with the young wood which would bear the next year's crop. We pleaded Brian's call-up and my hopeless inexperience, all to no avail, for each and every plea was met by the implacable reply: "The fact remains, you have failed to keep up the interest and repayment on your loan."

It was then that I first experienced the very real kindness of Papa Thornton, Secretary of the Land Bank for so many years. For on the Chairman's departure, I put my head down on his desk and wept. Papa, far from being embarrassed, patted my shoulder in the most fatherly fashion, saying, "There, there, Ducks, don't take on so, we'll find a way, in spite of that nasty old codfish." And we did.

At that time, coffee prices had fallen so low as to be uneconomic, for £25 to £50 per ton did not cover the cost of production with all the necessary manuring, pruning and spraying for Coffee Berry Disease and other diseases or pests, let alone the haulage of 60 miles by lorry to railhead. So with the help and wise advice of the Sotik Land Bank Agent, Colonel JK Matheson, I gradually took out the 135 acres of coffee, replacing it with pyrethrum, granadilla and fodder crops.

However, as the loans had been granted on the security of land with repayment to be from coffee crop sales, his advice was of necessity private and I had to agree to bear the brunt of the Board's displeasure when my action was discovered. This I did, blaming my ignorance of the terms of the loan, but before the blow fell we had a stroke of luck in the shape of an unexpected windfall of £800 from the estate of an elderly aunt. This saved the situation, for it provided the ready cash for the purchase of the dairy herd on which the whole of our future farming operations were to be based.

So, bolstered by Aunt Bertha's legacy and toughened by necessity, I was able to face the justifiable wrath of the members of the Land Bank Board. In fact with JK's approval, I was even intrepid enough to send in a proposition for their consideration: that I should reap the pyrethrum just coming into production and keep the newly-acquired Ayrshire cows on what was technically their farm, provided I in my turn agreed to pay them any surplus after wages had been deducted from the monthly receipts. Also, I was to agree that a first charge on the cattle increase would be the repayment of their loans.

Thanks to the backing of Jimmy Matheson and the special pleading of Mr Thornton, my proposition was accepted – although perhaps the threat that if they foreclosed I would plead my case before the Governor as the wife of a serving soldier may have provided added persuasion. Anyway, the first battle was over, though the campaign still had to be fought on the farm front.

We decided on Ayrshires as the poor man's breed, though as I was an Ayrshire lass it seemed appropriate. Brian got a few days' leave from

Cattle on Kipkebe

the OCTU to go over to Nanyuki and buy the first twelve Ayrshire in-calf heifers from the herd of Granny Bastard of Nanyuki. The Bastards were old friends of my cousins and ours. It was dear old Granny who had told me that my likeness to Brian was so great that our marriage must have been made in heaven.

These twelve heifers with their Australian background did us proud. I think I can claim the honour of being the supplier to send in the smallest amount of cream to the Kenya Co-operative Creameries, since my February cream cheque only amounted to Shs 28/-, but by July the cheque had risen to over Shs 1,000/-.

Our next batch of heifers, indeed the main herd, was bought from the Manager for the estate of Guest, Keen & Nettlefold in the Aberdare high country. These dainty in-calf heifers were of pure Scottish descent, while our bulls came from the well-known Kivulini herd. In my efforts to become a dairymaid I sat at the feet of 'Chub' Millington, and most of the credit for the building up of what proved a most successful dairying venture must go to him, the kindest and wisest and most upright of men, and for years the undoubted King of the Ayrshire stock-breeders. Many were the visits we have enjoyed under the hospitable roof at Kivulini.

On the advice of HS Smith, a grand Scot who lived on a well-farmed hill at Londiani, pigs were added to the farm population. But only enough to take up my surplus skimmed milk, for as Smith said in one of the best Scottish accents, "If ye don't lose your head when the price goes up and go in for tae many, nor cut them all out when the price goes doon, you'll no go far wrang." My twelve stalwart sows, rejoicing in the names of Daisy, Buttercup, Poppy, Glover, and other field flowers, kept the bacon sheds supplied with a steady population of between sixty to eighty baconers, which augmented the farming budget by some £800 per annum.

One of Kipkebe's bulls

My surplus on the first year's mixed farming operations was £160, but by the end of 1943 the farm's gross annual income garnered from dairying, pigs, pyrethrum and granadilla had risen to £2,800. And by the time Brian returned at the end of 1943 we had repaid £3,000 of the £7,000 outstanding on the Land Bank debt.

In fairness to my husband, I must make it plain that my success was due to the change-over to mixed farming, with dairying as a basis, which was made possible by the building of the tar macadam road, giving Sotik an all-weather outlet, and the guaranteed prices given to the farmers by Government to encourage production during the war years. Also, I must acknowledge my debt to so many of my kind friends and advisors including Mr WG Dawson, who, owing to an old head injury from the First World War, had unwillingly been forced to stay behind and act as one of the Group Farm Managers who were set up in all farming areas of Kenya under the Crops Production and Manpower Committees.

As a result of all this, and of the fact that Sotik was so depleted of manpower, I was elected to serve on Sotik's Farming Committee, although the farmers, having rashly landed themselves with a female Member, promptly decided that the safest thing to do was to hold all their future meetings at the week-end Kenya Defence Force Camp, when I couldn't attend.

About this time, one of Sotik's leading stock farmers, Mr RO Royston, asked me to help him start the Sotik Branch of the Stockowner's Association, which we ran together for many years. This was a very happy association, during which I learned to like and admire this delightful, humorous man.

All this talk of farming reminds me of an amusing incident which occurred during a visit of Sir Henry Monk Mason Moore, who had replaced Sir Robert Brooke-Popham as Governor of Kenya. I was acting as hostess when he came to Kipkebe for a tea-party given in his honour during a visit to the district, and having just introduced a couple of my neighbours, I escaped to talk for a few minutes to his young ADC, Frank Lloyd, whom I found much more amusing than HE. The young man asked me who had written the disgraceful article in the *Standard* criticizing His Excellency's speech announcing the Government's wartime agricultural policy. I had to admit I was the culprit, adding, "But you must realize that unless we shout here in Sotik, we shall never be heard in Nairobi, for the Kipsigis and the Sotik settlers are Kenya's forgotten tribes." To which the ADO, replied, "That may be so, but mercifully the Kipsigis at least do not possess a *Standard* Correspondent."

Before I leave farming, I should like to pay tribute to two men for their invaluable contribution to Kenya farming during the war years, in devising and setting up the District Agriculture and Production Committees, under the parent body the Board of Agriculture: Major Cavendish-Bentinck, later, as Sir Ferdinand, to become Speaker of the Legislative Council; and Captain FOB Wilson, a genial man and one of Kenya's most successful dairy farmers.

Their scheme changed the face of Kenya farming, particularly through the introduction of a Guaranteed Minimum Return to be paid on every acre ploughed and planted, regardless of the amount of the harvest. Because of GMR, many new acres were brought under the plough, and the directives of the Committees resulted in intensified production on existing acreages.

Of course, some of the farming community resented the regimentation of the Committees, but by and large it was accepted as an unavoidable necessity. The retention of these Committees after the War, in a slightly altered form, showed better than anything else that the farming community acknowledged their value.

These two men, so utterly dissimilar, made a good team. It was said that when you heard 'CB' speak you saw the townsman, but with 'FOB' you always smelt the manure. That was a fair comment, but it is only equally fair to record that on one occasion when Kipkebe was honoured by a visit from Major Cavendish-Bentinck as Minister of Agriculture, and I was showing him around, he appeared to be extremely bored until we reached the piggeries and I said, "Come and see my Field Flowers." On seeing my sows his whole face lit up and I discovered that he shared my passion for pigs. I have often thought in later years that perhaps it is the only thing we have ever had in common!

In mid-1941, I was asked to attend a meeting held in Kisumu, the main town of the Nyanza constituency, in order to discuss the formation of an Electors' Association.

I'll pause here for a moment to describe Kisumu. It was a pleasant, well-built town, situated at the head of the Gulf of Kavirondo on the shores of Lake Victoria, and was the headquarters of the Provincial Administration. From small beginnings as a lake port, Kisumu had grown as cotton growing expanded, and it became the centre of the maize marketing industry as well as the feeder port for Uganda and Tanganyika. As it was within thirty-eight miles of Kakamega, it shared the short-lived prosperity of Kenya's gold-rush [in the early 1930s], for then it seemed as if Kisumu, with its foundry and firms supplying mining machinery, had a golden future. When the gold petered out, Kisumu was compensated by becoming the headquarters of the Flying Boat Service. Alas, all too soon the claims of Naivasha, within easy reach of Nairobi, made Imperial Airways decide to bring these boats down on Lake Naivasha. So once again Kisumu lost out.

Before the Second World War it was impossible for us to reach Kisumu during the rains, for the road lay over the low-lying Kano Plains and was liable to be washed away with every heavy storm. But after 1939, when the 1st and 2nd Pioneers raised the road above the level of the Plains, we could travel to Kisumu in two hours, with the comforting certainty that although we might have a sticky passage back, we should be able to return to our home in the hills in the evening.

After the unprecedented rains at the end of 1961 and the completion of the Owen Falls Dam, the level of Lake Victoria was permanently raised. Some of Kisumu's docks were flooded, and what was a pretty place on the shore is now submerged. This is a tragedy, for this shady park bordering the lake was Kisumu's main beauty spot. Here one could sit under the shade of the enormous indigenous forest trees and, while enjoying a picnic, watch the fishermen leisurely pulling in their traps, or a hopeful cormorant sitting in the reed structure.

In this park grazed a tame herd of graceful impala, and one could also watch the many kinds of fish-eating birds. Often one had the fun of seeing a family of hippo disporting themselves, Mrs Hippo teaching the youngest member of the family to swim.

The lake on those early mornings was a pearly shimmering sheet of water, its surface hardly disturbed by even the faintest ripple, while the distant hills of Homa Bay were hazy with the portent of the heat to come. A beautiful and peaceful spot which we so often enjoyed that it makes me sad to know that it has gone forever.

The lake provided excellent sailing, although its treacherous waters needed a skilled yachtsman, for the placid morning surface could change as the afternoon storms blew up angry whitecaps. The change was so remarkable that even my small daughter noticed it, saying, "Oh Mummy look, the crocodiles have all woken up and are swimming hard" – the idea of serried ranks of crocs causing the waves by swimming just below the surface being a delightful one.

No description of Kisumu would be complete without a mention of her two leading citizens, two men whose far-sighted faith and hard work played so big a part in the development of the town, namely, John L Riddoch and James Maxwell, or 'Uncle Jim' as he was affectionately known.

John L Riddoch, an ambitious Scot, I believe arrived on the lake shores early in the 1900s with £50 in his pocket. Over the years, with the aid of a colony of good Scotsmen and true, imported by him, he has built up the flourishing firm of John L Riddoch, suppliers of all types of machinery, hardware, etc., and a chain of garages. In this way, while increasing his private fortune, he has provided a livelihood for many. 'John L' today must be a very wealthy man, although as I write these words, I can hear him say with his deprecating laugh and his Scots accent, "Ah, noo, weel maybe comfortably off." For John L has always looked after his fellow Scots, so that there have been times when even he has found himself fully stretched financially.

Life in Kisumu was often not too easy for the Sassenach outside the Clan. And thus St Andrew's Night Dinner was a big event of the year. On one occasion when the company had been bored by several rather pompous, pious and sentimental orations, a Roman Catholic padre, replying to the Toast of the Guests, made this delightful speech: He told the assembled Scots that his African cook had asked him with whom he was dining, and he replied, "With a *shenzi* (scruffy) tribe called the Wa-Scots who live up in the NFD of England." The cook, on enquiring "What do they eat?" was told by his master, "They don't eat much, they mostly drink, but when they do, they eat W'Haggissy." "What," asked the cook, "is a W'Haggissy?" and was amazed to learn that it was "a mincey" tied up in a *gunia* (bag) and that the Wa-Scots did not only eat the mincey but the *gunia* as well. Whereupon the cook said the Wa-Scots must be a very tough tribe.

To return to my discussion of the Electors' Union: Mr James Maxwell welcomed me on that day in 1941 when I, feeling very shy, the only woman in a gathering of strange men, was put at my ease by his courtly manners. The object of the Union, in a large and scattered province such as Nyanza, was to act as a two-way channel of communication between the Elected Member and his or her constituents. This private meeting was followed by a stormy public meeting where the Nyanza Electors' Union was well and truly launched, in spite of noisy opposition from a couple of wild young men known as the Robertson brothers. Ted and Struan Robertson were later to become two of my most persistent hecklers. But that day they had met their match in our newly appointed Chairman, Doc Parsons. This red-headed, stocky, fiery fellow, holder of a degree in Mining Science, was often described as a ginger beer bottle with the cork insecurely tied down. On this occasion he let the cork fly and when the Robertsons threatened to bust up his meeting, he replied in no uncertain tone, "You just try and I'll take one bound off the platform and throw you both out in a matter of minutes!"

In this manner was launched the first branch of the Electors' Union, which later played such a major part in the political life of the Colony, providing a forum for the free expression of European opinion and a training ground for European Elected Members.

The Electors' Union, agreeing that an election in wartime was most undesirable, decided to put forward a name for nomination by the Governor. Our unanimous choice fell on Commander Frank Couldrey, the popular ex-Naval editor of the *Kenya Weekly News*, a weekly paper which faithfully reflected settler opinion throughout the years. Not only were the editorials written in Frank Couldrey's bright and breezy style, but through the brilliant work of Mervyn Hill, Kenya's most able journalist, and the editor for many years. This weekly put the settlers' often incoherent though forcibly expressed opinions into well-reasoned thoughts written in the most polished English. Frank Couldrey was unanimously adopted as candidate and His Excellency nominated him to represent Nyanza, which he did well and truly up to his untimely death in 1947.

Since the days of our Sotik Ideal Homes Exhibition under the district Vice-Presidency of Mrs 'Moneiri' Haslehurst, the East African Women's League had become moribund. In November 1941 it was revitalised with a vengeance by the Colony-wide tour of Lady Baden Powell, who was now its President. Not to be caught napping, Sotik hastily reformed their branch, with the surprising result that a packed meeting welcomed the Chief Guide.

Lady Baden Powell, unaware that it was our first meeting for ages, said in heartfelt tones, "Although I do feel that the up-country branches ploughing their lonely furrow need cherishing, you must remember that you are vitally important to the life of the Colony." We preened ourselves, though feeling slightly ashamed of being such humbugs. Even so, Lady Baden Powell did that day rekindle a spark that has burned with varying intensity through the years until the 'Wind of Change' snuffed it out in 1963, when Sotik disappeared as a European settled district and the Sotik branch of the EAWL closed down.

Young farmers' wives who, added to the care of their children, are often expected to take charge of the dairy and the poultry and sometimes even do the accounting, are too busy to do outside work, and it says a great deal for the EAWL that it had branches in all the districts of the Colony. The League, since its formation in 1917, has a record of which it can be proud, for it has done much to promote the welfare of women and children of all races in Kenya. Since its formation, it has raised on average, the astonishing sum of £5,000 a year for various charities, chief amongst these being maternity and children's hospitals and a home for elderly pioneers. A very remarkable achievement.

I know how hard it is to raise any enthusiasm among farmers' wives for attending meetings, as the usual reaction to such suggestions is, "I don't understand politics and anyway I'm not interested." My reply was always, "But you must be interested in the improvement of our schools, hospitals, roads, etc. Perhaps you have not realised that politics in Kenya is the development of the country in which you have chosen to make your home."

It was not surprising that Sotik was not politically conscious, for we only saw our first Elected Member twice in seventeen years and it was not until we were represented by Lady Sidney Farrar [in 1937] that we knew what it was to have someone who fought for our interests. Lady Sidney concealed beneath her gentle charm a tremendous fighting spirit. At the end of her term of office in 1942, the First Aid Nursing Yeomanry claimed her. Before 1939 she had built up the FANY, the Kenyan equivalent of the ATS [the women's branch of the British Army] as a sister service to the Kenya Regiment, and she was its Colonel-in-Chief throughout the whole War.

CHAPTER 9

The Home Front

"But what good came of it at last?"
Quoth little Peterkin.
"Why that I cannot tell," said he.
"But 'twas a famous victory."
--*The Battle of Blenheim, by Robert Southey*

In East Africa, we civilians hardly knew the meaning of the word war. With the early collapse of the Italian resistance, our forces suffered comparatively lightly in the way of casualties, nor did our civilian population come under fire or ever know the terror of an air raid with its aftermath of horror. The King's African Rifles fought the nOturious monsoon campaign in the Burma jungle, part of the 14th (Forgotten) Army, under General Sir William Slim, but that was far from Africa.

All the war meant for us left behind was separation from our menfolk and hard work, for added to the routine job of running a home and looking after the children, the Kenya women took over and ran the farms. In this we were given the most marvellous co-operation by our African labour. A remarkable fact considering later events of the Mau Mau rebellion, but one which I believe proves that the majority of Africans are not anti-European if left undisturbed by the politicians.

We did not even suffer from a food shortage, though naturally many of the usual imported foods, chemists' goods and cosmetics were in short supply. (I remember making my own lipsticks by reshaping and reboiling the ends). No, perhaps the worst we farming wives suffered were occasional attacks of boredom, for the routine of running a farm or plantation was not as exciting as being a FANY.

Full of admiration for the tremendous courage and fortitude of our kith and kin in the United Kingdom, we often wondered whether, if we had to face such stresses and strains, we should come through the trial by fire as magnificently undaunted as did our British sisters.

Perhaps the disaster which brought the horror of war nearer to us in Kenya than any other was the tragic sinking [in 1944] of a Kenya troopship by a Japanese torpedo within one day of the ship's reaching Ceylon. She was carrying, as well as African troops, a large contingent of young Kenya nurses. She was struck amidships during luncheon and as she went down in seven minutes, most of the passengers were trapped below deck, with the result that these poor girls were all drowned. Many Kenya homes mourned that day and I have been told that the survivors amongst the African askaris sat and wept on the beach over the fate of so many young memsahibs.

The tragedy made the poster "Careless Talk Costs lives" only too true, for the information of her sailing had been leaked in a Mombasa bar.

As part of Brian's six months' course at the Officer Cadet Training Unit in Nakuru, every Cadet had to give a lecture twice a term. Brian called one of his talks "The Fighting Tribes of Kenya" and listed "The Settler" as the first amongst these. This caused much amusement, but quite apart from the fact that the settlers were always ready to fight the Government in peace time, almost every man answered the call-up when war broke out. As there were approximately 2,000 miles of unguarded border and only one battalion of the KAR, this was just as well.

When I came down for a week's leave and Brian drilled all day and danced all night, on one occasion he had no time to write his essay. The subject was "America's Role in European Politics" and as Brian was desperate, I wrote it for him. He dashed in at lunchtime, seized the essay, and after signing it, sent it in without even reading it. All was well until it was declared the Prize-Winning Essay and the Commanding Officer sent for Brian to congratulate him!

Another amusing incident on one of his leaves, this time in Nairobi, was our arrest by the Kenya Police for car stealing. A stupid Army regulation, made I suppose because of the shortage of officers, forbade officers on leave to live outside the camp, although they could join their wives in the daytime. The only way to get around this was to get some temporary appointment while on leave which prevented you from being on call. Brian managed to wangle a job as Welfare Officer to Hargeisa in British Somalia. This meant he had to wear a uniform, but we could be together and the only job his appointment entailed was buying four tablecloths for the Hargeisa Officers' Mess.

During these few days, our car was damaged in a crash and was in the garage for repairs. As we wanted to go out to the Prince of Wales School to put Michael's name down as a pupil for the following term, I suggested borrowing Brian's cousin's car. Sylvia was working as telephonist in No. 2 General, the Military Hospital in Nairobi, and she could not leave her switchboard, but told us we would find her little car parked at the front of the hospital with the key in the lock, the only small car amongst the Army transports. We found it just as she said and drove off.

The morning was spent in buying the tablecloths for Hargeisa and then, to celebrate Brian's return on leave, we foregathered with some friends to enjoy an excellent lunch at the Lobster Pot. Well-fed and happy, we returned to the place where we had parked the little car, only to find it surrounded by four European policemen, two on motorcycles. Naturally, we did not connect these representatives of the law in any way with us, but as my husband was about to step into the car, the tallest of the officers put his hand on Brian's shoulder and said, "Is this your car, sir?", to which Brian replied, "No, it's one I borrowed" – which turned out to be an unfortunate choice of words.

To our horror, the policeman said, "Stolen, I think you mean, for this car belongs to Lt Moore and was lifted from the back of No. 2 General this morning at 11 a.m.," adding, "I am afraid I must place you under arrest." Even though we knew we were innocent of intent, a cold shudder ran down our spines and this little incident has put me off a life of crime, which secretly I had always rather fancied. It was a new and awful experience to be under arrest.

Being ignorant of the niceties of behaviour under arrest, we waved the policemen into the back seat and proceeded to drive them to the hospital.

Afterwards, discussing the whole thing with a legal friend, the friend told us the police had made two mistakes: First, the officer had no business saying, "Stolen, I think you mean," for under British law a person is innocent until proved guilty; and second, they should not have allowed us to drive the car, for had we been the desperate criminals they supposed, we could have jumped out, left the car to crash and escaped.

Sylvia was rather astonished to see us marching down the long corridor with an escort of four tall policemen. We explained that the blunder had occurred as we had mistaken the back of the hospital for the front, and hoped that Sylvia would corroborate our story with the Inspector. She did, although she told me afterwards she was sorely tempted to say, "I'm afraid officer, there's some mistake, as I've never seen these people before."

This would have landed us properly in the soup, or more probably in the cells; even so, we were told that we could not be released until the car owner was found and the car had been handed back. Fortunately for us, he was located and within an hour was at the hospital. On seeing Brian, he said in tones of utter astonishment, "You!" It turned out that Brian had been the senior officer on the convoy which had brought them both down from Mogadishu a few days before – a most curious coincidence when you consider the number of military in Nairobi at that time.

In extenuation of our mistake, I said I was sure it was my cousin's car for I had noticed hair curlers in the cubbyhole, whereupon the young Lieutenant, who it transpired was newly married, blushed scarlet and said in dignified tones, "My wife's." Our apology, backed by a gallon of petrol, soothed his outraged feelings, though it was a little unfortunate for us when, as prospective parents apologizing for being late for our appointment, we had to tell the Headmaster that we couldn't help ourselves as for the past hour we had been under arrest!

Brian's leave came to an end, and he returned to take up his duties in Mogadishu once more. I was sad to see him go, for after three-and-a-half years in that hot and unhealthy coastal town, he was far from fit.

It was some comfort that Joseph, our second house servant, who acted as Brian's faithful batman, went with him. Poor boy, he died a few years later from cancer of the throat; he was a fish-eating Luo from the low-lying country near Lake Victoria, a simple soul who blamed a fishbone for his sickness. We took him to Mr Miller, the Kisumu Government Surgeon, who told us the cancer was far advanced and nothing could be done. But that was in the future. At the time I was happy to know that Brian would have Joseph to look after him until I could arrange to come to Mogadishu myself.

In June 1943 the District Production Committee granted me leave from the farm to join Brian in Mogadishu. Petrol rationing had not allowed for many jaunts off the farm, and both my mother and I were excited by the prospect of a holiday. She went off on a round of visits, the children were both at school, and our noble Group Farm Manager took over the farm.

The great day dawned and Oturi, my house servant and faithful companion, and I presented ourselves at Force Headquarters in Nairobi. We were introduced to the Officer Commanding Convoy, as in wartime the Somalia Mail travelled under military escort. Our fellow passengers were a Colonel and Mrs Horne and a Mrs Holman, going back after leave to join her Sergeant husband.

Colonel Horne, whom I later came to know well as Speaker of the Legislative Council, was returning to Mogadishu where he held a judicial post under the British Military Administration. Inevitably he was known as 'Trader' but he had some right to this nickname, for as a lad he had sailed before the mast, and indeed in his long and eventful life he had tried his hand at most things. His correct title was Mr Justice Horne as he was a retired Judge from Malaya, and later he was to become the most impartial and able Speaker under whom it was my privilege to sit in Kenya's Legislative Council. His wife, Marjory, was a daughter of Kenya's first Trade Commissioner, after whom the Jackson's Francolin was named.

The mailbags and masses of kit were chucked into the two lorries, and, heavily over-laden, we set off on our thousand-mile journey to Mogadishu on June 23rd, 1943. The Somalia Mail was nothing more than a three-ton lorry with an ordinary garden seat bolted crossways in the open back behind the driver's cab. Colonel Horne sat beside the Somali driver, while we three women were perched up behind, and after hours on this bench of torture our behinds were slatted like the seat. We found the only way we could survive with unbroken ribs and some skin left on our faces was to pack ourselves around with bedding and cover our faces with face cream.

Just after passing Fort Hall, a military car stopped us and told us our escort lorry had gone over the bridge, was smashed beyond repair, and all our kit was in the river. We hurried back to find the upturned lorry half down the bank and the kit strewn around but mercifully not in the river. The OC Convoy had hit his head, but seemed to have had a lucky escape, but the driver as well as the two askaris were badly hurt. Marjory, very agitated, started tearing up her bath-towel in strips, although apart from a cut lip, the injuries were all internal. I dispensed cups of sweetened tea from a thermos until an ambulance arrived and took the casualties to the Fort Hall Hospital. We picked up the personal kit and went on, arriving very tired and somewhat discouraged at the Sportsman's Arms Hotel at Nanyuki at 7 o'clock.

Next day, the Colonel phoned Headquarters to ask for instructions and was depressed to be told that the 'Mail' must tag on to a convoy of fifty new Army trucks not able to travel at more than ten miles per hour. This meant it would take us something like seventeen days to reach Mogadishu. Captain Nolan-Neylan arrived for lunch next day. He had seen no sign, either passing through Fort Hall or Nyeri, of our OC, and we decided that the Major must be suffering from loss of memory and delayed shock. We persuaded Captain Neylan to detach one of his lorries and to come with us, as OC Convoy, but just as we were about to depart, our own OC turned up. We finally left at 3 p.m., only to find that he had forgotten to fill his lorry's tank with petrol and had not even enough to go back the seven miles to Nanyuki, let alone the 1000 miles to Somalia.

Luckily, we were opposite the Phillips' farm and as it was now too late to leave, we let the Major go back for petrol supplies while the rest of us stayed with my cousin for the night. Isabel rose to the occasion magnificently, giving us a grand welcome which included hot baths and drinks as well as an excellent dinner.

On Sunday, after breakfast, the Major arrived and we set off once more, but as we only did eighty-two miles, failing to reach Garba Tula, we had to camp in a bleak and rocky spot on the roadside.

The country around Isiolo is rather gaunt, with its stretches of desert and lava rock, bounded on all sides by curious shaped mountains. Monday's run was through miles and miles of wait-a-bit thorn, the only vegetation in this desolate desert country. A howling gale was blowing and we came through several sand-storms. The entry in my diary adds, "The gallant Major nearly drove us mad, for as his top speed was ten miles an hour, it took us an eternity to do the scheduled 145 miles. We luckily found an old army site where we pitched camp. Oturi, as usual, had a fire made, the kettle boiling and a cuppa ready in no time – most welcome after the choking dust. He was thrilled to find an old stove and dumb-waiter, and with these civilized aids, produced a wonderful dinner. A good camp, though we were most anxious about our Major, who was delirious with a temperature of 102°."

We made a late start next day as it was difficult to control the OC, who was by now seriously ill and more gaga than ever. Trader took over command and as the road was good, we made Wajir by two o'clock, where we were fortunate in finding a European doctor on leave. He saw our poor Major and diagnosed concussion, delayed shock, laryngitis and bronchitis.

Wajir, with its Beau Geste Fort, startlingly white in the beating afternoon sun, was awaiting the advent of the Governor, so our arrival was distinctly inconvenient. We were given tea by a young policeman, an ex-white hunter, and enjoyed an hour's rest in his deliciously cool house. Ill as he was, the Major refused to be off-loaded without his case of beer, which was finally located at the bottom of the second lorry.

The road after Wajir, a track made through the dust by the South African troops, was grim, and we were thankful when Trader decided that he had had enough and we were allowed to descend from our perch at 6 p.m. I went to bed as I felt wretched, having developed an upset tummy and sore throat, the result of heat and dust.

From then on, every evening just before lights-out Trader would solemnly say, "Now ladies, an early start please, not one minute later than 5 a.m." I would set my alarm clock at 4.45 a.m., and Oturi, using a frying-pan as a tray, would take the OC his early tea. But when he touched his shoulder, such alarming rumbles would come from under the blankets that Oturi would hastily retire. Never starting before 7 a.m., we never reached the recognised campsite, to my mind a very good thing, as we were the first convoy to go through after the *shifta* [irregular local troops in Italian pay] had been active on the Abyssinian border. With no askaris, we were much safer blacked out in the bush at an unrecognised campsite.

Our dashing Somali drivers did their best, but they could not be expected to drive all day and guard all night. But to keep up the appearance of security, after one noisy martial march around the camp they would arrive shouldering their Italian rifles in front of the OC, salute smartly and say, "*Bwana, shifta mbaya sana – lakini shifta sasa hapana iko, kwaheri Bwana.*" (*Bwana*, the shifta are very bad but there are no shifta here now. Good night, *bwana*.) And so to bed for the four of us, on either side of a bush. These two little ceremonies were repeated night and morning, farcical though we all knew them to be.

Between Wajir and Bardera the road was appalling, scarred with wash-aways, ruts and holes, and strewn with boulders and rocks. Why our lorry did not break in two as we plunged on, regardless, goodness only knows.

The Northern Frontier District after the long rains was flowering for a few short weeks and the vivid green of the small thorns made a marvellous background for the beautiful bright pink Desert Rose, a black-stemmed succulent. The electric blue of the Vulturine Guinea Fowl, the Red-billed Hornbills and the gay little green and yellow lovebirds added colour to the scene. The country was teeming with birds and game, for besides hundreds of guinea fowl, there were spurfowl, plovers, sand-grouse and doves. Buck of the many larger varieties abounded, as well as pair after pair of the charming miniature dik-dik.

All these things we saw during our stops to cool the tyres in the heat of the day and when we were in camp at night, as during running time we had too much to do to keep our seats to notice anything. As we bumped and bounced from pothole to rut, we only managed to maintain our balance by bracing our feet on the bank of the cab and clinging to the iron supports of the canvas awning. We found that the only way to make the driver slacken speed was to shout to him, just as he drove, still in top gear, full tilt into a drift, "Look out for your plates or they will all be smashed!" - they being a present he was taking to his wife.

Poor Oturi was sure we were lost and was very relieved when we sighted Bardera and were shown into the cool rooms of the lovely house occupied by the Acting District Commissioner, Major Cusack of the British Military Administration. Oh, the pleasure of a bath, clean clothes, and, after a good dinner, boating on the Juba by the light of the moon.

From then onwards the journey was easy as the Italians had made the roads on their side of the border, and we eventually arrived in

Mogadishu on the 2nd July. Everyone there was getting frantic with worry about us, as the journey usually took five days and we were four days overdue. There had been no news of us and rumours were rife that the *shifta* had taken us all prisoner and that after roasting Trader slowly over a fire, had absconded with the women.

The morning after our arrival, Brian introduced me to the typist in his office, a beautiful Italian girl who minced forward on the highest of high heels, and, presenting me with a bouquet of flowers, said, "Ah, Madame, we have been waiting for you for days and days and days." Strangely enough, Brian was the only officer who had an Italian girl as typist. She was a student of anatomy, a redhead of eighteen with a lovely figure. Her fame had spread, and all the young officers used any pretext go visit the Town Major, so Brian's office often looked more like a café.

Mogadishu, when I saw it, was a lovely spot. The Italians had turned this strip of desert into an attractive seaside resort, which in its setting of palm-fringed beaches and blue sea looked like any of its counterparts on the Riviera. On the Lido, divided from the sand only by a carved stone balustrade, were to be found the marble palaces of the Fascisti hierarchy – beautiful houses of white coral rock trimmed with Italian marble.

I spent my leave in one of the biggest of these houses, which was approached by a flight of marble steps that would have done justice to St Paul's. Here in the beautiful high-ceilinged, spacious rooms, with their marble floors and shuttered windows, we lived in cool comfort. However, the wiring was dangerous and when turning on the bathroom light we always took the precaution of standing on an inner tube to avoid being electrocuted. Once Brian got a ghastly shock. On picking up the bedside lamp, it stuck to his hand. Fortunately, the pain made him jump and when he left the ground, the contact was broken and the lamp crashed to the floor.

Mogadishu was built on a simple plan. All the palaces were on the seafront. Behind them were the smaller houses and blocks of modern flats. Behind that again the poorer Italians lived in near hovels, divided only by a wall from the African quarter where the Somalis, surrounded by their camels and goats, lived in unbelievable squalor. The town under its Italian regime was a fly-infested plague spot, but the first thing the British did after their occupation was to clean it up.

When I was there, though the climate was still hot, humid and unhealthy, I found it an enchanting place for a holiday, and a pleasant change from the dull routine of three-and-a-half years on the farm. Although Brian was longing for a transfer, life for me was delightful, with the lazy days filled with fun and frolic. Our routine was this: an early breakfast for Brian, as working hours in Mogadishu were from 7 a.m. to 2 p.m.; home for a late lunch, followed by the universal siesta; then tea, after which we would play tennis, for by then it would be reasonably cool. This was often followed by a bathe from the lovely sands in front of the house, before changing and setting forth for a sundowner or drinks at the Officers' Club, where the wide veranda overlooked the sea.

Fraternisation was frowned on by the military authorities – rather ironical, as one of the former brigadiers had a beautiful Italian girlfriend known as 'La Carlotta.' She was the wife of an Italian doctor who had been one of the Head Fascisti. Like the portraits and statues of Mussolini and the Italian Royal family, the conquering British in their casual way had never bothered to remove him. Even the notepaper was still headed 'Governor della Somalia Italiana.'

As I did not come under military jurisdiction, I was allowed to 'frat,' so in the morning I used to ride downtown on the bus, with Oturi and my market basket, and have a happy time poking about in the little shops where so many lovely things were 'going for a song.' These included exquisite Venetian glass and china decorated with silver filigree which I longed to buy but which would never have withstood the terrible jolting of the Somalia Mail. It made me sad to think of the poor Italian women who were shipped back to Italy when their husbands were interned and had to leave their homes and beautiful possessions behind.

Brigadier Reid, who was the Commanding Officer and who acted as our host in Mogadishu, returned when peace came to take up his farming life in Southern Rhodesia.

We were relieved when Brian's transfer came through. He was far from well and also in considerable pain, having injured both his thumbs while practising unarmed combat. The military doctor, in civilian life an expert gynaecologist, had diagnosed arthritis and told him whenever he had a spare moment to sit and twiddle his thumbs. A most painful performance and no wonder, for on his return to Kenya after months of pain, Mr Bainbridge, the well-known Nairobi surgeon, discovered that both Brian's thumbs were dislocated. Had this been discovered at the time of the injury, it would have been a simple matter to put them back, but after a year the joints had become malformed and would not fit into the sockets. After three months with Brian in plaster, Mr Bainbridge finally had to operate, cutting out the joints. It was a year before Brian regained the use of his hands, and even then, with two jointless thumbs, he had little or no grip and now, alas, a good deal of real arthritis.

We travelled down from Mogadishu at the same time although not together. Brian was encamped twenty miles ahead of me in the bush each night as, thanks to Army red-tape, I was not allowed to travel in an Army convoy. Instead, I had to return by way of the Mail, in company with three strange men, military personnel of the British Military Administration. Brian left Mogadishu, his billet for three years, with no regrets, but I shall always look back on it with pleasure, for my month there gave me a very happy holiday.

For Brian, the war was virtually over. Transferred from Mogadishu on the grounds of ill-health, he was posted to duty in Nairobi, as the Army would not release him. I found it hard to go back to work on the farm, and although it was good to have Brian in Kenya, in a way our separation was harder to bear when he was as near as Nairobi. By Christmas, when he could hardly use his hands at all, he was finally released.

Peace came at last, and with it a return to our old life at Sotik. Husbands came home again, wives handed back the management of the farms, and life went on as before, with this difference: Mixed farming and wartime guaranteed prices had put the district on its feet financially, and Sotik never again had to face the slump conditions of the 1930s. Also, we ourselves had changed. Memories of the war years would always be with us – of how we had sat, hour after hour, glued to the radio during the Dunkirk days, numbed by the knowledge that Britain, and all she stood for, now faced the possibility of that dread unspoken word 'defeat.'

With Ann now a boarder at Limuru Girls' School, Michael at the Prince of Wales School in Nairobi, and no farm to manage, I, in company with many Kenya wives, felt rather adrift. Throwing myself into the work of the Nyanza Electors' Union, I was appointed a delegate to the Executive Committee in Nairobi and had the honour of being elected one of the three Vice-Presidents of the Union. I served under the Presidency of Major Freddie Ward, one of the most quick-witted and versatile men I have ever met.

The main task was to educate the electorate by providing a forum for public opinion. This the Union did through its annual conference, and through tours for their President, the Leader of the European Elected Members, and Government Ministers. As well as this, the local branches arranged meetings for their Elected Members in their constituencies, which was perhaps their most useful work. By these means the Union fostered the growth of an informed public opinion amongst the electorate.

The main event of 1946 as far as Sotik was concerned was the opening of the new Sotik Club. Sotik's only Club had been built by

Cattle on the Shaw's farm at Kipkebe.

the East-enders and was too far from the centre to serve the growing district. At first there was some opposition from members of the old Club, who felt quite rightly that a small district such as Sotik could not afford two Clubs. But this opposition was finally overcome and the supporters of the new venture were proved right, for situated just outside the township, the Sotik Sports Club provided a more convenient meeting place for the majority of the Sotik settlers. Also, the new Club lived up to its name, for a polo ground, a golf course and tennis courts were built there, as well as a hockey and football pitch. For some sixteen years it provided fun and games for young and old and fully justified its existence, though it has gone now. There was not enough flat ground for a racecourse, so the old Club became the Hunt Club and meets and race-meetings were held there.

In 1946 Nyanza suffered a grievous loss through the death of their Elected Member, Commander Couldrey. He was mourned by all Kenya's farming community as he was their champion, and the fearless way he fought their battles through the medium of the *Kenya Weekly News* won him a special place in their esteem. His death meant a by-election and Colonel George Maitland Edye, just demobilised, was presented by Sotik with a signed petition asking him to stand. George Edye had already represented the district on several committees and we knew his ability, and he gained general support throughout Nyanza because it was felt that as a farmer he was more interested in practical progress than in political practices. He was opposed by Lady Sidney Farrar and Mr TK Turton, but neither of these candidates presented a very serious challenge and George Edye had an easy win.

The visit of the new Governor, Sir Philip Mitchell, and Lady Mitchell was most welcome in the district. As they were personal friends of the Edyes, the Mitchells stayed with them, and their host and hostess decided to give a sundowner followed by a buffet supper in their honour. With an election to fight, this was not very intelligent. A tea-party yes, but a sundowner no; everyone could have been included in a tea-party and following Sotik custom the guests would probably have come with cake in hand. But because of expense it was not possible to invite the whole district to a cocktail party. The heart-burnings over the issue of the invitations can well be imagined.

George, seeing the danger signal, came to me in great distress, asking if, as Sotik's *Standard* correspondent, I would write an article stating how the chosen few had been selected. I unwisely agreed and wrote one of the most idiotic reports of my journalistic career. It read something like this: "During their visit to Sotik, Sir Philip and Lady Mitchell were the guests of Colonel and Mrs George Maitland Edye, who gave a delightful sundowner and alfresco supper, inviting the Chairmen and Vice-Chairmen of all the local Committees and their wives to meet the Governor and Lady Mitchell."

The Editor, thinking these details were unnecessarily clumsy, re-wrote the paragraph so that the published article read, "Colonel and Mrs Edye gave a delightful sundowner and buffet supper in honour of Sir Philip and Lady Mitchell, to which they invited all the important people in Sotik." That put the fat in the fire and by my efforts to retrieve an unfortunate situation, I had made matters a thousand times worse. However, in spite of this social (and political) *faux pas*, Colonel Edye won the election and represented Nyanza in Legislative Council until 1949.

In 1948 we turned Kipkebe into a Limited Company, in order to raise the capital to build a tea processing factory. The wet years we had had during the war had brought on Coffee Berry Disease, and our coffee was finished. On the advice of the experts, we planted tea. After the war Brian took out all that was left of the coffee and planted more tea. The dairy herd was kept on, and pyrethrum and passion fruit were grown to bring in some money until the tea bushes matured. Mrs Florrie Wilson, the pioneer aviatrix after whom Wilson Airport at Nairobi is named, became one of the earliest shareholders, and more capital was provided by the old Liverpool and Uganda Co., which at that time were cutting down on their holdings in cotton in Uganda and reinvesting in Kenya. Brian, as General Manager, was granted regular periods of overseas leave, namely five months every five years. We took our first leave in 1949.

Oturi at Kipkebe in the 1950s.

Michael had left the Prince of Wales School, Nairobi, in 1948, having won a Rhodes Scholarship to Oxford. When we sailed in June on the old Italian liner *Gerusalemme*, on what proved to be her last voyage, Michael came with us. At the Prince of Wales School, Michael had taken everything in his stride, and although in his final year he was Head of the School as well as of his house, captain of rugger and cricket, he never let success go to his head. I remember him once saying to me, "Mummy, if you're scared of doing something, you have no need to worry, but if you think you know all about it, it's then you need to watch out"– which showed an unusual wisdom for a sixteen-year-old.

It is fitting that Part I of this book should end with a description of some of the men who worked for us, especially Oturi, our Major Domo, whose devoted service has been the background to thirty out of my thirty-three years at Kipkebe.

But first to the kitchen. I have been called a talented cook, and if the number of young Kipsigis I have trained is a criterion, then I must be deserving of such a title. All I remember is that my early years as a housewife were made more difficult by the constant changing of cooks, because as soon as I had finished their training, they demanded a higher wage. As we could not afford to pay more, I found them posts with the more well-to-do Government officials and started all over again. My cooks have all come from the Kipsigis tribe, the Birir family being the chief suppliers. Arap Birir the second stayed with me for many years, before he graduated to the DC's establishment in Kericho, from where he rose still higher in the social scale, becoming, as he informed me with justifiable pride, "Cook to Lord Chief Justice." He was a charming 'Kip,' quick and intelligent, and when Sir Barclay Nihill retired, arap Birir took a course at Jeannes School and got his Gold Medal as a master baker. In company with several Kipsigis, he formed a co-operative, built a shop with a kitchen and large ovens, and set up the most successful bakery in Sotik. The opening ceremony was performed by Senior Chief arap Tengecha and myself, and arap Birir became a well-to-do and much respected member of the community.

Then came a period of stability, for Kiptamu was with me for twelve years. My last cook only left me after eight years because he refused to come to Nairobi when we moved there permanently in 1960. After that I trained a further two young Kipsigis who stayed for a while, though I lost one to the police for a period when he was arrested for brewing Nubian gin in the shrubbery in our garden. After serving a prison sentence of five weeks 'hard,' he returned so chastened and contrite that I took him back. After that there was no repetition of his short but highly profitable venture into illegal brewing: 36 shillings a gallon, and the police found over twenty gallons!

If our cooks were constantly changing, not so our house servants. Joseph was with us on and off from the time he was my hen *toto* until he died in 1947, a period of over ten years. My *dhobi* (laundry man), a Kisii named Miobi, clocked up fifteen, while Oturi of the same tribe has been the prop and stay of my household for forty years. Oturi came to us in 1933 as my pantry *toto* aged about ten years, and except for periods of leave, has been with us continuously ever since. An excellent servant, he

Tea at Kipkebe

knows his worth, and when we go on overseas leave, he hands over the care of my husband's clothes with the greatest misgivings, convinced that I shall ruin Brian's shirts with my inexpert ironing – and he is not far wrong.

Oturi, uneducated though he is, has a quiet wisdom far beyond learning, a simple dignity and a shrewd understanding. He knows the why and wherefore of everything, and this gives him his air of assurance. Oturi has his own set of values and a great sense of what is fitting, and often it is he who keeps us from falling below standard. If he decides that the occasion warrants a dinner jacket and lays out this garment, it is more than Brian's life is worth not to wear it.

Once, after returning from a visit to the Spiers at Njoro, where their handsome racing trophies are displayed in the dining-room, I found my sideboard covered with all my battered silver plate, entree dishes, teapots, toast-racks, the lot. When I asked Oturi why he had taken them all out of the cupboard, he replied in hurt tones, "Well, you haven't got any racings."

Once we nearly lost him through our failure to measure up to his standards. After he had been with us for about twelve years, I saw that something was troubling him. I asked him what it was, and he said simply, "I'm afraid I will have to leave and go to be houseboy to Bwana Edye, for there everything is so *maridadi* (smart) and his Head Boy wears a waistcoat and a turban." Dismayed as I was, there was nothing that I could do, but fortunately Oturi heard that the young Memsahib was reputed to be *kali* (fierce) and, on the promise of a fez and waistcoat, decided to stay.

As well as having a great sense of his own importance, Oturi has a charming smile and is extremely popular. With Brian's large family connections, coupled with my twelve years in politics, he is known in many parts of Kenya. Sometimes as we drive along and Oturi acknowledges some salute with a hand-wave after the manner of the Queen Mum, I ask, "Do you know that man?" and he replies, "No, he is only a Kipsigis, but he knows me."

During all the war years he looked after mother, the children and me, and Ann and Mike cannot remember their home without Oturi. He is called in to officiate at all family functions, acting as Major Domo at weddings, christenings, etc.

In Brian's absence, Oturi became, as well as Head Man, a combination of nurse and lady's maid, so it was natural that when I went into politics, Oturi went with me, leaving Brian's erstwhile batman, Joseph, to look after Brian.

He is the owner of a smallholding, and partner with his brother in a shop and a lorry in the Kisii Reserve, and he has sired and reared seven children – five girls and two boys. How Oturi squares being a good Catholic with polygamy, I have never discovered. Now that he is getting older, he likes the comfort of having his young wife with him, leaving the old lady to look after the rest of the family and to cultivate his small farm in Kisii. All the daughters, the eldest now well married in Mombasa, were educated at a Roman Catholic convent school.

As he has now become a man of substance, he only works for us for six months of every year, although he will always 'oblige' for a special family occasion. In this way we hope to keep him with us until we are all too old for work or for this world.

Peter Hill, in an article about Kipkebe, wrote: "African servants need constant supervision and no idle housewife could achieve the gleaming beauty of Kipkebe's interior, where the bowls of flowers are exquisite against their polished background." Maybe I was responsible for the bowls of flowers, but it was Oturi who provided the polished background, and his loyal service runs through our lives, as brightly shining as the silver and mahogany he has looked after with such pride, and polished so faithfully, for all these years.

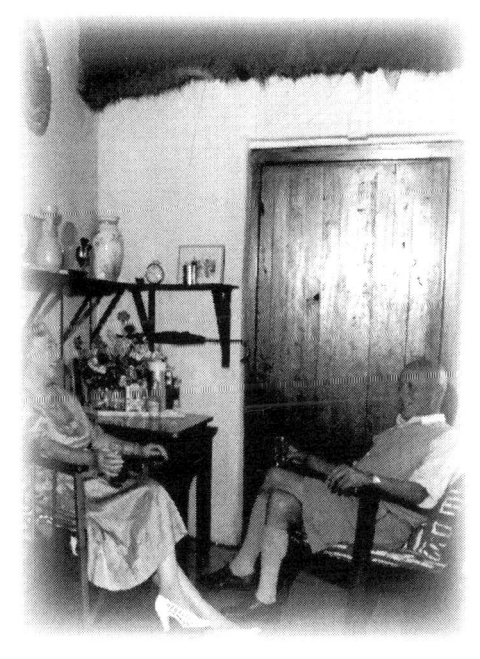

Agnes and Brian on their veranda at Kipkebe in the 1950s.

PART II

CHAPTER 10

Politics Beckons

*"If wisdom's ways you wisely seek,
Five things observe with care,
To whom you speak, of whom you speak,
And how, and when, and where."*
--Caroline Ingalls

Dull and responsible. Those were to be my watchwords for the next twelve years.

In June 1951, the Nyanza seat in the national Legislative Council became vacant owing to the tragic and untimely death of the Hon Terence Preston, who had won the seat in the 1949 by-election occasioned by the resignation of the sitting Member, Colonel George Maitland Edye. Edye had found it impossible to continue to represent Nyanza at the same time that he was supervising the development of his Sotik estate. Being the Member for Nyanza is no sinecure and there is no doubt that Terence's sudden death was the result of overwork and the strain of the immense amount of travelling involved.

My political career began when I contested and won the by-election and became a European Elected Member. On several occasions people had told me that I should stand for Legislative Council, but I should never have had the courage to do so had circumstances not forced my hand. Indeed, when I was considering standing again at the General Election of 1952, several people warned me not to, pointing out cheerfully that being Member for Nyanza had killed two men and brought a third to the verge of a nervous breakdown. It took a woman to survive!

On the momentous Sunday in mid-July which was to change the whole of my life, we were in the middle of a tennis party when, to our surprise, Mr R Pearce of Koru, the Chairman of the Nyanza County Council, arrived. Dick Pearce and I had worked together closely for several years as President and Secretary of the Nyanza Electors' Union, and I thought he must have come on Union business. He told me, however, that as no one had come forward as a candidate to fill the nine-months' gap until the General Election, he had been authorised by his Committee to ask George Edye, our former Member, to act for us again; but should George refuse, he was empowered to approach me. It was all sudden and unexpected, but the next hour seemed interminable. George Edye, hands clasped behind his back, chin sunk on chest in a most Napoleonic posture, strode up and down our lawn, trying to reach a decision.

I waited on tenterhooks; but at last he came in and told us his answer was No. George said that the reasons for his resignation in 1949 were still valid.

This being so, I was then asked if I would be prepared to accept nomination. Before giving my answer, I asked if there was no one with experience of Kenya and the interests of Nyanza Province at heart who would be willing to stand. I even mentioned Lt Gen Noel Irwin, although it was understood that while he would like to stand someday, he did not then feel that he had sufficient knowledge of Kenya or her problems, having been in the Colony under two years. Mr Pearce pointed out that if no one came forward, His Excellency the Governor would have to nominate someone to serve, probably from outside the Province. This would disgrace the Nyanza Europeans and make a nonsense of our claim as a community to leadership. I asked for time to consider all it would mean if I said yes. I was told that I could have just forty-eight hours; they would have to announce the candidate's name at the meeting of the Nyanza County Council to be held in Kericho in two days' time.

George Edye turned to me and asked, "What has all your political work been in aid of if you are not prepared to act even as a stop-gap for a few months? After all, you won't even have to fight an election." My husband agreed it was my duty to step into the breach, so in the end I said yes.

The Chairman and Members of the Nyanza County Council were kind enough to say they welcomed my decision and George Edye agreed to act as my proposer, giving me his whole-hearted backing.

Understanding that I was to be unopposed, I returned placidly to finish the annual repainting of our house. But my peace of mind was rudely shattered when, ten days later, the telephone rang. It was General Irwin. Our conversation went something like this:

Noel Irwin: "Have you heard the news?"

Me: "No."

Noel, in astonishment: "You have not heard?"

Me: "No", adding, "Our radio battery is flat and we've heard no news for a week."

Noel: "Oh dear."

Me: "Don't be so maddening – what has happened? Has America declared war on Russia?"

Noel: "No, nothing like that, only that I have decided to stand against you."

Me: "You said you wouldn't."

Noel: "Yes, I did, but I've changed my mind."

Me: "Surely changing one's mind is a woman's prerogative? Still, I wish you the best of luck," and I rang off.

I immediately phoned George Edye and asked if I could stand down now that the General had decided to stand. George's answer was an emphatic, "Certainly not." He pointed out that I had a great deal of support and if I stood down my sponsors would think I was afraid to fight an election. My answer was, "Too true, I am, not having the least idea how to begin." To which George replied, "That's all right, I'll be with you in ten minutes to give you your first lesson in planning an election campaign."

This he did, bless him, giving me there and then the first of many lessons and much valuable advice.

I also received a confidential letter from Major Freddie Ward containing a memo on "How to win an election in six easy lessons." This was based on the principle of "The last shall be first." Major Ward said that although a candidate cannot start early enough on the groundwork of setting up his committees, behind the scenes it was wise to "let your opponent enter the lists publicly first, let him be the first to send out his manifesto, then by the time yours appears his will have found its way to the waste paper basket, or been used to light the fires. There at least you will have the last word. Be content to let him be the pace-setter, but once you start, run your hardest until you pass him coming down the straight and win your race."

Extremely sound advice, which I followed faithfully in four out of my five campaigns, with success. I say four out of five, for in my first campaign for the by-election in 1951, I was really caught unprepared.

As I believed that I was to be unopposed until within a day or two before nomination day, I had made no preparations to fight an election, and so the General got off to a flying start. Changing his mind while on holiday at the coast, he had written his manifesto and had it printed on his way through Nairobi, which is 240 miles from Sotik. He had also had the foresight to collect his postal ballot papers from Kericho, the administrative centre, on his way home.

When I discovered that I would have to fight an election, there was no time to have anything printed, with our nearest town over 100 miles away. All I could do was to rapidly write a manifesto. I and my small band of helpers roneoed this and sent out 500 copies by hand from our Kipkebe sitting room. Many of my ballot papers were so late in being posted that they could not possibly reach the outlying districts of the province and be returned to Kericho in time for polling day. So, although it was through no fault of my own, I fell down this once on my groundwork and came near to losing the election. But if time was not on my side, undoubtedly luck was.

Distances being so great in Nyanza, General Irwin and I decided to hold joint meetings to save busy farmers having to travel twice to the various centres. A tour of ten meetings was planned. Before the war I had lived a life of complete dependence and had never driven a car out of Sotik by myself. The farm did not allow us to go away very often, so our circle of friends did not extend much beyond the Kericho/Sotik districts, Except for this small corner, I knew little of the province or its people, and it was with some trepidation that I set off with my faithful friend Oturi for the unknown country of the Lumbwa District.

Had I tried, I could not have chosen a more difficult district in which to fire the first shot, for the Lumbwa farmers, delightful individually, collectively provided some of the toughest audiences in Nyanza.

I chose at random a couple called Hudson, on whose support I had been told I could count, to visit first. I could not have done better; Geoff and Zara gave me a most friendly and heart-warming welcome and my visit to them did much to reassure me before I set off on my rounds. Not only did they map out my visits for me, but during that first evening they described many of their neighbours in a series of amusing little vignettes. With the background thus sketched in, the canvassing of complete strangers was made far easier.

I heard of a family who chorused, "Tha's right, tha's right," in the strongest of north country accents to everything that was said, even agreeing with their production chief when he told them that the 'shenziest' (worst) African farmer farmed better than they did. I learnt of a fierce Lancashire lad with a heart of gold on whose support I could count because he hated dictators; and of one local resident who was driven out of his house by a wife who fed him on nut cutlets and maddened him by reading Aldous Huxley aloud at the breakfast table.

At the end of this recital Zara asked, "How can you be afraid of such people?" This made me laugh and see things in their proper perspective. I was told, "If the General says he has 100% support in Lumbwa, his arithmetic is at fault." I felt comforted.

At last the dreaded hour arrived; I found myself on the platform with my opponent, Lt General NMS Irwin, DSO, MC, while the Chairman tossed a coin to decide which of us should speak first. The form was that while one candidate was speaking the other retired out of earshot until the time was up; each speaker had an allotted three-quarters of an hour. We could break this up as we liked, dividing the time between speaking and questions. I usually spoke for half an hour and devoted the last fifteen minutes to answering questions.

That first election was fought on personality, not policy. As to policies, there was fundamentally no difference between the two of us, for we both sincerely believed in the rightness and necessity of European leadership.

With agreement between us on policies, the only differences lay in the method of presentation, our approach to the job, and our vastly differing personalities. This was shown by the way we answered the same questions. For instance, asked if we considered that we would be delegates or representatives, Noel Irwin unhesitatingly replied, "a representative with full powers to act on your behalf as I think fit." I, too, said "a representative," but added that whenever time and circumstances permitted, I would return to lay the case before my constituents, and if I did not get a mandate of 75% on any vital issue, I would resign. I believe it was this sincere assurance, which I always tried to carry out, that won my first election.

In those years of unstable prices and lack of adequate transport facilities, most of the Nyanza farmers had a hard struggle to make their farms pay. The coffee slump had forced many of them to borrow from the Land Bank. Perhaps they felt that a Nyanza farmer's wife would have a greater understanding of their problems than a man who was a newcomer (even if he had been one of Churchill's wartime generals). The Kenya settler is an individualist, hating to be regimented, nor is he a respecter of VIPs, and certainly he has no inclination to roll out the red carpet even for a Lt General. So maybe Noel's Army background told against him.

My greatest handicap was that I was a woman, and Nyanza was a very conservative province. The General had a slogan, "Strong men for stern times and no petticoat government," while I had none. Many of the settlers were retired army colonels and I could hear them saying, "True, Mrs Shaw has lived here 25 years, but would we not be safer with a man? A woman is so unpredictable, often so indiscreet; and anyway is it not rather 'infra dig' for a virile farming community to be represented by a mere female?"

"I will never vote for a woman," was the uncompromising attitude of many of the older men.

Our methods of running a campaign differed, too. My opponent put his faith in the support of the most influential man in each district, while I relied on small private committees, consisting of two or three women who worked quietly behind the scenes, preparing my visiting lists and assessing my support in every district. Then guided by their advice I set off on my rounds. 'House to House' visiting, a game in psychology, can be great fun, but you must get your facts straight. So, card index in hand, memorising the essential domestic details, you approach the front door. Then after a question as to how Susan is doing at the Kenya High School, all you need to be is a good listener. There is no doubt that the most important factor in local elections is not the candidate's merit or ability but whether a personal call has been made. Each card should be marked For, Against, Possible, Probable, or Unknown, and it is the candidate's job to turn the Againsts into Fors, the Possibles and Probables into Certainties, and to assess the Unknowns.

This was largely done by guesswork in that first election, although in each subsequent campaign a growing number of people told me they were supporters. I never asked how people were going to vote, only stressing that they must exercise their right as citizens and vote; a candidate should be most scrupulous in respecting the fact that it is a secret ballot. If you are a good psychologist you can usually tell, although in some cases I do not know to this day how people voted, even after five elections.

Twice during the first campaign, the General's supporters approached my sponsors begging me to stand down. Otherwise, they warned, I would surely lose my deposit. Was this an election ruse or were they so badly informed that they really thought I should not poll even one-eighth of the votes? We knew it would be a hard-fought fight with a close finish, but we never thought it would be a walkover for either side.

In my first campaign, my habit of going down every signposted turning paid dividends. This was how I met the Very Reverend Bishop Hall and the Catholic Fathers. Seeing a large group of red brick buildings six miles from Kakamega, I turned in at the signpost saying 'Bishop's House.' I saw a clerical figure doing a spot of gardening. As I approached, the figure fled, leaving me standing hesitatingly on the small lawn. A few minutes later the Bishop came out wearing his stole and his ring of office, which he held out for me to kiss in greeting. In some embarrassment I explained that I was not one of his flock but only a candidate canvassing for the next election. With a charming smile and speaking in his delightful Irish brogue, he bade me enter and tell him all about it. I did so while the Bishop sat gently rocking in his latest acquisition, a much-prized rocking chair, a gift from American well-wishers.

Bishop Hall, a humane and most understanding man, could not have been more welcoming, putting me entirely at my ease. From that day we were good friends. Talking to Bishop Hall is always stimulating: Not only has he an up-to-date appreciation of the world situation but, from his racy account of some of his Church's difficulties, it was evident that he had his hand firmly on the pulse of African thinking and behaviour. On that occasion, saying goodbye and wishing me the best of good luck, he suggested with a twinkle in his eye that it might be worth my while to visit the Seminary. The young priests not only kindly gave me lunch and a warm welcome but also gave a great deal of help by addressing postal ballots to Fathers in outlying parts of Nyanza. I reached Kakamega just in time for a planned meeting. On arrival at the Club Mrs Irwin said, "Where have you been? We were behind your car before lunch but you disappeared just before Kakamega." I airily replied that I had turned off "to visit friends."

I was to tread this path many times in subsequent years: from my hometown of Sotik to Kericho, the headquarters of the East African tea industry, and from there by way of the 'Settled Area' to Lumbwa, Songhor and on to Kisumu. Then up 'Catholic Lane' to Kakamega and Bungoma, coming back by way of 'Church Missionary Society Alley,' where at Butere and Maseno you enter the Church of England stronghold. The main spheres of influence, Roman Catholic and Anglican, are well defined, although in this part of Kenya there are small offshoots of every known brand of Mission, from the American Church of God and the Holy Rollers to the world-wide Salvation Army.

My introduction to the Church Missionary Society at Butere was just as fortuitous and none the less warming. In a torrential downpour, Miss Bee Appleby offered me shelter and a bed. Miss Appleby, a great character, left her home in Australia to come to this country years ago and has spent her life as a missionary amongst the Abaluhya tribe, her great work being the translation of the Bible into the Baluhya language. Bee is a very remarkable woman, always cheerful and good-tempered, though she has few of the creature comforts which most people regard today as essentials. She lives her simple life in a small wattle and daub house, although she has now achieved her own car, a great joy, after many years during which her only form of transport was a pedal cycle. On this, Bee rode many miles through the African Reserves. A hard and often lonely life in a strange land, as a background for what must have been always difficult and often discouraging work. What selfless and dedicated lives these women lead. In this I include, as well as missionaries, nuns of all denominations. During my twelve years of office I was privileged to meet many of them and see some of the wonderful work they do amongst the African people. I was fortunate in gaining their support, for I badly needed all the 'Hail Marys' intoned and prayers said on my humble behalf.

The pattern of the meetings was much the same from the first one in Lumbwa to the final one in Kisumu. Opposition I had in plenty. Most of the vociferous heckling was provided by the Robertson brothers, that lively and amusing pair. Their tactics were anything but subtle and their noisy interruptions often gained me the sympathy of the audience and sometimes even their votes. I got my own back when Struan Robertson asked a question in front of a large audience at one final meeting in Kisumu. This enabled me to say, "Yes, Mr Robertson, I would be delighted to reply, but I thought that by now you would have known the answer, having asked me the same question at the last four meetings," which caused a roar of laughter.

Believing in the truth of a saying attributed to a famous actress that "Bad publicity is better than none," I made it a rule never to mention my opponent on my platforms. His policy yes, but nothing more.

At last the whirlwind campaign was over. Polling day came, and finally the count began in the District Commissioner's office in Kisumu. At 1 a.m. on August 29th, 1951, Mr Tom Watts, the Returning Officer, announced me duly elected by the narrow margin of four votes. I had won! But it was not over even then, for with such a photo finish it was necessary for everyone's satisfaction to have a recount.

If it had gone against me that night, I think it very unlikely that I should have stood again; but even two recounts on that hot August night could not change the result. It was clear beyond any shadow of doubt that, by a majority of four votes, the Nyanza electors had rejected the 'Strong Man,' preferring 'Petticoat Government.'

CHAPTER 11

Learning the Political Ropes

*"Nature has given women so much power
That the Law has wisely given them very little."*
--Samuel Johnson

I was sworn in by the Speaker, Mr Justice Horne, on 6th September, 1951, the final day of the fourth sitting of the third Session. Taking the Oath of Allegiance, I said, "I, Agnes Ramsay Shaw, do swear that I will be faithful and bear true allegiance to His Majesty King George VI, his heirs and successors, according to law, so help me God."

My first Sitting was a very short one; Mr Speaker, after taking the Chair at 10 a.m., adjourned the Council at 10.20 a.m. until 23rd October. This adjournment gave me six weeks in which to recover from the strain of that hectic election and to put both my houses in order: my home after four weeks' absence, and my new political house.

My first task was to prepare a working plan for the running of my enormous constituency. Nyanza being the size of Wales, a Member had to travel many miles to cover the whole province. With slow posts and often no telephones, it had been found impossible to run the constituency without a committee to provide a two-way channel of communication between the Member and his constituents. The Nyanza Electors' Union had been started with this objective. In view of my close association with the Electors' Union over the previous ten years, it was natural for me to decide to work through the Union's Executive Committee, on which sat delegates representing all the districts in the constituency.

This was common practice among the Elected Members, although it tended to make life difficult when most of the failed candidates, having entered the lists by way of the Union's 'Nursery School,' after their defeat took up Union work again as the best training ground for the next election. My ex-opponent became President of the Nyanza branch, which gave him the opportunity of getting to know the Nyanza people, as well as a means of making known his policies. He had a clear field while I was penned in 200 miles away in Nairobi, learning my job as an Elected Member – a most interesting job, hard work, but so diverse and varied.

My constituents could have been said to represent a cross-section of the British people in Kenya. In the large tea growing areas of Kericho and Nandi Hills you would find company directors and their estate managers, while in Kisumu, the Provincial administrative centre, there were Government officials as well as the commercial community. 'Wild Settlers' lived in the outlying district of Sotik and the farming areas of Lumbwa, Koru and Songhor, while in Kisii and Kakamega every known brand of missionary was to be found. This religious stratum was leavened by miners from the Rosterman, Lolgorian and Macalder Mines.

Forty-nine percent of my constituents were Government officials. Government placed a ban on administrative officers taking part in political associations, but did not deny them the right to vote. Nor were members of the administration allowed to voice opinions at public meetings in case those opinions might be contrary to declared Government policy. However, they were permitted to ask questions and many an opinion was in fact expressed, subtly couched in the form of a question.

My first nine months, during which the leader of the European Elected Members was that fiery old warhorse Major Albert Keyser, were the most exhausting and turbulent of my whole twelve years. The European Elected Members Organization lived from crisis to crisis, and hardly a week went by without our delivering yet another ultimatum to Government. The Budget Session of 1951 proved the highlight of these

The Legislative Council Buildings in Nairobi with the Ngong Hills on the horizon.

disruptive tactics. Bent on enforcing economy cuts on Government expenditure, we in the Opposition demanded a six-and-a-half per cent cut in all Government departments, pointing out that only the Directors could know where the economies could be made without impairing the efficiency of their departments.

[Note: Kenya at this time had a Legislative Council made up of a group of members appointed by the Governor and another group made up of elected Europeans and a small number of elected Asians. The European members frequently opposed Government policies and fought vigorously on behalf of the settlers. The first African elected representatives joined in 1957.]

This proved correct; but Government refused, saying that the proper course was to cut post-by-post during the debate. Left with no alternative, we blindly blue-pencilled all posts which seemed to us redundant. Seeing posts for 'Secretaries and Assistant Secretaries' and then others for 'Temporary Clerks (European),' we fell upon the item. We were gleefully supported by the Asian and African Unofficial Members, since European heads were falling on the block.

Moving the deletion of these 'Temporary Clerks,' Mr Gerald Hopkins, a retired District Commissioner, led off by saying, "Am I correct in presuming that this item represents the salaries of the lady secretaries which have recently started creeping into the offices of the District Commissioners?" The Chief Secretary, Mr Colin Thornley, answering in the affirmative, pleaded for their retention for confidential work. The Member for Aberdares reported that in his day, confidential matters were written out in longhand, and copies were locked away in the safe. At this point Michael Blundell sent an amusing note around the Opposition Benches which read, "This debate seems to be on whether we have 'flimsies' or 'floosies!'" Mr Hopkins stood his ground, replying that no matter how desirable these ladies were, they must go. We in the Opposition were in no mood to be denied economy, and go they did.

The ensuing clamour on the Government Bench woke Major Cavendish-Bentinck who was gently dozing. Realising what had happened, he interjected, "You can't do this, you're cutting out the confidential secretaries of the Provincial Commissioners and the District Commissioners." Even though CB sat on the Government Bench as a nominated Settler Member, we trusted him and listened to his advice, so we stopped. The Rift Valley Province's secretaries were saved, but alas, Nyanza's had been deleted.

Not having made my Maiden Speech, I was not permitted to take part in the debate. Even so, as I went out of Council everyone crowded around me saying, "You've only been Member a fortnight, but look what you've done – I'll bet your fan-mail will go up tomorrow." It did, for the morning brought telegrams and letters of protest from irate Government officials. Not only did those excellent secretaries lose their jobs, but the Provincial and District Commissioners all had to do their own typing – an outrage which confirmed all their gloomy prognostications as to what a woman Member might do. To make matters worse, this disaster happened just before Christmas.

After two months, all these desirable ladies were reinstated by way of a supplementary estimate. So much for our abortive attempt at economy, which nearly cost me my next election.

I chose to make my Maiden Speech on the Police – a strange choice for a woman you may think at first, but not so strange if you pause to consider. After all, to quote from my opening remarks, "Security must be the cornerstone of our development, for, without security and good security, the whole edifice will topple to the ground."

The European Elected members of LegCo in April 1952: **Back row left to right:** *Gerald Hopkins, Agnes Shaw, Stanley Ghersie, Clive Salter, George Usher, Laurence Welwood.*
Front row left to right: *Joan Shaw, Wilfrid Havelock, Albert Keyser, Shirley Cooke, Michael Blundell.*

The budget session opened on the 31st October, 1951, but we did not reach the Police until the 29th November. Yet I had to be ready to make my speech at any moment. Day after day I sat in an agony of apprehension. Would I lose my head or forget my words? Would I be inaudible? (The acoustics of the Memorial Hall were nOturiously bad.) All these doubts and fears assailed me daily as I sat and waited. At last the terrifying moment came. I rose to my feet and seemed to listen, as in a dream, to someone else making my speech. After two minutes I heard this strange voice – in reality my own – saying, "Though I am sure Honourable Members are above such things, still I wonder how many ordinary mortals have not at some time in their career indulged in some innocent form of law-breaking."

The laughter rang out and from that moment I had their attention. My ordeal was over; I sat down to Council's prolonged applause. Mr Speaker, as Chairman of the Committee, rose and said, and I quote from *Hansard*, "I am sure Hon Members will excuse my breaking away from precedents of the Chair, in expressing on behalf of the House what I am sure all Members feel on both sides of this Council, cordial congratulations to our new Member on her very excellent, comprehensive and ably delivered Maiden Speech." In all my twelve years as a Member of the Kenya Legislative Council, this was the only occasion when the Speaker rose after a Maiden Speech to congratulate a new Member.

It was a comforting memory down the years, but I never lost my nervousness in speaking in Council. Most Members will agree that it is a nerve-racking experience. If a speaker faces a hostile audience on a public platform, they usually give him a hearing so as to be able to heckle, but in Legislative Council all they wonder is how long will this delay the House. Technically you are addressing Mr Speaker, but unless you capture the Members' interest and hold it, they will yawn, fidget, talk to their neighbour, or even walk out, which can be extremely disconcerting.

'Ng'ombe' Williams, Provincial Commissioner for Nyanza for many years, finding the prospect of having to deal with a woman Member somewhat alarming, hit upon a splendid plan; he decided to turn all official parties into 'stag' parties and then there would be no need to include me. On being asked by Major Keyser if I had been invited to a dinner to be given to welcome Mr Alan Lennox-Boyd, the Colonial Secretary, in Kisumu, I replied, "No, it's a stag party." Albert Keyser, wondering if he had heard aright, said, "A what?" and I repeated, "A stag party," – whereupon he blew up. He had never heard of anything so ridiculous, so disgraceful, such a slight to the European community! He rounded off his tirade by turning to me and saying in a furious voice,

"What you've got to remember is that you're not a woman but an Elected Member," and with that parting shot he disappeared.

The line between our office and the Secretariat must have been red hot that day. Major Keyser came back a few minutes later, saying, "The Chief Secretary presents the Provincial Commissioner Nyanza's apologies if your invitation has gone astray. He asks me to say that a plane will be put at your disposal, you will be met in Kisumu and put up for the night," adding, "and you will go!" This occasion was to be my introduction to Mr Lennox-Boyd, the most charming and courteous of men, who put me completely at my ease, enabling me to enjoy what otherwise might have been a rather terrifying experience. These moments could be embarrassing, even though I was no longer a woman. I am glad to say that after that unpropitious beginning, Mr Williams and I worked together for several years and became good friends.

On a rather similar occasion, my first dinner at Government House, Sir Philip Mitchell, the Governor, turned to me after dinner saying, "As my Private Secretary is suffering from influenza and my Aide-de-Camp, worse still, from love, allow me, Mrs Shaw, to show you where to, I believe the phrase is, 'powder your nose.'" He added, "After the port we shall join our charming lady Member."

During dinner there was an amusing little incident. By the time the waiter reached Michael Blundell, who was well down the long table, there was no fish left, and when Michael complained, the old Government House African Major Domo said, "Sorry Sir, but one Hon African Member took five pieces." (The Member was a Luo from the shores of Lake Victoria, the staple diet of whose tribe is fish.)

On the 28th November, 1951, the Acting Chief Secretary announced the impending visit of Their Royal Highnesses, The Princess Elizabeth and The Duke of Edinburgh. He told Members that the Royal couple was expected to arrive on February 1st and that afternoon they would be present at a Garden Party at Government House, at which it had been arranged that Mr Speaker should present the key to Forest Lodge, the Colony's wedding present to them both. With what excitement we looked forward to that day! All Members of the Legislative Council were to have the honour of being presented to Their Royal Highnesses. The afternoon was warm and sunny and there was an expectant hush as we waited on the cool and shady lawns of Government House.

On the stroke of 4 o'clock Their Royal Highnesses appeared on the steps and the band struck up the National Anthem. The Royal couple walked slowly along the line of assembled guests, stopping now and then to allow for presentations to be made. Everyone was impressed with the grace, dignity and poise with which our young Princess moved. At last our turn came and on being presented to the Princess I was amazed to find that, in spite of her poise, she had an air of charming shyness. This made me realise what a great help her husband's easy friendly manner must be to this young girl, so soon to become our Queen.

Just before us in the queue were Sir Robert and Lady Shaw, and, as Joan was presented, Mr Speaker announced, "Lady Shaw, our elder Lady Member, and her husband, Sir Robert." Immediately afterwards he said, "May I present Mrs Shaw, our second Lady Member, and her husband, Mr Shaw," at which Prince Philip remarked, "How very confusing, don't you ever get mixed up?"

"Indeed we do, Sir," I replied. "Even my Maiden Speech was published in *Hansard* under Lady Shaw's name," to which the Prince exclaimed, "What a damned shame!"

I felt sorry for Joan Shaw on this score. Having been, to quote one of her colleagues, "the best man amongst them," she must have felt slightly aggrieved at the arrival of, not only another woman Member, but one possessed of the name of Shaw. If she did, there was no hint of this in the kindness of the welcome Joan extended to me. Naturally I was careful to give her precedence as the senior Lady Member and not in any way to poach on her preserves. Although differing in political thought, I grew to admire her clear-sighted approach to problems in Committee work and to value her judgment.

Strangely enough, our paths had already crossed several times throughout the years before we finally became fellow Members. During the war years when I was tied down by the farm, a certain Lady Shaw used to take our son, Michael, out with her son John for half-term. In 1942, when Brian was at home on leave, we attended a Father's Match at Pembroke House Preparatory School and discovered to my astonishment that Lady Shaw was none other than a girl whom I remembered at picnics in Scotland. Strange that we should both marry unrelated Shaw men and meet again through our sons, twenty-five years later, in Kenya. She entered Legislative Council four years before I became a Member in 1951.

Council was prorogued on April 8th. I had found the work intensely interesting, so did not take much persuading when asked to stand again at the General Election on the 12th June, 1952. There proved to be many compensating factors for becoming 'dull and responsible.'

CHAPTER 12

The Emergency is Declared

*"Let us be content in work
To do the thing we can, and not presume
To fret because it's little."*
--Elizabeth Barrett Browning

The 1952 General Election was fought between the growing liberalism of a section of the European community led by Mr Michael Blundell on the one hand, and the more diehard element typified by the late Group Captain Briggs on the other. Both men believed in the necessity for the continuance of European leadership; but whereas Blundell was ready to meet the inevitable African demand for advancement, Briggs was not prepared to yield an inch. His party were fighting a rear-guard action, entrenched behind the slogan of 'Merit and Ability.' During the campaign at a Sotik meeting I remember a young man saying, "But surely, Mrs Shaw, you won your last election on Merit and Ability?", to which I replied, "No, Sir, by the sheer luck of four votes!"

My campaign might have been bitter had it not been for the intervention of a third candidate, Mr Cyril Mayers, who provided light relief. He regarded the whole thing as a huge joke and often before he was due to speak he would say, "Oh, Aggie, I wish I felt better – my head aches so – I went to a terrible party last night!" While the General was speaking, Cyril and I comforted each other with the wishful thought that perhaps the applause at the end of the old boy's speech would be less than at the previous meeting.

The turn of the campaign in my favour came at Songhor, a stronghold of conservatism, where, after a speech interrupted by cat calls, I was subjected to half an hour of fierce heckling. I kept my temper and at the end thanked the audience for their "patient listening," adding that if I came through trial by fire in Songhor, no other meetings in Nyanza held any terrors for me.

Sympathy for me had been growing amongst my typical Kenya audience, who had the British instinct for fair play, and this statement was greeted with surprise and applause. At the end of the meeting a series of fierce arguments broke out all over the Clubroom. One enormous man bore down on me, saying, "Well done, Ma'am! I said I'd never support a woman, but by God I will, and publicly too."

In the light of present events, my 1952 political thinking as set out in my manifesto may be of interest and I quote: "Our aim must be to steer Kenya safely through the troubled political waters that lie ahead, and our goal to build this Colony which we have made our home, into a strong country where all her citizens, whatever colour or creed, can live and work together in peace and amity. For each in their own sphere must play their full part if we are to become a strong and united country and a worthy partner in a Federation. [At the time there was a move among white settlers in Eastern Africa to unite Kenya, Uganda, Tanganyika, Southern Rhodesia, Northern Rhodesia and Nyasaland. In 1953, the latter three did form the Central African Federation, which lasted ten years.]

"There is a grave danger that unless there is a closer political and economic association of these East African Territories, who look to Britain for their inspiration, tradition and principles, other ideologies may prevail in the not too distant future. Opposition to this Federation is, as you know, growing amongst educated African opinion from here to the Limpopo, and it is being fostered by self-seeking political agitators, led by ill-informed cranks. It is to be hoped that Whitehall will not let the clamour raised by those who wish to tread the Fenner Brockway [a liberal British MP] way, and are engaged in fanning the flames of racial hatred, stand in the way of a Federation of the Central African territories, which is the first step in the building of an East and Central African Dominion."

In an attempt to put Kenya's own house in order, the European Elected Members set up a committee under the chairmanship of Sir Alfred Vincent whose terms of reference were, "To receive and collate the views of the European community, as to the most desirable form of Constitution for Kenya." The objective was some form of responsible government under European leadership – a leadership which, if it were to be successful, must have the support of the other races. This, we acknowledged, could only be gained by the removal of their fears. I stated in my manifesto: "This fear is based on ignorance and it must be our tack to break this down and to make the other communities in Kenya realise, as Mr Blundell said, that the benefit of the acceptance of European leadership will far outweigh any advantage that can possibly accrue from the pursuit of political objectives which entail the abdication of the British Mission in Africa."

Sir Godfrey Huggins, Prime Minister of Southern Rhodesia, and Sir Roy Welensky of Northern Rhodesia were then looked upon as the champions of the white man's cause in Africa. When Mau Mau reared its ugly head, Kenya's settlers were much heartened by a statement from Sir Roy Welensky at our Royal Agricultural Show to the effect that he regarded Kenya's northern Frontier Province as his northern frontier. But even the formidable Sir Roy was unable to withstand the Wind of Change, or to save the Central African Federation from collapse.

In the nine months between the elections I had gained some ground. In my estimate I started from scratch, for although a sitting member can usually count on a lead of twenty-five per cent, as a woman I started twenty-five per cent down. Again a hard fought contest ensued, which I won by 145 votes.

The first Session of the newly reconstituted Legislative Council was opened by the Governor, Sir Philip Mitchell, on June 12th, 1952. A major portion of the Governor's speech was devoted to the Government's policy of preparing the way for constitutional changes, such as a wholly-elected lower Chamber. This must be done before Kenya could become self-governing. He even foreshadowed the creation of a Senate. The extraordinary thing was that Sir Philip's only reference to the emergence of Mau Mau was to say, "The Government views with concern the recent threats to law and order occasioned by the activities of proscribed societies. Urgent and continuous attention will be given to the task of maintaining the fullest confidence in the peaceful administration of the Colony."

I often wonder if his retirement has been haunted by his failure to acknowledge the seriousness of the spread of Mau Mau and to take effective Government action. The administrator's prayer of, "Give us peace in my time, Oh Lord," scarcely made sense when Sir Philip was planning to spend his retirement in Kenya. In a man with a long and distinguished career behind him, and a great knowledge of Africa and her peoples, borne out by his most able dispatch on Kenya's land and population, his behaviour was inexplicable. Well-warned by the field officers of his administration, who were greatly alarmed by the spread of subversion in the Central Province, backed by the intelligence reports flooding in which all told the same story of a threatened breakdown in law and order, he must have known all was far from peaceful.

The Electors' Union, then under the Presidency of Lord Francis Scott, gave him a full report of the meetings being held throughout the Reserves by Jomo Kenyatta. Evidence included the verbatim statements of three loyal Kikuyu, who although endangering their lives by coming, brought us reports of Kenyatta's speeches at these meetings. The effect of these speeches was that a very great many Kikuyu believed he was a god and indestructible. Kenyatta vowed he would lead his people to freedom and drive out the British Government and the European settlers who had stolen their land.

How all this was to be done was not specified, but the harassing of the settlers through the theft and destruction of their livestock and property, followed by a series of murders, was the direct result of the anti-European feeling aroused by these meetings. These statements were sent to the Governor and Attorney-General with no result. No satisfactory explanation for this blind spot has ever been found unless it were that Kenya was once again made to suffer for the whims of British party politics. The Labour Party then in power prided themselves on the liberalism and success of their Colonial policy and on the eve of an election, the last thing that they wanted was a rebellion in Kenya on their hands. It would not have suited their book at all, as a distorted sympathy for Africans and an antagonism towards the hapless European settler had become a main plank in their political platform.

In this book I do not intend to give a detailed account of the horrors of those years of the Mau Mau rebellion, the darkest period in Kenya's history. Many books have been written on the subject; in my opinion far and away the best of these, apart from the factual Corfield Report, is *Kenya Warning* by Christopher Wilson. He writes: "The mental and spiritual damage is incalculable. Its cruelty has seared the souls of men and left scars. Its treachery has shattered faith in those we knew, with whom we had worked in what we believed was mutual confidence. Its savagery has brought to the surface and renewed primitive characteristics which we hoped had disappeared."

This sums up the meaning of the tragedy of the Mau Mau rebellion for the European settler, but perhaps even more so for the missionaries, who saw their years of faithful work destroyed overnight.

Throughout the early months in 1952, many Kikuyu leaders denounced Mau Mau; many others at public meetings and in Legislative Council denied its very existence. The African Members were placed in a most invidious and difficult position, especially Mr Eliud Mathu, who as the Kikuyu representative showed the dexterity of a tight-rope walker during this period. In my opinion, he was one of the ablest debaters of any race who has sat on the Opposition benches. Eliud never failed to make capital for the African cause from any mistake made either by Government or by the European and Asian Unofficial Members. Most Members felt sympathy for his predicament: If he voted against the repressive Emergency Legislation brought in by Government, he would lose his seat, and if he voted for it, he might even lose his life. In these circumstances he decided discretion was the better part of valour, and whenever this kind of Legislation came before Council, 'flu unaccountably claimed Mr Mathu. I am sure that the fact that he was the Government African Nominee at that time explained why Mr Mathu did not become one of the top-ranking politicians of the 1960s.

Once, when Michael Blundell, Member for Rift Valley, in a burst of temper, gave vent rather forcibly to his feelings, Mr Mathu remarked that he was glad to see that all the volcanoes in the Great Rift were not extinct. The 10th of July was just such an occasion, when Mr Blundell, exasperated by Government's maddening attitude of smug self-satisfaction, moved his Motion: "That this Council notes the increasing disregard of law and order within the Colony and urges Government to take the necessary measures."

Mildly worded as the Motion was, in speaking of it the Leader of the European Elected Members was blunt, forthright and did not pull any punches. Underlining the aims of Mau Mau, Mr Blundell used these words: "Mr Speaker, Sir, there is in our midst today an element who, although nurtured and fostered and brought forward with the background and example of our Western views and Western freedom... which we call Democracy, intends to use those ideas to overthrow the State and in my view, we have got to be ruthless in dealing with the situation because it is not only the State that is under fire, but the happiness of every individual within the State." Mr Blundell went on to say that "the protagonists of subversive movements in this country have had the advice and backing and support of persons from overseas who are primarily interested in the destruction of this Government. They have also vocal support from fellow travellers, and from what I call the crackpots in our civilization."

I am certain that it was this failure of Government either to acknowledge the extent of foreign intervention, or to deal with it effectively, that allowed the Emergency to drag on for years. I was convinced that Asiatic Communism played a large part in organising and financing the Mau Mau movement. Could it be coincidence that the outbreak of Mau Mau found not only an Indian High Commissioner in Nairobi who was known to have had anti-British sympathies during the war, but also an Assistant Commissioner, an Indonesian, who with his wife was said to be an organiser of the Java and Sumatra riots?

To return to that July day in the old Memorial Hall, some of the faces on the Government benches showed expressions of shock, horror, and surprise when Blundell said that his information led him to believe that the Mau Mau target date "would be within the next nine months." During the 11 o'clock break that day, Government Members retired to their Committee Room to hold an Emergency

Meeting at which Mr Blundell was put squarely on the mat: "How dare he make such an exaggerated statement, bound to cause alarm and despondency," etc., etc. But within a few weeks the murders of Europeans had started. It is possible that Blundell's outburst may well have saved us from 'The Night of the Long Knives' as there is no shadow of doubt that the first Mau Mau attacks went off at half-cock. This was borne out time and again at the hearing of murder cases in the Court of Appeal.

The organisers of Mau Mau could no longer feel safe from discovery after the knowledge shown of their deep-laid plans by Michael Blundell in his speech. This made them feel that they must act quickly if their action was to retain any of the force of a surprise attack. They had been lulled into a sense of security by the obtuseness of Government. The days were gone when the District Commissioner was looked upon as the 'father of the people.' Moreover, visits to the local areas were infrequent, tied as the Commissioners were to their office desks by the ever-growing mass of paperwork, statistics to be supplied, forms to be filled, circulars received and sent.

How could one District Commissioner, two District Officers, plus twenty-eight police administer 400,000 people? But that was what they were expected to do in the Fort Hall district of the Central Province before the Emergency. Afterwards, with the introduction of closer administration, the staff was increased to one District Commissioner, twenty-six District Officers and 400 Tribal Police. Had this been the strength of the Administration in 1947 when Jomo Kenyatta returned, perhaps there would have been no Emergency.

Undoubtedly the cheese-paring economy of the Kenya Government as regards the Administration, the Police, and the Education Departments was a contributory cause to the conditions that caused the Emergency. Lack of adequate supervision enabled the Githunguri Teacher Training College to be used as a vehicle to pervert the Kikuyu teachers and indoctrinate them with Mau Mau teachings. Government had welcomed the action of the Kikuyu leaders in taking over the management of the Training College and the Kikuyu Independent School Association, but many of the schoolboys of 1948 became the Mau Mau of 1952.

At the end of August an Emergency Meeting of the European Elected Members drafted a list of proposed measures, which we considered must be introduced immediately to stem the ever-increasing lawlessness in the Colony. Mr Blundell, as Leader, asked for an interview with the Acting Governor to inform His Excellency that it was the considered opinion of his team that unless the necessary legislation were passed and a State of Emergency declared, there would be a complete breakdown of law, order and good government. Much to Blundell's surprise and relief, Sir Henry Potter agreed to fly to London to discuss the suggestions with the Colonial Secretary and the Governor Designate, Sir Evelyn Baring. Sir Henry himself was convinced of the necessity of these measures and finally obtained permission for the drafting of the required legislation, although it was considered wiser not to declare a State of Emergency until the new Governor was in the saddle.

This typified the struggle the European Elected Members had during the next few months to force Government to act; and in spite of the Elected Members' unceasing pressure, the powers granted were always too little and too late.

By October of 1952, hundreds of loyal Africans had been murdered including Senior Chief Waruhiu. On October 21st, Jomo Kenyatta, Fred Kubai and 81 Mau Mau leaders were arrested and a State of Emergency proclaimed. On 22nd October Chief Nderi Wang'ombe, who had spoken so courageously denouncing Mau Mau at the mammoth Nyeri meeting, was murdered, and on that day military reinforcements were flown in from Aden to Kenya.

On October 28th the Labour MPs Fenner Brockway and Leslie Hale arrived in Nairobi as the invited guests of the Kenya African Union, and hot on their heels came the Secretary of State for the Colonies, Mr Oliver Lyttelton, who toured the affected areas. November 11th saw the closure of the KISA schools, the channels for the dissemination of Mau Mau teachings, and on the 18th Jomo Kenyatta and five of his Mau Mau followers were charged at Kapenguria with the organisation of Mau Mau.

Whether after the arrest of Jomo Kenyatta and these other important leaders on October 21st the Mau Mau movement lacked direction will never be known. It is a fact that immediately after their arrest on October 28th, the first of the series of senseless, brutal murders of Europeans took place.

The first victim, Eric Bowyer, a gentle, kindly man, was hacked to death in his bath by his own servants; barely a month later Commander Meiklejohn and his doctor wife were attacked in their farmhouse and left for dead. The story of the wife's courageous drive, gravely wounded as she was, eight miles to the police station to get help is well known. There she was found, her face so slashed as to be unrecognisable, her eyes glazed, sitting in her own blood in her car. Then came the brutal murder of one of Kenya's pioneers, Charles Ferguson, and his young neighbour, Richard Bingley.

A few days later this was followed by an unsuccessful attack on those two remarkable women, Mrs Hesselberger and Mrs Raynes

Simpson. Before the month was out the Ruck family – father, mother and their six-year-old son – were hacked to death in a murder which was one of the most callous and brutal of the whole chapter of horrors.

By now nerves on the Kinangop were strained to breaking point and the growing alarm throughout the Colony culminated in a march on Government House on January 27th. The march was organised by the Nairobi leaders of the Federal Independence Party, and joined by many Kinangop farmers who brought with them eye-witness accounts of the savagery of the Mau Mau attacks. The horror of the Ruck murders, which had happened the day before, including the terrible death of their poor little son, who was the first European child to be murdered, brought things to a head. There was a growing feeling that Government was not taking the necessary action for the protection and defence of law-abiding citizens.

All this was cause enough for the Europeans to march on Government House demanding to see the Governor as the Queen's representative. The fact that capital was made out of the stresses and strains of the hour by a small group of rabble-rousers was beside the point. Eighty percent of that crowd of some 2,000 people, among them the Mayor of Nairobi, were respected citizens who had been led to believe that they had been asked to attend and give their support to their Elected Members who were known to be holding an emergency meeting with the Governor.

On reaching the Elected Members office the morning of the march, I found that the Government House staff were at action stations preparing for the siege. The gates were locked and oil drums had been placed up and down the drive. As we sat in the Executive Council Room discussing the effect this latest tragedy was likely to have on an already tense situation, an endless stream of Europeans came surging up the drive. When their numbers had swelled to over 2,000, they sang "God Save the Queen." These preliminaries over, the crowd kept up a steady chant of: "We want the Governor." This was very distracting to His Excellency. Finding it impossible to concentrate, he withdrew thankfully when a very harassed Private Secretary came in to ask the Governor if he would consent to see a deputation from the crowd.

Shortly after His Excellency left us, the crowd surged towards the House and we jumped to our feet and shot down the corridor. I found myself, together with others, helping to push the table used for the Visitors' Book against the door. I seem to remember Michael Blundell leaping on that table and shooting home the bolts of the great door. Meanwhile, the white-faced Government House staff were hurriedly closing the shutters of all the long ground floor windows.

With a shout of, "Come on you chaps, we are the only people who can stop this," Michael Blundell tore down the corridor with the rest of us behind him and out of the side door. Never have I seen Michael Blundell run before or since, but he certainly ran that day! He had advised the Governor that it would be wiser not to have African *askaris* on parade, and if he must have the Kenya Police present, then he would be wise to keep them out of sight.

Unfortunately, His Excellency did not take this advice. On reaching the front of the house the most astonishing sight met our eyes: a number of European policemen with their arms locked backed on to the great doors. Flattened against the police by the pressure of the crowd was Mr Vigor, the leader of the march, while over his shoulders a European woman was beating Government House door with a shooting stick. Around the front of the house was a thin cordon of bewildered African *askaris*, holding their truncheons at the ready, in the midst of this shouting, yelling mob of Europeans. To the askaris it was quite a new situation and they had no idea what to do. The racial tension was so strained by the horrible savagery of this latest of foul murders that had one European woman lost her foothold and gone down under the mob, hell might have been let loose.

Michael Blundell was quick to realise the danger in the situation, as many of the crowd were armed, and he did not hesitate to act. I was standing beside him and heard him turn to a young European policeman, ordering him to remove the *askaris*. The young man, to his undying credit, standing stiffly to attention in the midst of the swirling, shouting crowd, said, "I take my orders only from the Commissioner, Sir." Michael retorted, "Where the bloody hell is the Commissioner?" Turning round he saw Mr O'Rourke standing just behind him and said in the most peremptory tone, "Withdraw your men and I'll take the responsibility."

The Commissioner agreed, and European Members rushed in and out of the crowd shouting, "Back on the grass." Back they went and the frightened *askaris* were marched off to cheers from the crowd. There was still a good deal of noise and shouting. Michael called for a chair – it was impossible to speak to a crowd of that size from ground level. Out came a scarlet leather chair embossed with the gold 'George Rex.' Michael got hold of Group Captain Briggs, pushed him up on this precarious perch, and shouted, "Here's the man you want to hear – the man from the affected areas."

Poor 'Puck' Briggs, the last man to seek the limelight, was now the focus of all eyes. Rather nonplussed, he stammered out, "I thank you all, but in my constituency people are as steady as rocks." When he had repeated this several times the crowd became restive and started to shout again. Michael Blundell replaced the Member for Mount Kenya with Mr Humphrey Slade, Member for Aberdares, which included the Kinangop, the scene of so many of the murders.

Mr Slade is a Welshman of the greatest sincerity, to whom right is right and wrong is wrong, without compromise. A hush fell on the crowd and Mr Slade faced a silent and expectant audience, eager to hear what he had to say. Holding his lapels in the characteristic 'To Be or Not to Be' manner, Humphrey said in the gravest tones, "I do not thank you; I do not thank you for coming here and behaving like an undisciplined rabble." This was bad enough, but the crowd was incensed when they thought he said 'rebels;' after all, they *had* sung "God Save the Queen." This brought forth a howl of "How dare you," "Apologise," etc., until the crowd's attention was diverted by the unfortunate appearance of the Sultana of Zanzibar on the Government House balcony. This angered the crowd, and particularly the South African element, to see a coloured person in the innermost councils of Government.

All this happened in the space of a few minutes – some of the tensest I have ever lived through. By now Blundell, having got his second wind, leapt upon the chair, shouting, "Quiet, while I tell you what we've done." At last the crowd had got what it wanted and they listened attentively while the Leader of the European Elected Members told them that only that morning at our meeting with the Governor we had asked for three things: Firstly, the appointment of an overall Commander; secondly, European settler representation on the War Council; and thirdly, the introduction of conscription for both men and women. This announcement was received with applause. Michael, pleading the necessity of continuing our interrupted discussions with the Governor, walked towards the House, and the crowd peacefully and quietly dispersed.

I believe that when Michael (who was by this time pretty well all-in) went to report to His Excellency, he found Sir Evelyn Baring at his desk calmly writing a letter. On being given a much-needed drink, Mr Blundell apologised to Sir Evelyn, saying, "We had no previous knowledge of, nor have we been in any way responsible for, the events of the last two hours." He added, however, that it showed the state of tension in the Colony and the strain the Government had placed on the Elected Members.

In his short statement to the crowd, Mr Blundell had said, "Don't come here if you want to see us, come to our office at 4 o'clock," and sure enough when we got back to the Memorial Hall, there they were. Worse still, the Kenya Broadcasting Service, in their lunchtime broadcast, had announced in error that Michael Blundell would be available at 6 p.m. So once again, on our return from Government House, we found the shouting mob, several hundred strong, outside the Memorial Hall, blocking the traffic on Delamere Avenue.

Michael told us to turn them into a delegation, but that proved impossible. When we opened the doors of the Memorial Hall they poured in and banked themselves around the walls, leaving a small space in the centre. A number of Elected Members were grouped around Michael on the foot-high platform on which stood the Speaker's Chair. Again Michael told them what we had achieved. He then excused himself, saying he was due to see the Governor again at 7 o'clock, but that his colleagues would answer any questions. He strode off leaving Colonel Stanley Ghersie in charge. He, as the senior Member, attempted to take the chair. Every time he said, "Order, order, let's do this in a constitutional way," his voice was drowned by a roar from his audience. Although they were out to bait all the Elected Members, their anger was chiefly directed against Mr Slade and there were demands for his resignation.

At that moment, the Member for Nairobi South leapt forward and, shaking his fist at the crowd, cried, "I think you are all disgusting. Here you have a man like Humphrey Slade living under a terrible strain, with his friends being murdered around him, and because in a moment of stress he uses an unfortunate phrase you go for him." Someone in the crowd shouted, "That's right, it's a damned shame. Good old Slade," and there was a general "Hear, hear." Humphrey Slade was reinstated and their anger was turned in the direction of the other Elected Members. They shook their fists at us and demanded to know what any of us had done to help. We seemed to be in a tight corner, for the rabble-rousers amongst the crowd, denied of their first quarry, were determined to make a kill.

Just as things were getting somewhat tense, John Manussis, the racing driver, a little man, bounded into the small cleared space in the centre of the floor, pointed an accusing finger in the direction of the side door, and shouted, "Quiet, there's an enemy in our midst, a spy, a Communist." At that there was a general surge forward. A tall, pale-faced, red-bearded young man, dressed in a green velvet jacket and floppy black bowtie, was standing with folded arms trying in vain to make himself heard above the increasing clamour. In an effort to gain him a hearing, I took off my shoe and brought it down with a bang on the platform. It sounded like a revolver shot, and in the momentary silence Colonel Ghersie said, in the most dignified tones, "Your name, Sir?" To this the young man replied, "My name is Peter Evans and I am visiting Kenya in order to assist at a famous trial at Kapenguria."

This was too much for the crowd to stomach; they thought this must mean that he was helping Mr Dennis Pritt, QC, who was defending Jomo Kenyatta. With a roar of rage, they surged forward, our respected Chairman lost what little control he had, and Mr Peter Evans was picked up and thrown out of the side door. He turned out to be a journalist of rather pink, if not red, sympathies. That evening this unfortunate young man was again thrown out, this time from the bar of the New Stanley Hotel. A week later he was deported from the Colony. However, the Elected Members had reason to be grateful to this young Socialist, for he drew off the fire and fury of those other bearded and angry young men from our unfortunate heads, and we were able to escape in the melee. Here ended one of the most amazing days I had ever lived through.

Shortly after this, the Governor announced the appointments of General George Erskine as overall Commander and Mr Blundell to serve on the War Council, and the introduction of conscription. The march on Government House had achieved something!

In the midst of all this tragedy, one bright ray fell across the last days of the year 1952. Our daughter Ann was married to Donald Stewart Bush on 29th December.

Don Bush had come to Kipkebe as a pupil, to learn farming, three years previously, and when Ann returned home from her Art School in London, they fell in love. Both families, already connected by marriage, were delighted with their engagement.

Soon after the start of the Emergency, Don was called up to the Kenya Regiment, and was stationed at Karatina, in the Kikuyu Reserve. He was granted a fortnight's leave to get married. The Right Reverend Bishop J Beecher, who had confirmed Ann, married them in Sotik Church, and the reception was held in the house where Ann was born, Kipkebe.

The organisation of the wedding and reception was attended by the usual hitches, alarums and excursions so typical of our Sotik functions. The first and worst was that my sister-in-law, Joyce Vernon, and her daughter Jix, were left stranded at Naivasha by a forgetful young man. The loaves, rolls and pastries which she was to instruct him to collect en route were securely locked up in the Nakuru Bakery 100 miles away. The deep-freeze at the Tea Hotel, Kericho, broke down and the freshness of all my turkeys and hams hung in the balance, as being Sunday the engineer had gone off fishing. And last but not least, both our pump and hydraulic ram went out of action, and there was not one drop of water at the house.

Brian and Agnes Shaw at the wedding of Ann and Don Bush in December 1952

Ann's marriage to Don Bush in December 1952. Left to right: Brian, Agnes, Don, Ann, Michael, and Laura Cree.

I was frantic, with 300 or 400 guests expected at the wedding the next day. The final straw came when, in an effort to right some of these disasters by phoning my sister-in-law, every time we lifted the receiver all we could hear was the overture to *William Tell*. By ringing everyone on the party line, we finally located the culprit and my husband drove two miles to the next-door farm. He found the young manager sitting in his armchair, his feet up, oblivious to the trouble he was causing. He had taken off his telephone receiver so that he shouldn't be disturbed, and *William Tell* was blaring forth from his gramophone.

The saying that a bad dress rehearsal ensures a good opening proved true in our case. On the day, everything went without a hitch, and we shall always remember our daughter's wedding as one of the happiest of Kipkebe occasions. It was a family reunion as well; Michael, then doing his military service with the Black Watch, had flown out to see his sister securely tied up. The service was at 11 o'clock, the bride and groom went off in a shower of confetti and good wishes just after tea, and our last guest left at 5 p.m.

This was the signal for the twenty-five African farm *nyaparas* to sit down at the table in the children's luncheon marquee and finish off the feast. Many of them had known Ann from childhood and I was touched by the gifts of chickens and eggs they brought to me when they came to wish her well on her wedding day. A merry party they were, Kipsigis, Luo and Kisii, as they had been constantly toasting the young couple in champagne during the morning. A fitting ending to a Kenya farm wedding.

A week later Ann and Don came back to Kipkebe to spend the last half of their honeymoon mending tractors and ploughs and generally helping us on the farm, a wonderful effort, typical of Don. For since Don's call-up Brian had been single-handed. The week flew by all too quickly and our young people left us, full of high hopes, to start married life in a couple of mud huts in the Kikuyu Reserve. Poor darlings, little did they know then that they were to have eighteen homes in their first five years of marriage.

As a tailpiece to this family interlude, I would like to record an event which made the whole Shaw family very proud. This was the award of the MBE to Brian's sister, Irene Macdougall, in recognition of her fifteen years of devoted service as Matron of the Nakuru War Memorial Hospital.

Irene MacDougall having been awarded the MBE.

CHAPTER 13

Into the Forest

"Never in the field of human conflict was so much owed by so many to so few."

--Winston Churchill

The Lari Massacre on the night of the 25th March, 1953 was the turning point of the Mau Mau Rebellion. On that night more than 100 Africans died violent deaths. The horror of that massacre by the Kikuyu of their own brethren made a deep impression on the other African tribes. Indeed, that night a fear of the Kikuyu was born which was to prove a major factor in preventing the spread of Mau Mau to the other tribes.

Looking back, it seems strange that it was not until the following October that a motion on this subject was brought before the Legislative Council by the Member for Rift Valley. Mr Blundell moved, "This Council is of the opinion that the processes of justice on capital charges arising from the Emergency Regulations must be greatly accelerated and requests Government to introduce emergency procedures, whereby trial and punishment in such cases may be seen to be both swift and effective."

Speaking in support of the Motion, I reminded Council that we had been assured by the Attorney General that there was a law still on the Scottish Statute Book, although not operative since 1903, that could be invoked. By this means it would be possible to carry out a death sentence on a convicted murderer within fourteen to sixteen days from the time of sentence. These powers had not been used. Instead, six months after that terrible event, not a single Lari murderer had paid the supreme penalty.

Stressing that until we could bring home the fact that swift capture and speedy justice followed the committing of a crime, we should not be able to put down the rebellion. In conclusion I said that although I would not deny justice, I found it hard to regard with mercy people who reverted to such bestial barbarity, and had shown no mercy to their victims, often innocent women and little children.

After a long debate the motion was passed unanimously. Even so, only twenty-seven, out of a total of the 342 arrested and charged with murder in connection with the Lari Massacre, paid the supreme penalty.

Winston Churchill's famous words, quoted above, could well be applied to the young men of the Kenya Regiment, a European volunteer unit equivalent to the British territorials. At the outbreak of the Emergency, the Regiment was only about 450 strong, but the fact that the Kenya Government was able to call on such a well-disciplined force, whose loyalty was beyond question, probably saved a large part of the Colony from the reign of terror.

To quote *Hansard*, in a speech I made in Council paying tribute to the courage of these young men, I said, "The Kenya Regiment have borne the heat and burden of the day, having been on active service since the outbreak of the Emergency…These men of the Kenya Regiment, our Regiment, with their love of this country and their high courage, have proved the hard core of the resistance in the fight against Mau Mau. With their specialised knowledge they have succeeded in guerrilla warfare where more conventional army units were bound to fail. No words can tell what the law-abiding citizens of all races owed to the Kenya Regiment in those early days of the rebellion. As a European Unit they were our only striking force, while the older settlers in the Kenya Police Reserve held the fort on the home front."

To my mind the secret of their success was the fact that most of them had been born and reared in the Colony. Not only did they have a love of Kenya, which they looked upon as their home, but an understanding and liking for her people. It was this, more than anything, that inspired the Africans with a feeling of trust for the young '*Bwanas,*' their leaders, and out of dangers shared grew a strong bond of comradeship.

To continue a description of their work, with assistance from *The Kenya Police* by W Robert Foran, the main campaign against Mau Mau was mounted in the Aberdare mountain range and the foothills of Mount Kenya, home ground to the gangsters. The immense difficulties in containing a rebellion fought over terrain in which conventional forces were of little use made the task of necessity a slow one. The foothills consist of broken country made up of a series of gullies separated by steeply sloping ridges. On the top of these ridges would be perched the Kikuyu villages. One village would be under the sway of a chief well known for his unswerving loyalty, like Senior Chief Njiiri, while on the next ridge the people would be entirely in the grip of Mau Mau. There were few roads, if any, and the only way of reaching the villages was by hillside tracks. Higher up the slopes became steeper and more wooded, until you reached the forest. Here it was so dense that you could pass a gangster lying within a few feet and never see him – a sniper's paradise. Army lorries, manned by British troops complete with Army boots and encumbered with all their regulation equipment, were of little use.

'Item Force,' the detachment of the Kenya Regiment trained for this warfare in the forest, travelled light and knew that to crack a twig, or speak above a whisper, could be fatal. They were fed by airdrops, their rations sewn up inside the carcass of a sheep. After retrieving the welcome stores they would have to move on, as to feed near the drop would be asking for trouble. They also learned that to sleep where they had cooked and eaten might spell disaster. The strain of living under these conditions – sometimes the hunter, sometimes the hunted – was so great that after ten days they were usually relieved and returned to base camp for a period of rest. It was a hard campaign, but as the months lengthened into years, the security forces began to get the upper hand. They hunted and harried the gangsters with increasing success so that as the gangsters' casualties through death or capture mounted, their supply lines were cut and their morale began to crack.

At the time of his marriage, my son-in-law, Don Bush, serving in the Kenya Regiment, had been seconded to 'Ray Force.' He was stationed at the police post at Karatina, a market nine miles from the Government Boma of Nyeri in the middle of the Kikuyu Reserve. My daughter's honeymoon home was a couple of dilapidated mud rondavels, the living room being some 200 yards from their bedroom. Arriving in Karatina three months after the wedding, I found Don in bed, far from well. He had a high temperature and his legs were a mass of septic sores. Ann and I drove over to the Scots Mission at Tumutumu to ask the young doctor there to come over and see our patient. He diagnosed septicaemia and signed a letter recommending sick leave. That evening we entertained several lads of the Regiment who blew in for a drink and a little cheer and comfort before returning to some lonely outpost in the forest.

After they had left and we had attended to our patient, Ann called for supper. In response to a knock at the door, I was amazed to see my daughter pick up a loaded revolver before she called out to come in. In answer to my look of surprise, Ann said, "I have to do that, as you never know who may be behind the house servant." She added, "You needn't be afraid, Mummy, that Kamau will drop the chicken for he knows the drill." Poor children – they slept with a sten gun at their side. In the morning I was surprised to find about fifty ragged, dirty and sullen looking Kikuyu squatting around the huts, and was horrified to learn that they were Mau Mau who had been taken prisoner. Ann told me, "Don has sent for for barbed wire, but it has not yet arrived from Nairobi." She calmly continued, saying, "That's why they are loose, but don't worry, they're all right and jolly useful – they cut the firewood and dig our garden."

It was not until after the Mau Mau raid on the Naivasha Police Station that Government took the precaution of enclosing all police posts in a strong barbed-wire stockade. That raid, cleverly planned and executed by gangsters dressed as police askaris, besides releasing many imprisoned terrorists cost the Government heavily in the loss of arms and ammunition.

I went back to Nairobi on the Monday for a sitting of Legislative Council, happy in the knowledge that by that evening the children would be safe and sound at Kipkebe, Sotik.

Don Bush served with the Kenya Regiment for more than four years, at first in Ray Force and latterly being seconded to the Field Intelligence Service as District Field Intelligence Officer in charge of 100 square miles in the Thika district. This was a very hot spot, half-way on the supply route between Nairobi and Fort Hall, the centre of the Mau Mau kingdom. A good deal of his work was leading the 'pseudo gangs' [white-led government forces that adopted the style of the Mau Mau] to obtain information and to try and track down the terrorists. This proved an effective but highly dangerous method of breaking up the forest gangs, and for his services Don Bush was mentioned in despatches.

The year 1954 saw the build-up of the security measures which were to cause the eventual defeat of the Mau Mau rebellion. Chief amongst these were the formation of the Kikuyu Home Guard, 'villagisation" and the training of the pseudo gangs under the Field Intelligence Organisation.

Michael Blundell, as Member of the War Council, said that the Emergency would never be brought under control unless and until the supply of food, arms and ammunition could be denied to the forest gangs. In order to do this, he told the Council, it was necessary to introduce villagisation throughout the Central Province. The Kikuyu were accustomed to living in scattered huts either on the edge of the forest, or in clearings in the forest. This made it impossible to exercise any control over their movement, even by day, let alone by night. Once darkness fell it was a simple matter for them to arrange the supply of food to the gangs based in the forest.

The scheme conceived by Michael Blundell and supported by all the European Elected Members was for all these Kikuyu forest dwellers to be moved into villages. As Mr Blundell pointed out, once this was done it would be a comparatively easy matter to control arms running, and to stop the food supply lines. At first the Government turned down the suggestion of villagisation as being completely impractical, but after tremendous pressure it was finally adopted, and it proved the only way of starving the gangs out.

It was a gigantic task. The forest was cordoned off by the building of a high fence of wattle poles. To make the barrier more effective, a wide moat was dug on the outside of the fence and filled, not with water, but with vicious looking crossed spikes of wattle, like a porcupine ready to do battle. Even then, one village on the edge of Nyeri township, then a base for the Security Forces, was found to be feeding a gang night after night. To prevent this, look-out guard posts were built. Many villages had to be enclosed by these spiked moats. In addition, a curfew was imposed and the people warned that anyone seen by the guards attempting either to get in or out of the village would be liable to be shot. This system of villagisation was in the end highly successful, and had it been introduced when first suggested by Michael Blundell, it might well have shortened the Emergency by several months.

Government took a calculated risk in the formation and arming of the Kikuyu Home Guard, believing that such a force to defend the newly built villages from night attack was an essential part of intensified measures to bring the long-drawn out rebellion to an end. Looking back, it seems incredible that a loyal band of Kikuyu were successfully formed at a moment when thousands of their relations and fellow tribesmen were completely in the thrall of the Mau Mau leaders. How easy it would have been for them to defect, complete with their arms, to the gangs in the nearby forest. That this did not happen to any great extent I believe was largely due to the high morale, courageous leadership and spirit of comradeship that the young Europeans of the Kenya Regiment brought to the training of these units entrusted to their care. The same can be said of the "pseudo gangs" who were mostly officered by men of the Regiment. The biggest single factor in their success was the officers' liking for, and understanding of, the African.

In April 1954, the Commissioner of Police, Mr MS O'Rourke, retired and Col AE Young, CMG, Commissioner of the City of London Police, was seconded on loan to Kenya. The idea behind this move, which was to broaden the basis of the Kenya Police so as to enable the force more easily to meet the stresses and strains of an Emergency, was a good one, but the choice of Commissioner was amazing. Who could think the experience and training of a first-class London 'Bobby' would be of use in guerrilla warfare against forest gangsters? [Young had previously reorganized the Malayan police force during the independence struggle there.] The task proved quite beyond Col Young. Much of the carefully built up security was in danger of being undermined by his bringing charges against members of both the Kenya Regiment and the newly formed Kikuyu Home Guard. [Such charges were vindicated in 2013 when the British Government reached a settlement with Kenyan survivors of torture during the Emergency.] This action could so easily have resulted in this Kikuyu Force defecting to the forest, taking their arms with them, and it did cause many threatened resignations from both the Kenya Regiment and the Kenya Police Reserve.

The question was openly being asked, "Who are the Government fighting, the Mau Mau or the Security Forces?" The Governor, Sir Evelyn Baring, who also believed that much of the resistance which had been carefully built up over months was in danger of being destroyed, referred the whole matter to the British Cabinet. The price of quashing these charges was the offer of an amnesty for both sides [i.e. Mau Mau and Government forces], namely the famous (or infamous) 'Surrender Terms.'

The announcement of the Surrender Terms was made by the Government without reference to the European Elected Members. This provoked an extremely bitter debate in Legislative Council. Chief beneficiary under this Amnesty was a nOturious Mau Mau leader styling himself General China, who had been responsible for many brutal murders. His reprieve from a death sentence caused a Colony-wide storm of protest. Mr Blundell, who raised the matter as one of national importance in a motion on adjournment, ended his speech with these words: "Mr Speaker, I believe that the ordinary citizen of this country, of whatever colour or creed, will inevitably be convinced by this action that Government has become a party to these brutalities, to these murders and filthy oaths."

Blundell was supported in this motion by strong, forthright speeches from both Members representing the affected areas, namely the late Group Capt Briggs and Mr Humphrey Slade. Mr Slade, one of the fiercest opponents of the Amnesty, had placed "No Surrender Here" placards all over his Kinangop farm.

The Minister of Finance, Sir Ernest Vasey, spoke against the motion in defence of Government's action. Sir Ernest, always a champion of the African cause, was apt to be rather suspect in the eyes of the European Members of the Opposition Bench. He was an extremely able Minister of Finance as well as a shrewd politician, and the majority of the European farmers distrusted him, saying he was 'too clever by half.' So he turned his back on his own community and became the councillor-in-chief to the African Elected Members. He held his office as Minister of Finance until he was defeated in the election of 1956.

CHAPTER 14

Continuing Turmoil

*"This is the truth which you shall find
Good flourishes in all mankind,
And soon or late, some evil man,
Disgraces every sect or clan."*
--Edgar A Guest

The Mau Mau rebellion dragged on for seven long years. The cost to Kenya of this tragedy, not only in men and money, but also in the complete cessation of all development in every field, is impossible to assess. During these Emergency years, we in Kenya had plenty of time to try to discover the underlying causes of Mau Mau. Much thought was given to this by people well-qualified to understand the workings of the Kikuyu mind. During the short reign of terror in the early months, the savagery of the attacks gained sympathy for the many isolated farmers and their families, although very little of the real character of the uprising was understood in Great Britain.

In an attempt to enlighten all sections of the British public and capture their interest, if not their understanding, anyone who had any official position, if going home on leave, was asked to give lectures or even informal talks on the Emergency in Kenya. During my home leave in the summer of 1954, I spoke several times in places as far apart as London, Reading, Wedmore, Edinburgh and Ayr. My audiences, always appreciative, were as varied as the places, ranging from a House of Commons Committee through Rotary Clubs to Women's Institutes and schools. The object of my talks was to try and get across to different sections of the British people some understanding of the Mau Mau rebellion and its causes.

Kenya has always suffered from the spotlight of publicity and with the outbreak of the Emergency we became headline news. But too often it was only the violent side of the tragic phase through which we were passing that was written up for a sensation-loving public. If we suffered from publicity, we suffered even more from ill-informed cranks who thought they had a mission to champion the underdog. These misguided men and women ignored the bestiality of Mau Mau and would have had the world believe that the rebellion was a war of colour: black versus white. But what are the facts? During the Emergency only thirty-two Europeans were murdered while there were [about] 2,000 known Africans brutally done to death by their own kith and kin. So much for the theory of a colour war. But if it was not race hatred, what were the underlying causes of Mau Mau?

The Governor, Sir Philip Mitchell, while refusing to recognise Mau Mau as a rebellion, did not ignore the problems that arose from the rapid rate of increase of the African population of East Africa. The appointment of a Royal Commission under the chairmanship of Sir Hugh Dow in January 1953 was welcomed by politicians of all races in Kenya. The Commission was appointed to "examine forthwith the measures necessary to be taken to achieve improved standards of living, including the introduction of capital to enable present farming to develop and expand production, and to frame recommendations thereon, having regard to the rapid rate of increase of the African population and the congestion of the land in certain localities."

These wide terms of reference set the Commission quite a task and it is little wonder that they took over two years to complete the work. Before the report was presented, the African Members of Legislative Council clamoured for the publication of the Commission's findings, being convinced that these would underline the justice of their claims to the European White Highlands. In fact, the widely held view amongst educated African opinion was that the Royal Commission would advocate the throwing open of the White Highlands while keeping the African Land Units intact.

After publication it was found that the Commission's recommendations were that all lands should be thrown open, the rights of individual tenure replacing that of racial or tribal reservation. Their considered opinion was "that tribal and racial rigidities have brought about a situation of increasing tension, the basis of which is fear." In stating however that "access to new land can no longer form the basis of security for the indigenous population," the Commission stressed that the test of land needs must be replaced by the test of land usage. The truth of this would be proved after Independence; it would in fact be the acid test of the success or failure of the African Land Settlement Scheme.

The Royal Commission Report with its appendices, etc. runs to 482 pages and many thousands of words. It is a fascinating document and became the European Elected Members' stand-by as a book of reference. It is difficult to give a synopsis of this profound and detailed study of an immense problem in a book such as this. The Report's own summarised "Guide to the Main Conclusions" numbers some forty pages.

Acknowledging that the capital and enterprise which have contributed most to the economic development of East Africa came from outside these territories, the Report states: "The period within which the indigenous population has had close contact with Western civilisation has been short and the Africans are still ill-equipped to grapple with the complexity of problems which confront a people who have so recently entered into the intricacies of a modern world."

Another circumstance which had a profound effect on the African society, though most particularly on the returning askaris, was service overseas with the British forces in two world wars. The resultant awakening aroused new wants and the slowly dawning consciousness that only through wage-earning could these wants be satisfied. At the same time, it became evident that a tribal African society was unable to support any standard of living comparable to what they had seen elsewhere. It is probable that spending part of their lives outside East Africa's borders in the Army hastened the process, as the young men, dissatisfied with the narrowness of tribal restrictions, refused to return to their former way of life. This brought about the collapse of the tribal system before the adoption of any new order. The great increase in crime (which causes Government much concern) is largely the result of this too-rapid change; yet it is difficult to see how this could have been avoided.

The Commission stressed that, "Pressure upon fertile land leads to conflict, which is not essentially racial and could take place between African tribes, even if there were no non-African settlement." This is now being realised as it is demonstrated by tribal clashes over supposed spheres of influence in what was a European area.

Ever since 1951 when my work as an Elected Member took me into all districts of the Nyanza Province, I have realised that one of the greatest barriers to a better understanding was the fact that all three races lived in water-tight compartments. This was largely due to the system of land reservation, the Europeans living and working their farms in the 'White Highlands,' the Africans in their tribal reserves, while the Asians, denied the right to own land in either of these areas, lived mostly in the towns, forming the backbone of the commercial community in Kenya. Underlining this state of affairs in their chapter on social and economic co-operation, the Commission states categorically, "The isolation of the races in East Africa must be overcome, as without the closest economic integration of all their efforts the poverty of East Africa will continue."

It is this realisation that has caused many Europeans of the farming community to sell out and leave Kenya. They know that partnership with Africans is an essential factor for future peaceful co-existence, but they feel the gap between religious, social and cultural standards is still too wide to be bridged with any success. This fear, coupled with the knowledge that with the emergent millions of Africans there is little prospect of any future for their children, has led the majority of the 'settler' farmers to leave their homes in Kenya.

The overall conclusions of the Commission were extremely far-sighted, and Kenya has already felt the benefit of some of these recommendations, but perhaps its greatest value was that it gave the Colony a much-needed breathing space of two years.

In the summer of 1955, the European community were horrified by the senseless and brutal murder of Mrs Milton and her teenage daughter at their home at Lanet, near Nakuru. This double tragedy was not a Mau Mau crime. The facts of the case provided me with all I needed to support my plea that some form of documentation of domestic servants should be brought in to protect householders of all races. The murderer was a Luo tribesman, who in applying for work as a house servant the day before had used a stolen identity card. Government had earlier introduced an excellent system of registration of African employees, by requiring every African worker to carry a card which was a combination of identity card and a record of employment. This valuable document was known as the '*kipande*,' and contained a description of the holder as well as a complete record of his service, wage, capabilities, and character. Although there was no photograph, there was a thumbprint.

As a result of organised political agitation amongst the Kikuyu, who publicly burnt their *kipandes*, the bill which had ordered all men over eighteen to carry this comprehensive record was repealed. The small buff card which replaced the *kipande* gave only the barest details. As it carried no description or photograph of the holder, and no thumb print, it was easy to steal or even to buy a card with good references. Thus, with no means of identification, there was no means of checking, and the Miltons were not to know that the man they had engaged with such good references had in fact a criminal record of robbery with violence. All windows and doors in the house, except for the back door, were kept locked as an emergency precaution. Coming in from the garden Mrs Milton and her young daughter found the Luo man prizing open a drawer in the kitchen where money and valuables were kept. Caught in the act, and seeing his way of escape barred, he seized a poker and struck them down, killing them both in sheer panic.

Such a tragedy aroused public anger and I had solid support from householders throughout Kenya. Many members of the East African Women's League were present while I was moving my Motion. I told Council that as a result of political demonstrations organised by the Kikuyu leaders, the excellent system of identification of domestic servants provided by the *kipande* and its successor the Red Book had been discarded. In the face of this noisy agitation, as was so often the case, the Colonial Government weakly gave way to African demands, showing more concern about assuaging political clamour than ensuring public safety.

The Parliamentary correspondent of the *Kenya Weekly News*, reporting on the Week in the Legislative Council, headed his article: "End of Term – Mrs Shaw carries the prize," and summed up the debate in these words: "To Mrs Shaw must go the honours of the week for hers was undoubtedly the most important motion debated; the Member for Nyanza spoke well and *Hansard* records that Mrs Shaw sat down to prolonged applause." The only evidence of disapproval was apparent on the frowning face of Mrs Barbara Castle, the Labour MP from Britain, who was sitting in the Distinguished Visitors' Gallery.

The terms of the Motion were: "It is essential that a system of identification of domestic servants be introduced without delay." After a long debate it was with some relief that Council heard Mr Aede, the Minister of Labour, acknowledge the necessity of doing something about the domestic servant situation in view of the recent double tragedy. As the Mover, I gladly accepted the enabling amendment put forward by Government, namely: "That a Select Committee be appointed to examine the whole field of Domestic Service, and to recommend in what respect existing legislation should be amended, or fresh legislation be introduced, in order to provide a sound basis of mutual confidence between employers and employees."

The Committee was appointed and sat for months. At last, in spite of opposition from the African Members, they finally produced their report, only to see it blown away by the Wind of Change. By then the gale was so strong that no Colonial Government could successfully have launched the required legislation. The result has been that the Kenya householder still has no protection from unwittingly engaging someone with a criminal record. Even more serious is the fact that the good servant is placed on a par with the unscrupulous imposter. This has been responsible for a tremendous increase in house-breaking and robberies, over fifty per cent of these crimes being committed with inside information, if not with active assistance from house servants. [IDs for all Kenya citizens over age eighteen is now compulsory.]

CHAPTER 15

The 1956 Elections and the End of the Lyttelton Plan

*"For Forms of Government, let fools contest;
Whatever is best administered, is best."*
-- Alexander Pope

The new multi-racial Government that had been established under the Lyttelton Constitution [which modified but didn't destroy the concept of European leadership] in 1953 came into force in May of that year. Multi-racial government was not new in Kenya, where members of all races had sat together in Legislative Council for several years. What *was* new was that, under the provisions of the Lyttelton Plan, elected representatives of the Opposition [elected Legislative Council members as opposed to those appointed by the Colonial Government] were enabled to cross the floor of the House to take up ministerial office. This put into effect the avowed colonial policy of the British Government: "That the power should pass progressively into the hands of the people on the spot." The experiment was working well, although it was evident that something must be done to right the numerical imbalance between those on the official and unofficial sides of Council. This was the result of three Europeans, three Asians and two Africans crossing the floor to take up ministerial posts. The creation of nominated members to sit on the Government bench further strengthened the Government side. From an unofficial majority of two, the pendulum had swung to a Government majority of sixteen.

In spite of being modelled on the Westminster pattern, the Lyttelton Constitution was not in any sense a true democracy. The Opposition had a useful part to play, but to do that effectively it had to be sufficiently strong to be able to bring pressure to bear. Since the introduction of the Lyttelton Plan, the Opposition was weakened numerically and, with its unity of purpose undermined through sectional interests and racial antagonisms, it could no longer play an effective part. This produced a dangerous situation where the Government could afford to disregard the attacks of the unofficial side. To quote from an article written by Oliver Wood, correspondent of the London *Times*, on his return from Kenya in May,1955: "The multi-racial Government established under the Lyttelton Constitution is working. There is a new spirit abroad which is penetrating outside the council chamber into social life, and is gradually making inroads on the colour bar...yet it would be unwise to ignore the underlying tensions." That, then, was the situation before the General Election held on September 28th, 1956.

The choice before the electorate was bewildering in the extreme. [At the time there were four European settler parties.] It really lay between the isolationism of the diehard Conservative Federal Independence Party and the co-operation preached by the United Country Party under the leadership of Michael Blundell. To befog an already confused issue, two further parties entered the election arena, both breakaways from the two main bodies: the Independent Group, a moderate off-shoot of the FIP, and the Capricorn Society, a party of extreme liberalism. The position which faced the European electorate was briefly this: On the extreme right were the reactionary settlers of the FIP; on the extreme left were those who believed in the Capricorn Charter. Side by side in the middle were the moderates: a little right of centre were the Independent group; and a little left of centre the United Country Party.

Fortunately for the future of Kenya, although one or two of the FIP were elected, after the election they merged with the right-wing moderates of the Independent group. No Capricorn candidate was elected, for although the Europeans had moved some way along the road to liberalism, there were few amongst them who were as yet prepared to embrace African nationalism.

Living now in an independent Kenya with a purely African Government, it seems impossible to understand how we of the United Country Party could really have believed in the success of our policy, which in 1956 seemed to us to embody the most liberal thinking possible. To illustrate what we thought then was sufficiently left-wing to be acceptable, let us examine the basic principles of policy to which the two main parties subscribed.

Their supporters, led respectively by Mr Michael Blundell and the late Group Captain Briggs, were agreed on three fundamentals: the preservation of the White Highlands; the rejection of a franchise based on a common roll; and agreement that multiracial education should not be introduced below University level. Where they differed was in their attitude towards greater African participation. The United Country Party supported a multi-racial policy because we sincerely believed it offered, through co-operation with the Africans in a Coalition Government, an acceptable alternative to African nationalism. It seems difficult to understand how we could have been so politically blind, yet at the time the policy was put forward in all good faith.

The Independent group claimed to support a 'non-racial' policy. They stated rather pompously, "No man should be denied any position of responsibility solely by reason of his race, and conversely, no man shall be given a position of responsibility solely by reason of his race." The criterion was to be one of 'Merit and Ability.' Their brand of liberalism in the glare of harsh reality appears even more blind than ours, and perhaps their faith was not so 'good.' Even at the time it was obvious that the high-minded ideal was to be used to ensure that an all-European Government could be safely entrenched behind the slogan of Merit and Ability for years to come. Strange that so few noticed the stirrings of the gentle zephyr which was in so short a time to become a roaring hurricane. The Independent European leaders, convinced as they were of the rightness of their liberal thinking, were perhaps the blindest of all. And yet perhaps not so strange: There are none so blind as those who do not wish to see.

The great majority of the European electorate were farmers from the White Highlands, and farmers the world over are not very interested in politics. In Kenya this was true unless the settlers felt that their security was threatened. Then overnight they would become one of the most politically noisy communities in the world. Throughout the years, whenever a crisis arose, the farmers rallied behind leaders such as Lord Delamere, Lord Francis Scott, and later Michael Blundell.

Since the days of the 'Boston Tea Party,' political clamour has paid dividends in any struggle with the mother country. Britain, always sensitive to world opinion, especially where the administration of her colonial territories was concerned, could be counted on to give way, under pressure, rather than face the publicity of a showdown. This policy encouraged rebellious behaviour because, if public opinion could be sufficiently aroused, appeasement would be the result, and the dissident colonialists were likely to emerge from the struggle stronger than before. In this way, over the years, the European community, through astute leadership, had increased their influence in the Government of Kenya until they represented an extremely powerful minority.

The farmers lived a long way from Nairobi (a beastly place), and if forced to go down for a meeting of the Land Board or an agricultural conference, they would get back to their farms just as soon as they could. Sometimes, if they were lucky, their business would coincide with the races, or a game of polo, and after a good afternoon's sport, husband

and wife would enjoy an evening at Muthaiga Club. There they would meet many up-country farming friends, or even their Elected Member. They might realise the old 'so and so' was pretty worked up about some political kerfuffle, but after all it was his job to sort it out. Surely that's what the fellow was elected for wasn't it? In any case how could they be expected to understand the ins and outs of politics?

Hadn't they enough to worry about already? The drop in prices, the increase in stock-thieving, not to speak of the ever-rising cost of production. The constant demands of the farm labourers for more pay for less and less work. The threat of strike action used to blackmail the farmer by these tiresome jumped-up chaps in the Trade Unions. No one could tell where it would all end. That was their real worry, not whether Kenya should have a new Constitution or not. Who cared about that as long as they and their children could continue to live in Kenya? Had not the Colonial Secretary, during his last visit, admitted the British Government's responsibility for the encouragement of European settlement in Kenya after both world wars? What's more, he had assured them that H.M.G. would honour its pledge to the 'settlers.' Old 'so and so' had met him at a sundowner at Government House and said that he was a charming chap. Then surely there was no need to worry about what a few African politicians shouted from a platform at Makadara Hall on a Sunday.

For years the European community had demanded self-government, yet many of them did not seem to realise that the introduction of the Lyttelton Plan was the first step in the transfer from the Colonial Office of real responsibility for government to the people of Kenya. Not understanding this, there were many European settlers who were out to destroy the newly set-up coalition government. On the other hand, according to a statement made in the *East African Standard* of 16th August 1956, the three European Ministers (Blundell, Wellwood and Havelock) were prepared to work with any group of individuals who supported the main principles of the Lyttelton Constitution. These were the progressive substitution of 'unofficial' ministers for civil service ministers and the participation of representatives of the main races in a coalition government.

Again my right to represent Nyanza was challenged in 1956 by Lt General Irwin, now a supporter of the Independent Group. I still followed the lead given by Michael Blundell. This time my opponent was defeated by a combination of personality and policy – at least that is what I like to believe.

In common with most of the European electorate, my constituents were sick of party strife and my policy of co-operation found favour. I said the situation was too grave and the issues too vital to allow personal antagonisms and party bickerings to destroy our leadership, adding, "Everything we hold dear is at stake, time is running out. The pattern of our nationhood emerges and therein lies the challenge. A challenge which can only be met by a strong and united party giving clear and definite leadership."

The lesson the 1956 election taught us was that the electorate demanded unity from their elected representatives. Pledged to this, the first action of the successful candidates [should have been] to agree to give up all party affiliations and declare one loyalty to the European Elected Members Organisation.

The split over the Lyttelton Plan and all the bitterness it had caused was a tragedy. In allowing differences over the Constitution to widen the gulf between the parties, the Elected Members had done the European community a great disservice. After all, the Europeans were all working towards the same goal: to safeguard our minority position and ensure a future for our children and grandchildren in Kenya where we had made our homes. At the final meeting of EEMO, just before the dissolution of Council, our Chairman, Sir Alfred Vincent, made a plea for unity. He added, "After all, you know, it is just possible that some of you may be returned." To which Michael Blundell retorted, "Yes, Sir, Mr Slade and I have glimpsed that very gloomy possibility."

If our organisation of European Members was recognisable in spite of a slight face-lift, the team of African Elected Members thrown up by the first African Elections certainly was not, as both the previous Nominated African Members lost their seats. Mr Apollo Changa's defeat had been expected. A Government nominee, he had been appointed Minister in the face of a good deal of opposition. In fact, his opponent went so far as to threaten his life and Mr Changa showed considerable courage in taking up the post. Mr Eliud Mathu's defeat, on the other hand, did come as a surprise, although the vote was weighted against him on a purely tribal basis. The Kikuyu at that time were more often feared than liked. To be permitted to stand at all as a Kikuyu, under the Emergency Regulations, he had to be a proved loyalist. This Mr Mathu could claim to be, and his defeat was a great loss to Council as in mental ability he had been far in advance of his other African colleagues.

The new team were unknown quantities, with the exception of Mr Tom Mboya, the up and coming Secretary General of the Kenya Federation of Labour. The Kikuyus failed to win a single seat, a result caused perhaps through the realisation by the other tribes of the harm the Mau Mau rebellion had done to the African community. Whatever the reason, the Emergency certainly gave the Nyanza Luo their chance in the political field.

With the exception of Tom Mboya, the African Members were politically immature. For most of them it was their first appearance on the political stage. As the acknowledged leaders of the opposition, we were careful not to do or say anything which would prejudice our good relations with our new colleagues.

Sir Evelyn Baring opened the first Session of the Eleventh Council in October 1956. The Governor gave a full review of the 'Emergency position, telling the Council that the security forces had begun to obtain results against the forest gangs, as distinct from the Mau Mau rank and file.

In his speech, the Governor told Legislative Council that of the fity-one major gang leaders, only two remained at large. His Excellency said, "All branches of the Forces had been responsible for this, working as a coordinated team under the capable leadership of General Lathbury." Indeed, Lathbury had succeeded so well that the Governor was able to recommend that the Kenya Police should now take over control of operations from the Army, and in support of the Provincial Administration they should resume responsibility for the maintenance of law and order. However, the Members were informed that the War Council was to continue to sit and the Army would remain in support of the Police. It was estimated that there were still several hundred terrorists living in the forest, but faced with inevitable starvation, it was hoped that many would surrender.

The new year was ushered in with thankfulness. The worst was over, as gradually the situation was returning to normal.

Since the African elections held in March, 1957, the European Elected Members had made it plain that they would welcome co-operation with the other racial groups. To facilitate this, we had a joint meeting with the Asian and African Elected Members to examine the possibilities of resuscitating the Unofficial Elected Organisation. In the past this organisation had dealt with all business and matters of common interest coming before Council. Our attitude was that if the Opposition in Legislative Council was to prove effective and do any constructive work, some such organisation was essential.

We made it plain from the start that we were not prepared to discuss the African demand for extra representation as an isolated issue, but only as part of a negotiated Constitutional Settlement. Mr Mboya made it equally plain that his attitude was one of uncompromising demand and that he had no desire for, or any interest in, achieving a negotiated

Agnes tending her roses.

settlement. Whatever may have been stated to the contrary, the European Members made repeated attempts to gain the Africans' confidence, but Mr Mboya's influence was too strong for our counsels to prevail.

In October 1957 the Secretary of State for the Colonies, Mr Lennox Boyd, paid a visit to the Colony and held talks with the three racial groups, starting with a three-hour meeting with the European Members. The primary talks were most encouraging; we found the Colonial Secretary's reaction to the African demands was the same as ours. In fact, he had already stated in the House of Commons that the question of increased African representation could only be considered as part of a negotiated constitutional advance. This would embrace other points such as Africans taking up Ministerial office and safeguards for the minority communities. He added that Her Majesty's Government intended to stand by that statement.

Mr Lennox Boyd made this clear throughout his negotiations with all races, but, as far as the African Members were concerned, his words fell on deaf ears. Mr Mboya continued to demand 20 extra African seats, while at every meeting Mr Odinga chanted with monotonous regularity that as far as he and his colleagues were concerned he, "must make it perfectly clear, Sir, that the Lyttelton Plan was null and void." Exasperated by these tactics, the Colonial Secretary turned to Mr Odinga, saying. "In that case, Mr Odinga, as you yourself are a child of the Lyttelton Plan, you too must be null and void." At this the Honourable Member got very excited, shouting. "No, No, No, that is not true."

Throughout the frustrating fortnight's talks, the two African Leaders, Mr Odinga and Mr Mboya, adopted the same uncompromising attitude. This effectively barred the way to a negotiated settlement between the

Agnes and Brian reading in the shade at Kipkebe in the late 1950s.

racial groups. It only remained to decide whether to rest on the Lyttelton Plan [seen as an interim reform meant to last until 1960], or to make it possible for the Colonial Secretary to take the initiative forthwith. If such a deadlock continued over the next three years, it would not only prejudice any hope of a reasonable settlement in 1960 but could cause serious injury to the Colony's economic progress. We decided to give the Colonial Secretary the power he needed.

The initiative was entirely ours, and it was the deliberate action of the European and Asian Ministers in handing in their resignations which killed the Lyttelton Plan. The Africans were delighted for they thought that this would mean an immediate return to direct Colonial administration. You may ask what they hoped to gain from that. I would reply that they were banking on a Labour Government's being in power after the British Elections. If this occurred (with voters misled by British political fanatics of the left wing) the African Members foresaw a straight road through to Republican status.

What actually happened was the last thing they dreamed of or wanted, namely the imposition of a multi-racial Constitution, on much the same pattern as the Lyttelton Plan, for a period of ten years. This was a constitution whose provisions favoured minorities more than any which could have emerged from a negotiated settlement. Hoisted by their own petard, having previously steadily refused to negotiate, they then clamoured (backed by a chorus of their advisors) for a 'Round Table Conference.'

This, then was the background to the enforced Lennox Boyd Constitutional Settlement, the introduction of which we considered a triumph. Not only did it correct the numerical imbalance and other weaknesses of the Lyttelton Plan, but it was to be enforced for a period of ten years. This gave us time, which was our greatest need. After all, the Colonial Secretary had given us his word, and we had not yet learned to doubt the good faith of the British Government.

The Lennox Boyd Settlement was introduced at the new session of the Legislative Council. Although boycotted by a walk-out of the African Elected Members, the change-over was smooth enough. On April 23rd, the Legislative Council (sitting as an electoral college) voted for members to fill the new 'Specially Elected Seats.' This ballot also passed off without incident.

Sir Ernest Vasey stood for one of these seats. With African, Asian, and Government backing, he should have been completely safe, and Members were amazed when it was announced that he had tied for the only remaining seat with Mr Humphrey Slade. Oddly enough, under the provisions of the Constitution, the two names had to be written on two slips of paper and put in a box. Then one of the names was drawn by Mr Speaker. The moment was tense. In a hushed and expectant silence the house waited while Mr Speaker drew and read out the name of Mr Slade. There was tremendous applause. Sir Ernest felt his defeat bitterly, and shortly afterwards left Kenya to become Tanganyika's Minister of finance.

Refusing to recognise the new Constitution, the African Elected Members organised opposition to its introduction in the form of public demonstrations outside the Council. They also boycotted all sessions of the legislature. Everyone was tired of these disruptive displays, and the business of the House was conducted with such expedition without them that we grew to welcome their 'walkouts.' This was very human, yet as it proved, very foolish. But who would have thought that by these immature tactics, the African Members could throw out the new Constitution, and that within three years force the British Government to break its pledge to the Europeans and accede to the African demand for a 'Round Table Conference?'

By the summer of 1958, after two years of continuous political effort, my brain had reached saturation point. I had to get away from Kenya and her apparently insoluble problems. Campaigning for the 1956 elections had been followed by long months of constitutional negotiations. Before the introduction of the Lennox Boyd Constitution in 1958, two visits from the Colonial Secretary had been necessary. So it was with a sigh of relief that at midnight on June 6th I stepped into a

Britannia and turned my back on it all, for three glorious months' leave in Europe with my husband.

The person who made this possible – a thousand blessings on her clever head – was Mrs Christian Rawson-Shaw of Songhor. A Magistrate, and an active member of my political committee, she kindly agreed to act as my stand-in during my absence. That day, after Council had adjourned, Christian lunched with me at the Parliament Buildings, and after lunch was formally introduced to my colleagues of the European Elected Members Organisation. The Budget Session was in progress at the time and it was rather an ordeal for her to be plunged into the middle of it. But knowing my stand-in I had no doubt that she would be able to cope.

Returning to a colder climate for a few months on leave restores more than physical health; one also regains a sense of proportion and mental balance. Thus, thanks to my good friend, I returned from leave refreshed in body and mind; in fact, ready for anything. Just as well, for on November 4th I plunged straight into work again, with a six-week session of Council which took us up to Christmas. Fortunately for me, the Council did not sit again until February 18th. This gave me the opportunity to tour my constituency. To tour Nyanza took me about a fortnight, and I had to travel several hundreds of miles, over indifferent roads, to hold ten or twelve public meetings.

Looking back over that period, from the 1956 election until the year 1960, there seems to be a curious feeling of urgency running through all my speeches – a sense that time was running out. Nor was I the only person who was aware of this. For instance, in 1956 I had an informal meeting with a highly placed administrative officer from an adjoining territory. In answer to my question as to whether union with the Central African Federation was a possibility, or only wishful thinking, he unhesitatingly replied that not only did he think it was possible, but also that it was the only hope for Kenya, adding that we had only twenty years at most to achieve it.

It seems strange now to think that this was the considered opinion of a man whose position gave him access to all sources of information on colonial policy throughout the British Territories in East Africa. Thus, at that time even he failed to realise that Kenya was already caught up in the march of world events and would be unable to resist the pressures from outside, as well as from within her borders.

The pattern of events became all too familiar: vociferous demands by local left-wing politicians, often supported by members of the British Labour Party, followed by strikes and threats of civil disobedience. This phase usually resulted in the appointment of a Royal Commission. After that there followed, as inevitably as night upon day, the calling of a Constitutional Conference.

CHAPTER 16

On to Lancaster House

*"There are no hopeless situations:
There are only men who have grown hopeless about them."*
--Clare Boothe Luce

One happy memory which I shall always carry with me is of the 1959 visit to Kenya of Her Majesty Queen Elizabeth, the Queen Mother. On her arrival, her first act was to pay a visit to the Parliament Building. Not everyone could leave London in mid-winter, fly some 4,000 miles, and appear unruffled, less than twenty-four hours later, in a delightful summer ensemble in her favourite powder blue. This wonderful woman took it in her stride. She had a charming smile and a word for all the members of the Council who were being presented to her. During her stay she toured many parts of Kenya, and wherever she went she won the hearts of all races.

For us the highlight of her visit was the reception given at Government House by Sir Evelyn and Lady Mary Baring. This was attended by members of the Legislature, Her Majesty's Judges, the Consular Corps, Navy, Army, Air Force Chiefs, and Administrative heads of Government. It was a brilliant scene. The men in uniform, wearing decorations, and the women *en grande tenue*, the sparkle of their beautiful jewels offset by their graceful long gowns. I believe this was one of the last of such occasions. There was an air of hushed expectancy as the distinguished guests waited in the ballroom.

On the stroke of nine, the band struck up the opening bars of the national anthem, the double doors were thrown open, and there, poised on the bottom step of the great stairway, stood the Queen Mother, a glittering figure. The spotlights struck sparks from her ruby and diamond parure and sequin-embroidered gown. I shall never forget her graceful carriage as, the anthem over, she stepped forward, escorted by our handsome Governor and followed by Lady Mary. Later, as she moved amongst the guests, all were to feel her personal magnetism, as her charm of manner put everyone at their ease. When she paused to speak to us, my husband said: "I was privileged to meet you, Ma'am, during your first visit to Kenya, in the early Twenties, with your husband." The Queen Mother's blue eyes filled with tears, and with a sad little sigh she replied, "Ah, those were my happiest days." A great and gracious lady.

Entering the Parliament Building on the morning of April 2nd, 1959, I sensed something unusual was afoot. Wilfred Havelock, then Minister of Local Government, said, "Aggie, we've asked Michael Blundell to meet us in the Uganda Room; you must be there as it is very important."

Sitting at the enormous Round Table, under the shadow of the lifelike portrait of Sir Francis Scott, were legislative Council Members of all races, from both sides of the House; moderate men of goodwill, ready to sink their differences and work together, in the belief that only in this way could Kenya achieve her nationhood. Thus was born the New Kenya Party.

At the opening of Council that day, Michael Blundell asked leave of Mr Speaker to make a personal statement. Mr Blundell informed the House that a group of Members had asked him to resign from his Ministry and to cross the floor, in order to become Leader of a new Party. Michael, always an emotional man, spoke with deep feeling, saying that while he would leave his Ministry with a great sense of loss, he felt it his duty to resign to undertake this new task.

Sir Alfred Vincent then rose to announce, on behalf of those Members who, by becoming signatories had accepted the policy of the

Agnes Shaw (centre) chats with Kenya's Governor Sir Evelyn Baring.

New Kenya Party, that they warmly welcomed Mr Blundell. On the rising of Council there was a buzz of conversation, as Members gave their views on Michael's action which, according to their political thinking, they considered right or wrong. But whatever their opinions, I think that there were few, if any, who did not admit that it was a courageous step to take. For many of us it gave promise of a new hope – a hope not to be fulfilled – and yet I wonder. For was it not the understanding which grew from the co-operation of the three races working together for the good of the whole which laid the foundation for a smooth transfer of power at Kenya's Independence?

To enable you to understand the policy of the New Kenya Party, I cannot do better than to quote from a speech made by Mr Blundell during his tour of the Colony in his capacity as Leader of Kenya's first truly representative multi-racial Party. Answering his own question of "What are the Facts?", Michael Blundell sketched the Kenya political scene in these words: "If we accept the facts upon which our existence is built, the vastness of the African Continent, the numbers of its tribes, the complexities which arise from our fragmented society with its varying races, and its competitive cultures, there stand out ahead of us two roads and two roads only. One, to perpetuate into the distant future the differences in culture and in education, in tradition and ethnic origins, which today divide the people of this country, with all the attendant possibilities of hate, mistrust, envy, and fear which such a course engenders; the second to attempt, however laboriously, however painfully, to move towards an ideal which will transform the diverse mosaics of our country into a single pattern, secure in itself, constant in its various elements.

"We have accepted the second of these roads, fully aware of the difficulties, aware of the problems, but equally in the full knowledge that to reject the challenge must leave us with the mounting and increasing hatreds of a society which is trying to perpetuate forever the differences within itself. The ultimate goal which we have placed before us is the creation of a nation here welded from the kaleidoscope of our people by the ideas and outlook of the British Empire, and firmly entrenched within the Commonwealth."

Among the Members who joined to form the New Kenya Party that day under Michael Blundell's leadership were, as well as Sir Alfred Vincent, Wilfred Havelock, Humphrey Slade, Norman Harris, and my namesake, Lady Shaw. [A total of six of the fourteen European elected members, including Agnes Shaw, became members.]

With the departure of Sir Evelyn Baring in the autumn of 1959, an era in Kenya's political and social life came to an end. On the political side, the ending of the State of Emergency heralded the dawn of a new era, a period of reconstruction, and an all-out effort to repair the ravages made to our economy by the Mau Mau Rebellion. If some of the restrictive measures, such as closer administration, were to be projected into the new era, so, too, were many of the constructive schemes for development, which were to provide the solid foundations for an Independent Kenya. The principal of these was Land Reform.

Sir Evelyn had come to Kenya at a most unfortunate time, for with the tensions bred of the stresses and strains to which the farmers were daily subjected, any Governor was bound to reap a degree of unpopularity. Our leader, Michael Blundell, came to know Sir Evelyn well, and rated him a great man.

On the social side, too, the departure of the Barings marked the passing of an era. The well-known American writer John Gunther described government in Kenya as being suspended in air, out of touch with reality, and the Governor and his aides as apparently having stepped down from their Edwardian frames. Out of touch with reality it most certainly was not, although Sir Evelyn, being very conscious of the dignity of his position as the Queen's representative, did bring a certain formality to Government House functions. This required no conscious effort on the part of the Barings, who came from a line of administrators, and although Sir Evelyn may have been humble in assessing his own worth, he was an aristocrat born and bred.

Kenya, one of the last strongholds of conservatism, still provided the settler farmers with the way of life of a bygone age, and they rejoiced in a Governor who upheld these traditions. The essentials for gracious living were still ours, essentials which, once lost, no amount of money can replace. In Kenya we had been fortunate in that we had been able to preserve this delightful way of life longer than in most places in the modern world. Lulled by our very isolation into a sense of false security, the awakening, when it came, made us feel we had been betrayed.

The arrival of Sir Patrick Renison did little to warn us of the danger threatening our valued security; rather it tended to increase our complacency. Sir Patrick's Speech from the Throne, made to Legislative Council on November 10th, shortly after he took up his post as Governor of Kenya, declared the State of Emergency officially at an end. He concluded by describing himself as "strangely hopeful" ahead of a forthcoming London conference at Lancaster House.

The members of the New Kenya Party, too, were strangely hopeful. Early in 1959 we learnt that there had been a conference, held at Chequers, attended by the Governors of Kenya, Uganda, and

Tanganyika, in order to discuss with the British Government the future of these territories. From what our leader, Mr Blundell, had gleaned during a brief visit to London to see the Prime Minister in May, the outcome of the Chequers Talks was an agreed policy for all three: There was to be a gradual transference of power from HMG to the people on the spot over the next ten to fifteen years. This was so completely in line with the thinking of our Party that confidence in our future in Kenya was somewhat restored.

Today when we know the facts, it is difficult to understand why the new Governor was not made aware of the speed-up of the timetable before he took up his appointment. Although most of the European community put the blame on the new Colonial Secretary, the late Mr Iain Macleod. I have always felt that the Prime Minister, Mr Macmillan, was the person responsible. I am equally certain that our friend Mr Alan Lennox Boyd, now Lord Boyd, must have been very distressed by this change in British policy, which amounted to a breach of faith as far as the Kenya settler was concerned.

I am not in a position to know the true facts, but I feel sure that the granting of independence to the people of Kenya within two years was dictated by world pressures, over which Britain had little or no control. In Mr Macleod, Mr Macmillan found a Colonial Secretary impervious to unpopularity, and sufficiently strong to carry through the new policy which aroused such dreadful bitterness amongst the European farmers in Kenya.

It was only too obvious, at the first Lancaster House Conference, that Sir Patrick Renison had not been put fully in the picture, for during those frustrating weeks, to use his own word, he was often seen to be 'groping.' In fairness to Sir Patrick, I must record that on his return to Kenya he managed to keep the Colony boat on an even keel, although it was buffeted by many political storms.

On a warm January night in 1960, all the delegates to the 1st Lancaster House Constitutional Conference left Nairobi together. The New Kenya Party was represented by its Chairman, Sir Wilfred Havelock, along with Michael Blundell, Norman Harris, Lady Shaw, Humphrey Slade, and myself. Laurence Wellwood went for the Independents, Puck Briggs and Mr Roberts represented the Federal Independence Party, and Chunilal Madan, the Asians. The African delegates were Tom Mboya and Oginga Odinga, with Ronald Ngala as their leader. We arrived next day to find London blanketed with snow. The members of the Blundell party had agreed for greater convenience to all stay at the same hotel. Our choice fell on the Reubens, an old-fashioned hotel, which had just been taken over for modernizing.

Unfortunately, the new owner was under a cloud over his involvement in an alleged swindle of some three and a half million pounds – a charge which was finally not substantiated. On arrival, I rang my bell and asked the Irish maid for a face towel, and I received this odd reply, "Well, Ma'am, it's this way: if I give you a face towel, the lady next door goes short." Puzzled, I asked why. The maid replied in her delightful Irish brogue, "You see, the poor gentleman who's just bought us has not been able to even spend a sixpence since his little spot of bother with the Court."

I got my face towel in spite of this financial stringency, although it was true that a Government Receiver was stationed at the cash desk during the whole of our stay. We were made most comfortable, and on our return visit I was very touched to find a vase of roses on my dressing table with a card saying, "Welcome back, Mrs Shaw." So I personally had a soft feeling for the 'poor gentleman.'

The formal opening of all these Conferences followed a similar pattern. The public and the press were admitted, and the batteries of cameras, TV and flash, were terrific. The delegates being assembled, the Colonial Secretary arrived with his entourage.

He then formally opened the Conference with a welcome to all delegates, which called forth a formal reply from all groups. This

Agnes Shaw attended the Lancaster House Conferences, to determine the path for Kenya's independence.

was usually followed by what was termed the keynote speech by the Colonial Secretary, which set forth the Government's reasons for calling the Conference. After this formal opening, the Conference got down to its business behind closed doors. An agreed press statement was issued each day, at the end of the sitting.

My first Conference was an exciting experience, though I should have been very surprised if anyone had told me then that I would spend fourteen weeks of my life in Lancaster House (a mansion built for the 'Grand Old Duke of York'). In spite of its magnificent facade, Lancaster House is only three storeys, because of the immense height of the rooms on the first and second floors. Sir Charles Barry, my brother-in-law's great-great-grandfather, left his mark on the house, as he did on so many London buildings, by designing the graceful stairway.

Both Kenya Conferences, in 1960 and 1962, were held in the beautiful and stately rooms on the first floor. These were decorated in the rococo style of the Georgian period, and in moments of stress I would feast my eyes on the overflowing cornucopias and the garlands of flowers of the exquisitely carved and gilded cornices. In the great ballroom, which had been set aside for our leisure moments, mirrors

John ole Konchellah (third from the left) and Justus ole Tipis (far right), both wearing lion skin hats, were two Kenyan delegates to the second Lancaster House Conference.

decorated the walls, while between the tall windows were small marble console tables, supported by cupids. Remarking to Michael, during a coffee break, that the long dead decorator must have foreseen the multi-racial character of the Conference, as the cupids were suitably black and white, Michael pointed out that not only that, but he must have been a man of great political perception, as the white cupids had supported their black brethren on their shoulders for all these years!

On the third floor, in a rabbit warren of domestic quarters, were the committee rooms for delegates. Here the Coalition headed by Mr Wellwood, the African Group, the Asian Members, and the Blundellites – all the diverse pieces that made up the mosaic of Kenya politics – had their offices, and planned their campaigns behind closed doors. The windows of our committee room, which overlooked Clarence House, brought some delightful distractions. The bark of a corgi dog would bring us all to the windows in the hope of seeing the Queen Mother, and one day our patience was rewarded, as there she was at her drawing room window, smiling up at us as we waved excitedly back. Then too, the sound of the fife and drums always got us to our feet, and no matter how cold it was, up would go the window and out would go our heads. One day at the 2nd Lancaster House Conference, during a New Kenya Party Meeting, we were thrilled to hear the bagpipes. There were cries from the African Members of, "Come on Aggie, it's your tribe today," as they made way for me at the window!

My memories of the 1st Lancaster House Conference are chiefly of the appalling intransigence of the African Elected Members, of their impossible demands, and their obstinate refusal to meet any other group in the early stages. But we were so used to these tactics by now that we were not seriously alarmed. Even their boycott of the opening session did not worry us unduly. This was caused by our refusal to accede to their demand that the Kikuyu 'Freedom Fighter' Mbiyu Koinange should be admitted to the conference room, which caused quite a stir in the left-wing British press.

Rightly, our confidence was not shared by Michael Blundell, the Leader of the New Kenya Party, as was shown by his letter written to the Colonial Secretary in December of that year, and since published in his book *So Rough A Wind*. But Michael Blundell had access to sources of information which were not available to an ordinary Member.

Ronald Ngala, whom we later came to know so well as the Chairman of the Kenya African Democratic Union, (KADU) was then Leader of the African Elected Members. Chosen, I imagine, for his moderation, he must have had a difficult time holding the balance between Oginga Odinga and Tom Mboya who, although both of the Luo tribe, were bitter opponents. Two more differing characters it would be hard to find: Odinga, a patriarchal and colourful figure who drew his support largely from the elders of his tribe; and Mboya, a modern Luo, a progressive Trade Unionist, who appealed to the younger and more educated section of the Luo.

The strain these conferences placed on the leaders of the different parties was very great, while for the rest of us, the endless hours of waiting in our committee rooms was wearying in the extreme. We were not allowed to leave the building but had to be on call. Sometimes these doldrums would last for several days, but they would be punctuated by periods of intense activity, when some solution had been found to remove a deadlock, and we went forward again until the next breakdown.

The conference hours were long, from the daily briefing at 9 a.m. until we adjourned at 5 p.m. Nor was our work over then, for the evenings were filled by cocktail parties given in our honour by various political bodies such as the UK branch of the Commonwealth Parliamentary Association or the Liberal and Labour Parties. At the majority of these functions, the political thinking was far to the left of our own, ranging from the palest pink to the fiercest red, even amongst the Conservatives. Added to its flavour, from a pinch of the pepper pot, would be men of the "lunatic fringe," and this *pot-au-feu* would be served to us at boiling point nightly, garnished with a sprinkling of die-hard Tories.

On February 1st, Black Monday, the blow fell [a reference to Colonial Secretary Iain Macleod's declaration that there must be majority rule in Kenya regardless of the wishes of the white settlers].The terms of the first draft came as a terrific shock to the European, Asian and Arab Members. Mr Macleod had leant over backwards to appease the African Nationalists, and the rest of the delegates held their breath while waiting to see what their reaction would be. It was a flat refusal. There is no doubt that this came as a great surprise to the Colonial Secretary. If the proposals were a staggering blow [to the Europeans], the fact that the Africans found them "totally unacceptable" was equally staggering. But what a relief! For the proposals, as they stood in this first draft, would have meant the total eclipse of the moderates, and an end to any European influence. The conference appeared to have finally floundered.

Next morning at the opening of the Session, Mr Blundell asked the Colonial Secretary three questions.

Firstly: Did he not think that before he set up committees to decide the numbers of both the Council of State and the Legislature that we should go into a committee of the whole council to decide the form of franchise?

Secondly: Was HMG's mind irrevocably made up on this point? If so, we might as well go home. Or was HMG prepared to consider suggestions?

Thirdly: Did not Mr MacLeod think there might be some merit in an adjournment, to enable some members of the New Kenya Party to have private talks with an equal number of Members from the African Group, led by Mr Mboya?

Mr Blundell rounded off this questionnaire by stressing that "Everyone had agreed that the ultimate goal must be self-government, and equally admitted that it only remained to decide what steps should be taken next towards this goal."

The Colonial Secretary replied to the first two questions with a Yes and a No, and said that as to the third, it would be up to the delegates to decide [whether to have talks]. Ronald Ngala refused on behalf of his group. Nothing daunted, Michael repeated his offer in writing, and as soon as the conference broke up we all retired to our committee rooms.

We were told later that there was a prolonged and bitter discussion in the Africans' committee room. After hours of noisy argument, Mr Mboya had to give way. A series of talks began on February 4th and lasted eight days. But still no solution [to the impasse over how majority rule was to come about] was found.

At this juncture, when the whole thing seemed about to end in a stalemate, the Prime Minister sent for Mr Blundell and the Members of the New Kenya Party. It was a cold and frosty evening and I shall never forget the beauty of the branches of the leafless trees, patterned against a darkening sky. As we walked across St James's Park to No. 10 Downing Street, the glowing face of Big Ben seemed to be beaming down on us with a fatherly benevolence. According to our differing outlook and our personal reactions to the Colonial Secretary's proposals, we felt angry, betrayed, or frustrated; but all, after the strain of those weeks of argument, felt weary, and many of us thoroughly despondent.,

Mr Macmillan greeted us all by name, and after shaking hands with everyone, gave us each a large whisky and soda, after which the atmosphere became distinctly warmer. When we were seated, the Prime Minister, in welcoming us, had this to say: "I have asked you to come and see me in this famous room where 300 years of British history has been enacted because I have the greatest admiration for your leader Michael Blundell – a great leader, if I may say so. Also, for you of the New Kenya Party, for forming the only Party in the whole continent which has had the courage to try the multi-racial experiment. By your action you may well change the face of Africa."

We all knew this was complete nonsense, but all the same it made us feel terrific. Mr Macmillan finished with these words: "On the wall behind you is the portrait of Horace Walpole, the first Englishman to hold within his hands the power of Prime Minister. I commend his motto to you all." (Which, being translated into English means, "Don't tempt Providence too far.") Thus did one of the most plausible and persuasive of men give us warning.

After Michael had spoken, the Prime Minister called on some members of the New Kenya Party to speak at random. His choice fell firstly on an African, secondly on an Asian, and then on me. Excepting for our Leader, I was the first European whom he had asked to speak, and as I might be the last, I decided to speak from the European standpoint as strongly and forcibly as I could.

In my opening remarks, I told the Prime Minister that his saying it would be difficult to put across the changes in the Constitution was a gross understatement. On my return to Kenya, I explained, I would have to move my constituents' thinking to where I had been blown, as it were, by the blast of a bomb – from the middle of the road to the far left-hand corner where I found myself with my back against the wall. Mr Macmillan remarked, "Is it as bad as that?" I replied, "Well, Sir, you have telescoped fifty years overnight for the Kenya settler." Nodding his head, he said, "Yes, I suppose we have." I told him that after the initial shock was over, I still thought that we could persuade them to agree to the changes, provided they could be assured of two things.

These were, firstly, that Britain would guarantee that there would be a Colonial Office hand on the steering wheel for the foreseeable future, to ensure that all that we had built up in Kenya during the last sixty years would not be swept away overnight by an immature African Government; secondly, that if the multi-racial experiment failed, Her Majesty's Government would compensate the settlers and buy them out. The Prime Minister listened attentively and when I had finished, commented "a valid point," before turning to ask other Members to speak.

Just as we were leaving after our two-hour session, he beckoned Michael and me into his study, saying, "About your valid point: I can assure you that my Government admits their responsibility for the European settler in Kenya and will honour that commitment if the need arises. But to do as you ask and to compensate the European farmer now would bring about the very situation we are trying to prevent. There would be a mad rush to off-load, with the resultant collapse of Kenya's agricultural industry, on which the Colony's economy is largely based. It would give the world the impression that the British Government did not believe in the success of the multi-racial experiment, which is far from the truth." Then he added, "Lastly, and perhaps most dangerous of all, it would lead the African to suppose that we did not wish the European to stay in Kenya." I had to admit the validity of his answer.

Most people will agree that it would be difficult for any man to follow in the footsteps of Sir Winston Churchill, the greatest Englishman of our time; but in spite of Macmillan's many detractors, there are those who think that he acquitted himself well. History alone will be the judge. All I know is that I went down to No. 10 that evening with hatred in my heart, and a sense of complete betrayal, but came away feeling that the PM might well be right.

As to our predicament, I think it was then that we Europeans of the New Kenya Party realised that there was no alternative to acceptance. Mr Macleod made it clear to us that refusals would bring an imposed Constitution, which might be infinitely worse, whereas acceptance would leave us with some room for manoeuvre. There and then we set about getting the best terms we could for the minorities, through checks and balances and various safeguards entrenched within the Constitution. Another condition of our acceptance was that the African members of both parties should be made to take up ministerial posts, believing as we did that only in that way would they become more responsible and be trained to take over the reins of government. And so, perhaps wiser, but certainly very much sadder, we returned to Kenya.

Had we not already realised what hostility we as a party should have to face on our arrival in Kenya, the welcome prepared for Michael Blundell by the wild men of the Federal Independence Party would have left us in no doubt. Poor Michael! To the accompaniment of cries of "Traitor!", thirty pieces of silver were thrown at his feet as he walked towards the airport building.

That demonstration was a sample of what he, and to a lesser extent all the Europeans of his Party, would be subjected to in the coming months. Our reception at the Parliament Buildings was colder than charity and a few days later, as a gesture of protest, Sir Ferdinand Cavendish-Bentinck resigned his post as Speaker. His resignation seemed to me an admission of his inability to fit into the new scheme of things, but it was hailed by the great majority of European settlers as a noble and selfless action. Their feeling was summed up in one item in the press: "Elder Statesman quits honoured position to lead European Community to safety." Like drowning men, the shocked and badly frightened settlers clung to CB. Nearly every one of them felt that his leadership was now their only hope.

Only about twenty-five per cent of the Europeans still supported the New Kenya Party but we stood firm, convinced that an acceptance of The Wind of Change was our only hope of survival as a community in an independent Kenya. I went straight into battle, holding the first of my tour of ten meetings, in my hometown of Sotik, within a few days of my return. Knowing I was in for a tough time, I realised that the only thing to do was to tell my constituents the plain and unpalatable truth. Even then, I found the extent of their bitterness, caused by the British Government's breach of good faith, and the anger aroused through fear for our future, almost unbelievable. I was told after the meeting that many of my neighbours had said, "Aggie's meeting is on Wednesday, and her funeral on Thursday."

Facing a packed meeting that day at the Sotik Club, I started to speak to the accompaniment of boos and hisses. This made me angry, and I decided not to pull any punches but to give it to them straight from the shoulder. I told them that they were living in a 'Fools' Paradise' if they thought that in some miraculous way we in this country could stand out against the changes taking place in the rest of the world. Kenya had offered escape for many people from a changing world where neither the accident of birth nor of wealth could any longer ensure privilege. Now our right to leadership, our very way of life, was being challenged. If we were to survive as a community in Kenya, we must wake up and face this force, this African nationalism, which was sweeping the whole continent like a prairie fire and had reached our very borders.

As I spoke, driving home my points with all the strength of which I was capable, my audience quietened and gave me a most attentive hearing. I continued by saying that even though our security, our land, and perhaps even our lives were threatened, to talk of armed resistance was crazy. What a handful of early settlers had done in the 1920s was not possible today. With the dice of world opinion loaded heavily against us, and without the backing of the British Government, we should be fighting against tremendous odds and there could only be one outcome to such a struggle: total failure and the loss of all that we held most dear.

I asked them if they wished to turn Kenya into an Algeria with all the useless bloodshed, misery, and resultant bitterness this would bring in its wake. At the end of two hours, several people spoke in support of what I said. My chief political opponent, Lt Gen Irwin, proposed a vote of confidence on their Member's action in accepting the proposed Constitution, which was carried by 135 votes to 5.

Meetings in all parts of Nyanza Province, followed much the same pattern, and in each case, after I had spoken, and answered questions, I asked for and gained a 'vote of confidence.'

After fourteen days of touring I came home, victorious but utterly exhausted, with no fight left in me. The first round of what was to prove a long and bitter battle was over, as threats of violence gave place to saner counsels.

CHAPTER 17

The March Toward Independence

*"My son, despise not race nor clan;
Pass judgement only on the man.
Make friends or enemies by deeds,
Never by boundaries or creeds."*
--Edgar A. Guest

After such a turbulent start, the rest of 1960 passed more quietly. So perhaps this is a good place to break into this history of public affairs with a short account of some of the changes in our private lives.

In the autumn of 1956, Brian and I were alone at Kipkebe, my mother being in England for a few months and the Bush family in India. For the first time we were free to give some thought to our own future. Talking things over one evening, we realised that as our farm was now a company, were anything to make it impossible for Brian to continue to manage the estate we should be homeless. This came as something of a shock. We decided that some time, when in Nairobi for a sitting for Legislative Council, I should start house hunting.

Within a week the opportunity came, and I set out, accompanied by a friend. On being shown with pride what the young agent described as a gentleman's residence, a ghastly suburban villa in Muthaiga, overlooking and overlooked by others of the same breed, I exclaimed, "I couldn't live surrounded by all those houses!" Surprised, but determined to humour this crazy woman, he then took us to a dark, dank and dismal dwelling of Grecian design hidden in an acre of jacaranda. As these alternatives were all he had to offer we decided to try another house agent.

I was introduced to a delightful man, who said, "What type of house had you in mind?" He listened while I described what I wanted and then asked, "How much are you prepared to pay for this perfect place?" My reply was, "Not a penny more than £6,000."

Looking at me in amazement, he said, "My dear Mrs Shaw, sorry if I sound rude but I think you must be mad. I don't believe such a

Hardy House in the Langata area of Nairobi, to which Brian and Agnes Shaw moved after leaving Sotik.

place exists even at £30,000." Then suddenly he exclaimed, "By Jove, it does, and at your price! But you mustn't go to see it today." I asked why, and was told the house had been standing empty for some time and there were bats in the basement and bees in the bathroom. Excited, saying I wanted to see it at its worst, I took the keys and drove out the ten miles to Langata. As a friend and I drew up at the front door, my friend exclaimed, "Look, oh how lovely!" There, rising above the garden wall, framed in a tumbled mass of golden shower and tea roses, was Mt Kilimanjaro. Her huge dome, 100 miles away across the plain, towering above the clouds, was coloured by the rays of the setting sun. We stood spellbound by her beauty. At last Audrey said, "Don't bother about the house, you can do something with it, but you have got to buy that view." And that is just what we did.

Hardy House, built in 1938, is a two-storeyed, grey stone house of no known architectural design. Though dilapidated, it was basically sound and well suited to our purpose, as the whole second storey was built as a self-contained penthouse. This provided me with a delightful *pied-a-terre* in Nairobi for sessions of the Council for the next three years, as well as the security of having tenants below and insurance against burglary while I was up-country. When Brian retired from Kipkebe in 1960 we made our home there, and during my last four years in Council, I had the pleasure of entertaining there with my husband and repaying some of the wonderful hospitality we had enjoyed. In that year we reversed our position, moved into the main house downstairs, and let the penthouse. But upstairs or downstairs or in my Lady's chamber, we lived in 'a room with a view.'

And what a view! To our right the beautiful Ngong Hills, their seven peaks forever changing, and to the left, over miles and miles of African plains, always the hope that Kilimanjaro, that dreaming mountain, would show herself in all her splendour. She is more capricious than any woman, remaining hidden for months only to reappear suddenly, more beautiful than ever. The grandeur of the view was softened by a foreground of forest, where the grey and green of the indigenous trees was relieved by the pink of the flowering Cape chestnuts.

The garden had been claimed by the African bush and only traces were to be found, with a poinsettia bravely pushing up through a tangle of undergrowth here and there; but as one of our most expert landscape gardeners exclaimed, "What a background for a garden." Sitting at the window of our penthouse, gazing out over the fringe of forest to the hills and plains beyond, he suddenly said, "Don't speak for fifteen minutes and I'll draw your garden for you." Too good an offer to miss from the Master Craftsman, so even I was silent while he sat and sketched. What fun it was reclaiming the five acres and transforming that rough sketch into a colourful garden, where African and English flowers blended in perfect harmony. Near the house was a formal rose garden, and borders gay with phlox, delphiniums, antirrhinums and sweet-smelling stock, while brilliant bougainvilleas edged the green lawns which sloped gently down to meet the forest.

A lovely peaceful spot, which was for me a refuge from the frustrations of my busy political life. The Psalmist who wrote, "I will lift up mine eyes unto the hills," showed a profound wisdom. As I set out each day and returned each evening, the beauty of the Ngong Hills meant to me a renewal of strength and refreshment of spirit. Perhaps the Maasai are right in their age-old belief that it is a holy place, as they believe that God descended on the highest of the peaks to create the world.

Before we finally left Sotik to move to Langata and the house with the view of the hills, I had yet another election to fight in Nyanza Province, and many preparations to make.

The election was to be held in 1961, and the election machinery was clumsy. All European candidates had to fight a preliminary election in which only their European constituents voted. Any candidate who received at least twenty-five per cent of the votes cast was eligible to go forward to the main election, in which both Africans and Europeans voted, and for which the franchise qualifications were so low that they almost amounted to universal suffrage. The purpose of these preliminary elections was to prevent any left-winger from standing for one of the European constituencies in the 'White Highlands' and being elected by a large African majority, against the will of the majority of European voters.

This pre-selection was a clumsy device which caused great bitterness amongst the European settlers and did not please anyone. In the multi-racial constituencies set aside for European representation, the more liberal members of the New Kenya Party, led by Michael Blundell, were defeated by men from the Cavendish-Bentinck Coalition. This did not prevent the New Kenya Party members from going forward as candidates to the general election providing that they had polled the required twenty-five per cent in the first election.

Many of our supporters, normally rational-minded men and women, were driven through fear to join the ranks of the "Last-ditch die-hards" of the Coalition Party. Thus, the majority of the settlers did their best to throw out their former leader Michael Blundell and very nearly succeeded, as Michael only scraped through the primary with twenty-six-and-a-half per cent.

Fear breeds hatred, and the feelings aroused in this bitter campaign were so intense that Blundell's life was often threatened both at public meetings and by anonymous letters sent through the post. All his followers suffered to a lesser degree, although I was lucky enough to gain thirty-seven per cent, which was the highest percentage polled by any member of the Blundell Party. The unbelievable bitterness of the campaign was such that, when members of the New Kenya Party won their seats at the general election with overwhelming African support, many Europeans felt that they had been disenfranchised. It was not a happy position for either side.

Realising that the aftertaste of this bitterness was bound to poison the political scene for some time, it took more courage to go forward after the preliminary to fight the general election than to resign then and there. Two things persuaded me to go on. One was the loyalty I felt for Michael Blundell, and the second was the sincerity of my belief that the only hope of survival for the settlers in Kenya was through the adoption of a more liberal policy. I was comforted by the fact that many of my constituents told me that although they had voted against me at the preliminary to show their disapproval of my policy, at the general election they intended to vote for the Member they wanted to represent them. In other words, they did not want to exchange their 'Universal Aunt' for a little-known 'Uncle.'

We were given a short breathing space between the two elections, but not long enough to allow us to do more than to get our second wind. This time my opponent was Titus Oates, a settler turned Government officer who had been in the Colony for many years and farmed in the Kipkabus district of the neighbouring province. Being a prominent member of the right-wing Coalition Party carried him to victory in the first round, when he polled sixty-three per cent of the European vote; but this was to count against him with the Africans and Asians. Three other factors undermined Capt Oates's chances. The first was that Nyanza distrusted 'carpet baggers.' The second was that many of the Nyanza electorate saw the too-familiar hand of General Irwin on the steering wheel of the Oates campaign. And the third was the unfortunate choice of an electoral symbol – no, choice is the wrong word, for it was merely the luck of the draw.

Our first joint action was to appear in the District Commissioner's office at Kericho to be given our electoral symbols, necessary for an electorate many of whom could neither read nor write. The District Commissioner showed us the various signs: a bicycle, a motor car, a cock, etc., before asking us each to draw one out of the hat. My luck was in: I drew the maize cob, which is not only the basic foodstuff for most Kenya Africans, but also symbolises fertility. Saying, "I hope I don't get the bunch of bananas," my opponent put in his hand, and out came the bananas! Bad luck for him as that fruit, although the staple food of many Uganda Africans, means very little to the Kipsigis tribe.

My symbol was a good omen for the success of my campaign among the Africans – not that I lacked support in that direction. I knew I could count on the Kipsigis anyway, having lived amongst that warrior tribe for over thirty years and therefore being well-known to them. However, leaving nothing to chance, I had already visited Senior Chief arap Tengecha. He was holding a *baraza* [meeting] for all his chiefs and headmen, and I arrived just five minutes before their meeting began. As I shook hands with Tengecha the others gathered around, including the District Officer. The preliminary courtesies over, I asked my old friend if I could count on his support and that of his people at the general election. With a beaming smile the old Chief took hold of the lapel of my dress and laying his head upon my breast, said, "*Bibi* Shaw, we are your children and we shall suckle you like our own mother." Very gratifying, but slightly embarrassing, especially in front of the young British Administrative officer!

African and European elections in Kenya were quite different. To take one instance, in a European campaign the various candidates would often all address the voters at the same meeting, but no two African meetings could be licensed to be held in the same town or even district on the same day. This was because a clash between rival factions would surely have resulted, which could have developed into a major riot. As before, my small committee (organised by my charming and most able secretary Meg) did sterling work behind the scenes, but at this election I had to employ African agents as well. This was necessary to ensure that my manifesto reached the African electorate, especially those working on farms. It was short and simple, printed in English and Swahili, as well as four other African vernaculars. It carried my photograph, the picture of the maize cob, a short statement, and a detailed explanation of how to vote. The bitterness against Michael Blundell and his party was so intense that in the campaign, many European farmers had no scruples about destroying any election literature sent to their farm post boxes, to prevent its reaching their African employees.

Above all I owed my success in the election to my good fortune in having the support of Mr Richardson, the Manager of the East African Tea Packing Factory in Kericho. With his help and shrewd advice, I planned my campaign. Not only did 'Dickie' know everyone of importance in the African/Asian world, but he had his finger well and truly on the political pulse of the province. Through his varied sources of information, I was warned of the many pitfalls that await the unwary. Thus forearmed, I entered the hustings, brandishing my maize cob and shouting my slogan, "Aggie for Action," and "No Votes for Oates!"

This campaign was to be the most exhausting I ever fought. Instead of the usual combined meetings, I had to hold two meetings a day, outdoors in the morning or early afternoon, and an evening meeting in the local hall or cinema. In market places I usually stood on a table or the bonnet of a Land Rover to address a crowd numbering anything from a few hundred to several thousand.

The technique at these meetings was totally different. At the outdoor gatherings, my listeners were largely illiterate and I used my settler-brand Swahili; whereas in the evenings I spoke in English to an intelligent and mostly well-educated, multi-racial audience. For the first time in my life I came to appreciate the Old Testament. I found the only way I could make myself understood to my all-African outdoor audiences was by the use of parables. Statements were illustrated by the simplest stories and points driven home by the use of popular slogans, such as *"Uhuru na Haki,"* *"Uhuru na* KADU," *"Uhuru na Bibi* Shaw." Each shouted slogan would be followed by a roar of applause. Hard on the voice, but no strain on the intellect!

I usually spoke for half an hour and then answered questions for at least an hour, or until my patience was exhausted. For as well as having to deal at question time with the professional heckler or political smart-aleck, I would have to cope with the old Nandi man who would say, "Memsahib, I will vote for you if you will promise to get my *Bwana* to allow me to keep one of my cows on his tea estate – tell him only one please." Nor could he understand my refusal, even though I carefully explained that this would mean everyone would want to do the same. The result would be over a thousand cows and the Manager would find that he was no longer running a tea plantation but a large-scale cattle ranch.

During this campaign the Asian community found themselves in a very invidious position. From private talks with the heads of the different sections, I was confident of their support, but only if I did nothing to compromise their good relations with their European customers in Kericho. So I exercised the greatest tact and only visited their shops in the lunch hour or after closing time. Then, if by any chance a late shopper came in, I would be hustled into the office or behind some packing cases, safely out of sight. So successful were these tactics that, two days before the polling day, even the Police 'Special Branch' did not know which of the two candidates the Asians were backing. But I did!

The election was on a Monday, and on Saturday night, after all the Europeans were safely in their homes or at the Club, I held a large meeting of Hindus, Muslims and Sikhs in the Hindu temple in Kericho. That night I was given the most vociferous support. On the licence I was listed as the only speaker, but after I had spoken the meeting itself took over, and there were speeches in English, Gujarati, Hindi and Urdu. All the leaders of the different sections felt compelled loudly to voice their support. Each speech was greeted with roars of applause and approval and Brian rounded off the proceedings with an excellent impromptu effort in Hindustani, much to everyone's delight.

There was one very amusing incident. The Sunday before, my opponent had addressed a similar meeting in Kericho, and the next day two young Asians came to see me. They appeared much distressed and told me that they had taken great exception to something my opponent had said about me in his speech. They asked me to correct, at my meeting the following Sunday, the impression given by what they considered to have been an offensive remark.

This was rather a poser, but I decided to let the mood at the meeting dictate my reply. After such encouraging support, I felt able to deal with the remark at question time. I told my audience that Mr

Oates had apparently caused offence, having referred to the possibility of my being elected to Legislative Council by asking: "What would one woman do amongst fifty-four men?" This was greeted by a roar of laughter. Assured of an understanding, though unexpected, sense of humour, I said, "I could think of many things!" This answer produced more laughter and applause. And so happily to bed at midnight, certain of being able to count on more than 700 votes.

Polling day was without incident. Confident in the knowledge of the majority support of both the African and Asian voters, I never doubted the result, but the size of my majority – over 2,000 votes – surprised and pleased me. With the primary and general election, both the Europeans and Asians had fought two campaigns within two months, a pretty exhausting business. We hoped for a short rest, but none of us ever imagined that it would be over two months before a Government was formed.

On the African front, the election was fought between the main political parties, the Kenya African National Union and the Kenya African Democratic Union. KANU, the bigger of the two parties, drew its support chiefly from the two largest tribes: the Kikuyu, with their satellites the Embu and Meru; and the Luo. These two tribes happened to live close to two of the largest towns in Kenya, Nairobi the capital, on the edge of Kikuyu country, and Kisumu on the shores of Lake Victoria. KADU, on the other hand, was a grouping of the smaller tribes who banded together in an attempt to withstand pressures from the power bloc which had come into being with the alliance of the Kikuyu and Luo tribes. KANU could therefore claim a far greater proportion of educated Africans amongst its members than KADU, whose greatest support came from more warrior tribes such as the Maasai, Kipsigis and Samburu.

The people of the coastal strip and of the northern part of Nyanza, who feared the incursion of the Kikuyu and Luo, threw in their lot with the Democratic Union. KADU was led by Ronald Ngala, an honest and sincere African, ably supported by his two Lieutenants, Daniel arap Moi, the acknowledged leader of the Kalenjin, and that astute politician and outstanding figure amongst the Africans of north Nyanza, Masinde Muliro. Although there were a few other men possessed of the qualities of leadership amongst the KADU ranks, the party did not have the numbers of experienced politicians which KANU could muster – men such as Joseph Murumbi and Mbiyu Koinange, of outstanding ability, whose years of exile from Kenya had served to broaden their outlook and education and to act as an apprenticeship in the political field. On the Luo front Tom Mboya had done much to build up the Trade Union movement as General Secretary, looking to the USA for his financial backing. Far out on the left wing the patriarchal figure of Oginga Odinga saw his way to power through an alliance with the Peking Eastern bloc. All these men of KANU had travelled widely, and could count on friends and finance from outside Kenya's borders for what they liked to call their fight for freedom.

As a party, KADU gained the support of the great majority of Europeans, but that did not make up for the lack of educated Africans to provide the required leadership, nor did they possess the funds necessary to finance a campaign. Thus, out-generalled and outbid, KADU entered the lists. Although the party put up a brave fight, many of their candidates being successful, they could not hope to win the election in the face of such overwhelming odds. KANU's victory was a certainty, and everyone expected them to form a Government. But the expected seldom happens in African politics, and after two months of stalemate, when Kenya was without a Government, His Excellency the Governor, Sir Patrick Renison, finally asked the defeated party to form a Government.

This was a direct result of the biggest blunder ever made by Tom Mboya in his meteoric but turbulent political career – a blunder which, I believe, lost him the chance of ever becoming Kenya's Prime Minister. The Governor's stand was that until a Government was formed, there was no question of releasing Jomo Kenyatta; whereas Mr Mboya insisted that the Kikuyu leader's release should precede the formation of any Government. KANU took up the battle cry of "No Government without release," and His Excellency stood firm on "No release without a Government," a position from which it was impossible for him to retreat.

Had Mr Mboya been a shrewder politician, he would have realised this, and in the knowledge that Sir Patrick's word was his bond, he could have seized his great opportunity by saying: "Well, Sir, provided you give me your promise to release Jomo Kenyatta immediately after the formation of a Government, I will form that Government." At that moment most of the Kikuyu leaders were either still in detention or prohibited immigrants overseas. Mr Mboya was the unchallenged leader and could have become Kenya's first Prime Minister.

Faced with Mr Mboya's obstinate refusal, His Excellency had no choice but to send for Mr Ronald Ngala, the leader of the KADU opposition party, and invite him to form a Government. Unable to secure a sufficient majority amongst his own party to enable him to govern effectively, Ngala approached Michael Blundell, leader of the multi-racial New Kenya Party, to discover if some of the European and Asian members of his party would be prepared to join a KADU government.

This was a logical step, as the two parties were closely allied, many Africans being members of both, and the resulting coalition between KADU and the NKP was an obvious solution. Even then, this did not give them a sound working majority, and throughout its life the KADU Government had to rely on the support of the European Coalition Party, who took up their position together with some of the more moderate-minded Asian members of the Cross Bench.

Secure in their own strength, and confident of their power to force the Government to accede to their demands, KANU must have been dismayed by this turn of events. This was plainly demonstrated by the filibustering tactics adopted by the opposition benches during the whole period of the KADU Government's short term of office. These noisy demonstrations, disguised as points of order, whose object was disorder, were aimed at the defeat of the Government. Childish as these disruptive tactics were, they imposed a great strain on the Government. Ronald Ngala and the other KADU leaders had constantly to be on their guard. No motion was allowed to go to the vote without cries of "Divide, divide," as the opposition forced division after division upon the House. And although the Government always won, it meant endless vigilance on the part of the Whips to see that all Members were in the Parliament Building, ready to obey the strident summons of the division bell.

An amusing incident occurred as a result of these KANU pressures. In May, early in the life of the new Government, we had unprecedented rain, and many of the Members in the outlying districts of Kenya were

Brian and Agnes Shaw in the late 1950s.

literally stuck in the mud. This was KANU's chance. Knowing the danger that threatened, KADU held an emergency meeting. An anxious count of heads confirmed our worst fear: that with the unavoidable absence of so many Members, our voting strength was so depleted that we would be certain to lose should a division be forced on a vote of confidence. To save the Government from defeat the Members must be brought back, but how? Communications in Kenya are not very rapid at the best of times, but now, added to the vagaries of the most temperamental posts and telecommunications service, we had the forces of nature: torrential rains, bridges swept away by flood waters, roads a sea of mud, telephone wires down or damaged by gales. District Commissioners were alerted by radio, messages went out by Land Rover or (where bridges were down) by African runner, to bring Members in from the outlying districts to the nearest Government Boma or Police Post, where a plane would be waiting to fly them to the capital. Those of us who were already in Nairobi were told that whatever happened, we had to stage the biggest filibuster of all time and keep the debate going, avoiding a division at all costs until the absent Members arrived. Even so, it was a close call as the distances to be covered were terrific.

Members looked around to see if they could not persuade some of the Opposition to absent themselves. It so happened that one of the KANU members had gone on leave, and acting as his stand-in was a young man who was studying at the Ministry of Administration. One of our African Ministers got hold of this young man and said: "I understand you are studying to be a District Commissioner." "Yes," replied the young man. "Well," said our Minister, "as a District Commissioner, wouldn't one of your first duties as a loyal Government servant be to support Government?" The answer was an emphatic, "Yes."

The unfortunate young man was then asked if he thought voting for a vote of no confidence in Government could be considered support. Reluctantly he admitted he did not, and asked what he should do. He was told that his best course was to go back to Kabete and his studies without delay. Fearing damage to his chance of a Government career, he took this advice and the opposition lost the vote. This was the most crucial moment in all those trying months, but the KADU Government, through the loyalty of its Members, survived, and all attempts of the KANU opposition to bring our Government down failed.

During the ten months of the KADU Government's life, I held a post as Parliamentary Secretary to the Ministry of Health and Housing. A most interesting position, where even if I did not contribute much, I learnt a great deal about Kenya's health services. As I developed a better understanding of the immense difficulties under which the Department worked to raise the standard of health by teaching home hygiene to Kenya's ever-growing population, my admiration for their work increased daily. My Minister, Mr Bernard Mate, was a pleasant personality, and during my term of office I was lucky to work with one of the most efficient Permanent Secretaries I have ever known.

With my uninhibited settler attitude towards the ponderous Government machine, I must have been a sore trial. But my welcome by the Department was so friendly that I had no feeling of being an intruder in a closed shop, and it is with gratitude that I record the help and advice I received from so many members of what is one of the finest Government departments in Kenya. The high quality of their selfless service will, I hope, prove a spur and inspiration to those who have taken over the Ministry of Health in an Independent Kenya, initially under the leadership of Dr Njoroge Mungai.

My first meeting with Dr Mungai was rather unfortunate, as this story against myself will show. One of my first official engagements, just after my appointment as Parliamentary Secretary for Health, was to accompany Mr Mate, then Minister, to a cocktail party given in his honour by the Kenya Medical Association. On being introduced to Dr Mungai, I said, "Before you entered Legislative Council, I had always wanted to meet you, as I gathered you have done a great deal medically for your own Kikuyu people," adding, "but I must admit to disappointment when I heard your maiden speech." Dr Mungai asked why, to which I replied, "Well, if you remember, you said you feared that KADU would implant some radioactive material in the stones of the house which they were building for Jomo Kenyatta, which would cause the death of your beloved leader, and cause his two beautiful daughters to become as vegetables. Do you expect me to think that an intelligent man like you can really believe such utter rubbish?" The doctor laughed and shrugged his shoulders and said, "No, but my constituents do."

What was my horror a few minutes later, when Dr Mungai rose to introduce Mr Mate in an able and witty speech, to learn that as President of the Medical Association, Dr Mungai was our host! After the Minister's speech Dr Mungai introduced me with a few graceful words.

Saying our goodbyes and thanking our host for a delightful party, I said that I thought after my earlier remarks it was most forgiving of Dr Mungai to introduce me to the gathering in such a charming way. Dr Mungai replied, "Not at all, it was a pleasure, but Mrs Shaw, apropos our conversation, all I ask is that when you visit our beloved Mzee in his new home at Gatundu, you bring a Geiger counter."

CHAPTER 18

The Pace Quickens

*"If there is negotiation, it must be rooted in
mutual respect and concern for the rights of others."*
-- J.F. Kennedy

Mzee Jomo Kenyatta was released from detention on the 29th July 1961. This event, hailed with joy by some and viewed with misgiving by others, passed off without incident. Ten years is a long time for anyone to be shut away from any contact with the world, and to stage a Rip van Winkle comeback must be a rather shattering experience.

On his release, Kenyatta did not appear to be a dynamic leader, but rather a bewildered old man. People who came in contact with him, noting the change, said he had lost his magnetism. I did not believe this, for surely the sudden transition from a life of captivity to being not only free but the centre of the Kenya stage was quite enough to account for the difficulty he found in adjusting himself to the changed circumstances of a modern Kenya.

Thus for a time Jomo was content with his role of Mzee Kenyatta, accepting the high place his martyrdom had won for him in the regard and affection of his own people, the Kikuyu. His acclamation as a freedom fighter only caused the faintest ripple on the sea of world opinion. After a period of over two years, he regained his fire and fervour, and since taking over the reins of Government as Prime Minister at Independence he has stood head and shoulders above Kenya's other political leaders.

It is nothing short of remarkable that he should have achieved this high standing after making the initial mistake of re-entering the political arena as an ordinary member of the Opposition in the Legislative Council. The KADU Government welcomed his action gleefully; they foresaw that for Kenyatta to be subjected to the cut and thrust of debate as an ordinary Member was bound to cut him down in size. That is why there was little if any opposition to his attendance at the 2nd Lancaster House Conference.

That the KADU leaders were right was proved by the lamentable showing Kenyatta made with his first speech at that conference [which began in February 1962]. Unfortunately for the KANU delegation, their

President opened the debate for their side. How could his speech be otherwise than a string of outworn phrases and clichés? Oginga Odinga rose to speak next and completed the destruction with a ranting, raving speech in the best Odinga tradition, which shocked the members of Her Majesty's Government to their Civil Service core. We felt sorry for Tom Mboya that day as he rose to try and salvage something from the wreck.

Our mood in the New Kenya Party was not one of hope, but one of grim determination. Banded together as we were in the KADU Government, representative of the minority tribes in Kenya, we knew what we were up against and had no illusions left. Our faith in Her Majesty's Government had been badly shaken, but at least the man seen as the instrument of our betrayal was no longer in office. In his place, as Secretary of State for the Colonies, was Mr Reginald Maudling, a man whom we had met on his first visit to the Colony in November and whom we all liked and felt we could trust.

On arrival at London Airport we had had to undergo the usual press conference with its battery of TV cameras. Standing next to one of the Maasai Members of Government, I overheard a conversation which reflected little credit on the Kenya pressman, but said a great deal for the quickness of the shrewd reply.

In the most objectionable tone, the pressman asked, "Why can't your leaders – Kenyatta, Mboya, Odinga – agree?" He added in a sneering tone, "After all, they are only black men." Without a moment's hesitation the Maasai warrior, splendid in his colobus monkey skin cape, drawing himself to his full height, replied, "If you, Sir, can tell me why Kennedy, Khrushchev and Macmillan can't agree, I'll answer your question."

KADU attended the Conference as the Government Party. This gave them an official status. Also, the multi-racial aspect of their membership and the moderation of their views found favour with the Bow Group, then the strongest faction within the Conservative Party.

This collection of young Tories had emerged after the Second World War, and their go-ahead and liberal thinking was in tune with the mood of a post-war Britain. Their views were often more left than those of the Labour Party. Believing that unless the Conservatives could be jolted out of their traditional rut the Party was doomed, they were imbued with a sense of urgency and grew in strength. At the time of the first Lancaster House Conference, the Bow Group, led by the new Colonial Secretary, Iain Macleod, had been a force to be reckoned with. In fact, so powerful had they become that the more conservative backbenchers of the Party grew alarmed. Shaken out of their comfortable complacency by these young men, the right-wing die-hards rallied under the able leadership of Lord Salisbury. Thus organised, and with the financial backing of the City of London, they acted as a powerful brake on the Bow Group.

But at the time of the 1st Lancaster House Conference, this had not been the case; and the Kenya settlers had failed to gain the support of the right-wing Conservatives on which they had counted. By 1962, it was too late, for the Kenya ship was firmly set on a course for an early Independence. Although by then the Salisbury Group was a well-organised and powerful body, with solid financial backing, all they could do was to use their influence to secure the best terms for the compensation of the European settlers.

The majority hoped for the best terms on which we could continue to live in Kenya. Alas for many of our farmers, it meant the best terms on which they could sell out and go. Whether the settlers are amongst those who hope to stay or those who have gone, their gratitude to Lord Salisbury and his colleagues must be recorded in history. By their untiring efforts, the British Government has been shamed into honouring something of their debt to the men and women who were encouraged by that same Government to leave the Motherland so many years ago in order to colonise this small corner of what was then thought of as 'darkest Africa.' Nothing can ever compensate these settlers, now in the third and fourth generation, for the loss of their beautiful and gracious homes, for the sadness of leaving Kenya, and the break-up of beloved families; but at least the cash compensation has given some of them the chance to start life afresh.

The tensions which built up over the weeks of negotiation at [the second]Lancaster House were terrific, but there is no doubt that the strain lay heaviest on two men: Ronald Ngala, Leader of the KADU Government and Chief Secretary in all but name; and Michael Blundell, President of the New Kenya Party. On their shoulders rested the burden of decision. This was no new thing for Mr Blundell, but for Mr Ngala it proved almost too heavy. Poor Ronald, a sincere and peace-loving man, a member of that happy tribe the Giriama, was not meant to carry such a load. The sympathy, especially of his European colleagues, went out to him on several occasions when at our daily early morning meeting he admitted to being unable to sleep.

We all lay awake for long hours, wrestling with our problems and wondering if we were right in holding out for this or that, and the pressures from all sides were intense. But hold out we did, for eight weeks of long drawn out argument and counter argument. After two weeks of complete stalemate, the final phase was a weekend of intense activity, when, after meeting all the Parties privately to ascertain their views, Mr Maudling felt able to assess the measure of agreement. On the Monday, the delegates were told that a sitting of the full Conference had been called for the next day, at which time the Colonial Secretary intended to make known the decision he had taken, in consultation with Her Majesty's Government, on the proposals for constitutional advance for Kenya.

At a meeting of the KADU Party, Michael Blundell reported that he had good reason to believe that KADU had gained many of their points, but he cautioned that whether we felt relief, dismay, anger or joy, we should receive the statement in complete silence, giving outwardly no hint of our inward feelings. The Government Party acted on this advice, and although as we listened we realised we had come out of the conflict extremely well, we gave no sign, and after a formal expression of thanks, filed out in silence.

Not until we reached the privacy of our committee room at the Reubens Hotel did we show our feelings. The relief, after weeks of anxious strain, was intense, and the excitement in our moment of victory was tremendous. As I entered the room at the Reubens I found myself caught by my friend Musa Amalemba, who seizing me by my arms, danced me around saying, "Aggie old girl we've won; isn't it wonderful, we've won!" After the burst of enthusiasm had died down, Ronald Ngala called us to order, reminding us that our victory was only the beginning of what would be a protracted struggle. All we had achieved was the bare bones, and the task on our return to Kenya must be to put flesh on this skeleton.

The next day we were to learn how right he was, when the Colonial Secretary informed us that the price KADU must pay for victory was to agree to resign, in order to form a Coalition Government. Mr Maudling stressed that Her Majesty's Government felt that through participation in Government, KANU would learn to shoulder responsibility. He said that only in this way would men nurtured in extreme nationalism become reasonable citizens, capable of governing an independent Kenya. This was true, and the British, past masters in compromise, put forward their case with consummate skill. KADU, having no alternative, accepted, swallowing the bitter pill, sugar coated though it was, with good grace. So ended the 2nd Lancaster House Conference, which prepared the way for Kenya's Independence eighteen months later.

Back in Kenya, the KADU Government resigned, after deciding what Ministries should be retained by KADU and which should be offered to KANU, and the struggle for power began. Both sides had their political advisors: chief amongst these on the KADU side was Michael Blundell – the man who had the vision to see that the only basis on which the Europeans could remain in Kenya was to win the trust and goodwill of the African leaders and the people they represent. It would never be won by standing in the way of their advance to Independence, a goal they had determined to achieve at whatever cost. This had been made clear at the 1960 Conference; but no one could foresee the speed with which these changes were to be thrust upon us.

That Michael Blundell still hoped for a gradual transference of power over a period of years is shown by his letter to John Morrison, published in his book. Summarising the British Government's intentions he wrote:

"As I see the position the proposals of the Secretary of State do in effect mean that Kenya is irredeemably set upon a path of African-influenced government immediately, and ultimately largely one of African domination. In the next few years we should do our utmost to train the Africans to accept responsibilities for all races on a national rather than a racial basis, so that they come to regard the Europeans as an element in society which it is to their advantage to maintain. The Proposals themselves will, of course, be a tremendous shock to the European opinion and in order to soften them it is essential that the Secretary of State realises the need for a Land Development Board, whose function it will be to purchase farms from those who are unwilling to accept this future and offer them (the farms) for redevelopment to the best economic advantage of the country."

I have quoted this letter because it proves that not only did the leader of the New Kenya Party sincerely believe that it was intended to introduce these changes gradually over a period of years, but that he saw the necessity for Great Britain to acknowledge her responsibility to the Kenya settler. To honour that debt, the British Government would be required to undertake to buy out and compensate all those European settlers who felt unable to accept the new order, or those who believed that an independent Kenya would offer neither security for them nor a future for their children. This point should be made if only because of the repeated claims of the Coalition Party that they alone were the only people who fought for compensation. The members of their Executive did fight hard on this issue, and the pressures they brought to bear on Her Majesty's Government through the leader, Sir Ferdinand Cavendish-Bentinck, with such men as Lord Salisbury, did bear fruit. This is not denied; and all the farmers who have taken their compensation and gone owe much to the untiring efforts of the Coalition's leaders on their behalf.

But Michael Blundell fought their battles too, although perhaps it is true to say that he was more concerned with reconditioning the thinking of his fellow countrymen in order to make it possible for them to stay in Kenya.

To continue on the subject of Michael Blundell, immediately after the 'Swearing In' of the Coalition Government formed by KADU and The New Kenya Party in 1961, at their first joint meeting, Michael Blundell proposed that Ronald Ngala should be the leader and Chairman of the KADU Parliamentary Group. It was no easy thing for him to subordinate his ebullient personality to the leadership of Ngala, but the secret of his success was that he was able to do so. In this way Michael Blundell was not feared as a rival, but rather was welcomed by the leaders of KADU as a valued and trusted supporter. This enabled Michael to retain his influence with such men as Ngala, Muliro, Daniel arap Moi, and ole Tipis, all ardent African nationalists at heart, placing his long political experience at the disposal of the KADU cabinet.

And did not Michael Blundell's multi-racial party lay the foundation for the racial co-operation which exists in Independent Kenya today? This was founded on his sincere belief that "No Government in Africa can function if it is based on the suppression by Europeans of the legitimate advance of the African people." He said, time and again, "I believe this not only to be impossible but to be morally wrong." Not a popular opinion at a time when many of the European settlers were living under the strain of the Mau Mau terror, which threatened their families, their homes, and indeed their very existence. But this did not deter Michael Blundell nor destroy his faith in the ultimate success of a multi-racial society in Kenya. Racial bitterness was at its height, fanned by fear of the Mau Maul terrorists, and this could well have dealt a death blow to any hope of racial co-operation in the future. That this did not happen was, I believe, due to two men: Michael Blundell, who even in those dark days clearly saw the pattern of the future; and Jomo Kenyatta who, remarkable man that he is, was able to rise above bitterness and instead of seeking revenge sought the co-operation of the Europeans, and indeed of all races, in the building of an independent Kenya.

Many people call Michael Blundell's withdrawal [from politics after Independence] a tragedy. But was it really a tragedy? Was it not the wisest thing that he could do? And is his valuable experience of a lifetime in this part of Africa really lost to Independent Kenya? History will give the answer to these questions, but one thing is certain: It takes a great man to be able to step out of public life, at the height of his power, when even the Premiership of Kenya was within his grasp.

To be able to give it all up, willingly, without bitterness, and return happily and with immense enthusiasm to his farm, is to me not the measure of failure but of the man's greatness.

To return to the aftermath of Lancaster House: After the strain of the 2nd Constitutional Conference, I was exhausted and suffering from a surfeit of politics. I was thankful to be able to resign my office as Parliamentary Secretary, but I was still, of course, an elected Member of Legislative Council. In order to take leave, I had to find someone to take my place as representative of the Nyanza Constituency.

This time Mr Duncan Wilson came to my rescue, acting as my stand-in during my period of absence. Duncan was Kenya born, of Scots farming stock, and a sound farmer himself who had grown to be much respected throughout his district for his public-spirited work on various local committees. He was rewarded by being elected Chairman of the Nyanza County Council, a signal honour for so young a man.

Knowing the constituency was in good hands, I stepped into the East African Airways Comet for a tour of Europe, feeling tired but relaxed. On arrival in Rome, we found the Eternal City suffering from the noisiest of election campaigns. We were glad to escape on Monday, flying over the Alps into another world.

On arrival in London the first thing we did was to attend the annual East African Dinner. Lord Boyd and his charming wife were our host and hostess, and the guest speaker was the Colonial Secretary, Mr Reginald Maudling. To me it was a vivid reminder of the stresses and strains of the previous two years, with their fateful conferences. This event is always a pleasant occasion for the opportunity it affords of reunion with old friends, but that year, answering eager and anxious questions as to how things were in Kenya, I knew I was tired of it all. On our return to Kenya in October this feeling persisted, and during the succeeding months as the Europeans of the New Kenya Party retreated step by step into the background, I realised the days of our political influence were over. We Europeans must now step down, and hand over to the new leaders of the country, as Michael Blundell had done.

My political career in Kenya, and that of all the other European elected members except Bruce McKenzie and Humphrey Slade, ended in 1963 with the coming of Independence. Bruce McKenzie was nominated a Member of Parliament in Independent Kenya and appointed Minister of Agriculture in Mzee Jomo Kenyatta's Government, a post which he held for several more years. Mr Humphrey Slade remained in Parliament as Speaker until his retirement in 1970, a figure much respected and beloved by the new generation of Parliamentarians.

In 1964, with the full support of its members, Ronald Ngala dissolved the KADU Party, a courageous step, taken in the interests of a wider unity. Thus Kenya has followed the example of all her African neighbours in becoming a one-party state.

Ronald Ngala and the KADU leaders can comfort themselves

that many people are as convinced as I am that had it not been for the interim period of the KADU Government, followed by the Coalition, there might have been another Congo situation in Kenya. If, after KANU's overwhelming victory in the 1961 Elections, Mboya had formed a Government and attempted to force the one-party issue, the result could have been bloodshed. Tribal feeling at that time was running high, intensified by the fear of domination by the Kikuyu/ Luo alliance. The bid for supremacy made by some of the Kikuyu through the Mau Mau Rebellion was still fresh in the African mind. The interim KADU federal-type Government, followed by the Coalition between KANU and KADU, led by Jomo Kenyatta, did much to allay these fears, and a great deal of credit for this lessening of tension must go to Mzee Kenyatta himself. Through his untiring efforts, his country-wide tours and public meetings, and his repeated calls for "Harambee," Mzee Kenyatta did more than any one single man to unify the Africans and lay the foundations for nationhood in Kenya.

CHAPTER 19

After the Storm

"Out to the undiscovered ends"

It is tempting, although perhaps not very wise, at the end of any phase of life to take stock. This requires courage, especially when the debits appear to outweigh the credits. But even if most of what one has helped to build disappears, has not the builder learnt much in the building? And perhaps what has been created has served its purpose.

Over half a century ago the Sotik Salient was opened to European settlement to act as a 'buffer state' between four warring tribes. This small island of white settlement, set in the midst of four African land units, certainly achieved its purpose; and I like to think that a great deal of what has been accomplished by that handful of British colonists will remain: the civilizing influence, the good husbandry of the land, but above all the understanding and friendship which has grown throughout the years between the Kipsigis tribe and their European neighbours.

After Independence, most of the farming land in South Sotik was bought by the Kenya Government through the Settlement Schemes. These farmers, some of the first to be compensated, left Kenya to seek 'fresh fields' and their farms were divided up into smallholdings and sold to Africans of the Kipsigis and Kisii tribes.

Thus, the land cut out of the African Reserves, this buffer state, returned after sixty years to African ownership. That this did not happen in North Sotik, which was under tea, was due to three factors: first, that the Government was not prepared to pay the compensation asked by the tea companies; second, that the revenue brought in by way of tax was too valuable; and third, that the tea companies provided much needed employment for the local Africans as well as roads, schools and hospitals.

As a family, we were more fortunate than many of our Sotik neighbours, for, as I have recounted, we had turned our farm into a company in the 1940s. When Brian retired, Don Bush stepped into his shoes and carried on with the work of development for a further five

Agnes reading with grandchildren Graham and Tish at Kipkebe in 1959.

years, bringing the acreage of planted tea up to 600. Thus the dear old thatched rondavel house continued to be home to our family, and we had the happiness of knowing that our grandchildren spent their childhood in the house where their mother was born.

The 2,000 acres my husband bought in 1927 grows ever more productive, giving employment to hundreds of Africans, and it is comforting to know that all the hard work he put into development Kipkebe is not lost.

What of my twelve years as a European elected Member of Nyanza Province? Many of the districts which I represented have been handed back to the Africans. Their former owners have accepted their hard-won cash compensation and have left to seek a livelihood elsewhere. Their farmhouses stand derelict, and their pretty gardens have been swallowed up by the African bush. Gone are the well-farmed lands, the mown lawns, the fenced paddocks and the herds of pedigree and high-grade stock. The acres of coffee are now divided into small plots, to form parts of peasant holdings. Sad, you may say. Yes, it is heartbreaking, but is it not only a phase? Will not these same acres be brought back into full production someday, under the Kenya Government's plan for co-operative farming?

In the early days the pioneers of farming in Kenya made many mistakes, trying out first this crop and then that. Men such as Delamere, the Cole brothers, FOB Wilson, and scores of others lost large sums

Ann, Agnes and Brian at Hardy House in July 1965.

through experiments and through depredations to their stocks from both lion and unknown diseases. In a new land, where little was known of climate or soil, the road to success was no easy one, and as the farmers who came out to settle in Kenya learnt the hard way, so must their African successors. In one respect they are more fortunate than the pioneers, for today they do not start from scratch. Over the years, the Kenya Agricultural Department, with their teams of experts, scientists, technologists, and their complement of Field Officers, have learnt a great deal. This wealth of knowledge is placed at the disposal of the African farmer. The farming districts now are well served by road and rail, and adequate distributing and marketing facilities have been built up by bodies such as the Kenya Farmers Association. Also, what the African farmer lacks in capital is being made available through the various banks and Government settlement schemes.

In this way, through co-operative societies, I believe African farming can in time be raised from its present subsistence level to become a revenue-producing industry. This is essential if the gap in Kenya's economy caused by the departure of the European farmer is to be filled. There is no better way of ensuring the stability of an independent Kenya than through creating a prosperous African farming community. Men with something to lose seldom become revolutionaries!

On the political side much of what we of the New Kenya Party fought for has been thrown overboard. Our attempts to safeguard a democratic system of government, through the federal-type constitution known as *majimbo*, have been nullified by the passing of the Constitutional Amendment Bill. A one-party system has been introduced.

In 1964, when Kenya became a Republic, much else that we of British nationality held dear disappeared forever. In the shifting sands of African politics, where change is the order of the day, it is difficult to assess what has been achieved. But of one thing I am certain, and that is the lasting value of the understanding which grew out of Africans, Asians, and Europeans working together in the New Kenya Party towards a common goal. As we got to know each other, fear and suspicion were allayed, and friendship grew. In our committee meetings race was forgotten and colour consciousness disappeared as we worked together daily as a closely-knit team. That we became friends is shown by the warmth of the welcome I find from my former colleagues on the few occasions when I have revisited the Parliament Buildings. Asked once why I no longer attended the Commonwealth Parliamentary Association dinners, I replied that as a left-over of the Colonial days I was out of place. They assured me this was not so, and said, "Aggie, we'd like you to come to the dinners." Touched by their obvious sincerity I said that perhaps I'd come to the next CPA dinner, and on bidding them goodbye, I caused much laughter by saying, "Call me a Colonial if you like, but don't you dare call me a neo-Colonial!"

Today in Africa it is fashionable to decry everything Colonial, and although many hundreds of intelligent and educated Africans must realise the tremendous amount Britain achieved in Kenya in a short sixty years, few if any, dare say so. If now and then a voice of truth is raised, it is soon drowned by the popular choruses of vilification and abuse. The passionate desire of the African people for equality makes them afraid to acknowledge past indebtedness. Perhaps someday they may come to realise that it is only a mature nation that has the generosity to pay tribute to its former teachers. Whether or not the African will ever have the courage or honesty to do so, the true record of Britain's achievement as a foremost colonial power has already passed into world history. To quote that great Englishman Sir Winston Churchill, I would say of the wind, "Let it roar, let it rage, we shall come through."

Kenya does not owe me anything, for she has given me a lifetime of happiness. Indeed, I owe her much, and should like to feel that in my years of life and work in this lovely land I have repaid my debt in part. Those of us who owe Kenya so much offer our prayers for her future, her peaceful progress, and the happiness of all her people, as they march along the Uhuru Highway, chanting the cry of "Harambee" out to the undiscovered ends.

Endnote

I finished writing this book in 1964. Some of the opinions herein may seem out of date, some of the questions I posed may have been answered, but it remains a true record of my life and times in Kenya as I saw them.

Now, in 1973, ten years after Kenya gained full Independence, we are still here. We left Hardy House and moved to a smaller house on the ridge above the Mbagathi River, at Karen, the Nairobi suburb which took its name from Karen Blixen. Her house still stands, less than half a mile from ours, but the red soil ridge on which she grew coffee is now cut up into residential plots and a fine golf course. The Mbagathi River, in its steep valley, bounds our plot on one side, and from it we pump water to irrigate the roses which do so well here, and which we grow commercially. A strip of indigenous forest still borders the river, not much changed since Karen Blixen wrote of it in *Out of Africa*. It is so close to our small house that the bush babies play in the trees in the garden of an evening, and we have tamed a family group, who come at dusk every evening to a tree just by the house, and feed on the bananas we leave for them on a lighted platform.

Agnes and Brian at Comfort Cottage in 1969.

Not far away live our daughter Ann and her husband Don. They left Kipkebe in 1965, of their own choice, and Don has become a chartered accountant, learning his profession and taking his exams at the same time as he held down a full-time job to support his family. Michael, who now practices law in Nairobi, is married. His wife is the daughter of 'Tiny' Kingsford, who first came to Lamuria to be a pupil on the Shaw family's farm there, on Brian's father's advice. So their children are the second generation born and bred in Kenya on both sides. This of course, enables them automatically to be Kenya citizens. Michael Blundell, completely retired from politics, still lives and farms very successfully at Subukia, and wins many prizes at the annual flower shows. His garden was always a show place and still is.

Tea is still grown on Kipkebe but the General Manager, since the Bushes left in 1965 is no longer a member of the Shaw family. Still, thirty-eight years in one family is not a bad record for a farm in Kenya.

In spite of the doubts expressed by many European friends, after nearly fifty years we are still living a full and happy life here in Kenya, with the accent no longer on politics, but on roses. We are extremely well treated by all Kenyans, from the highest in the land to the lowest, as welcome guests in the country. We receive an invitation each year to attend the Independence Celebrations, and this year were honoured by being allocated seats in the President's pavilion. We have made our home in this country that we love, and we are happy and grateful to be allowed to stay here.

Agnes and Brian in their garden at Comfort Cottage in 1970.

Oturi serving supper to Agnes at Comfort Cottage in March 1971.

Printed in Great Britain
by Amazon